# DATE DUE

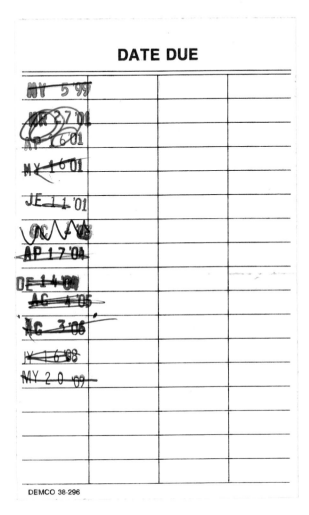

| | | |
|---|---|---|
| MY 5 99 | | |
| MR 27 01 | | |
| AP 16 01 | | |
| MY 16 01 | | |
| JE 11 '01 | | |
| OC   03 | | |
| AP 17 '04 | | |
| DE 14 03 | | |
| AG 4 05 | | |
| AG 3 06 | | |
| MY 16 08 | | |
| MY 20 09 | | |
| | | |
| | | |
| | | |
| | | |

DEMCO 38-296

# Modern Critical Interpretations

*Modern Critical Interpretations*

# LORD OF THE FLIES

*Edited and with an introduction by*
## Harold Bloom
Sterling Professor of the Humanities
Yale University

## CHELSEA HOUSE PUBLISHERS
Philadelphia

© 1999 by Chelsea House Publishers, a division of
Main Line Book Co.

Introduction © 1999 by Harold Bloom

Printed and bound in the United States of America

10  9  8  7  6  5  4  3  2  1

∞ The paper used in this publication meets the minimum
requirements of the American National Standard for
Permanence of Paper for Printed Library Materials,
Z39.48-1984


Library of Congress Cataloging-in-Publication Data

Lord of the flies / edited and with an introduction by
Harold Bloom.
         p. 272    cm. —(Modern critical interpretations)
      Includes bibliographical references and index.
      ISBN 0-7910-4777-6 (hc.)
      1. Golding, William, 1911–      Lord of the Flies.
   2. Survival after airplane accidents, shipwrecks, etc., in
   literature.    3. Adventure stories, English— History
   and criticism.    4. Islands in literature.    5. Boys in
   literature.    I. Bloom, Harold.    II. Series.
   PR6013.O35L635           1998
   823'.914—dc21                              98-23884
                                                 CIP

# Contents

# *Editor's Note*

This volume brings together a representation of the best critical essays available on William Golding's *Lord of the Flies*. My Introduction questions the aesthetic achievement of the book, while conceding its ongoing usefulness as an allegorical warning against latent human violence.

The critical essays commence with Claire Rosenfield's Freudian reading of Golding's boys, after which Bernard F. Dick rather boldly compares *Lord of the Flies* to *The Bacchae* of Euripides, a somewhat more formidable literary achievement.

Bernard S. Oldsey and Stanley Weintraub take at high moral value Golding's fable of Original Sin, while Robert C. Gordon is content to identify Golding's use of themes from Homer and Euripides.

Golding's imaginative flexibility is praised by Mark Kinkead-Weekes and Ian Gregor, after which Leighton Hodson centers upon the pervasive metaphor of darkness in Golding's tendentious tale.

Howard S. Babb culminates by praising Simon as the redeeming character in the novel, while Jeanne Delbaere-Garant finds in *Lord of the Flies* an expanding and outward-going relevance that can be applied to nearly everything.

In Arnold Johnston's interpretation, Golding's first novel retains a mythic power that compensates for its limitations of design and execution, after which Philip Redpath contrasts the linear structure of *Lord of the Flies* to the more adroit circular shape of Golding's *The Inheritors*. James Gindin compares the same two works, rightly seeing them essentially as preparations for Golding's best and most original novel, *Pincher Martin*.

Patrick Reilly, courageously evoking Swift and Camus, takes *Lord of the Flies* as a morally persuasive fable of evil, while S.J. Boyd returns us to the saving grace of Simon. To L.L. Dickson, Golding is commendable for attempting to portray a mixed nature in his characters, while John F. Fitzgerald and John R. Kayser are quite Augustinian in hailing Golding's revelation that Original Sin and Pride are one.

In this volume's final essay, Lawrence S. Friedman accurately judges *Lord of the Flies* to be "a spiritual vacuum," in comparison both to Euripides and to Sartre.

# Introduction

Popular as it continues to be, *Lord of the Flies* essentially is a period piece. Published in 1954, it is haunted by William Golding's service in the Royal Navy (1940–45), during the Second World War. The hazards of the endless battles of the North Atlantic against German submarines, culminated in Golding's participation in D-Day, the Normandy invasion of June 6, 1944. Though *Lord of the Flies* is a moral parable in the form of a boys' adventure story, in a deeper sense it is a war story. The book's central emblem is the dead parachutist, mistaken by the boys for the Beast Beelzebub, diabolic Lord of the Flies. For Golding, the true shape of Beelzebub is a pig's head on a stick, and the horror of war is transmuted into the moral brutality implicit (in his view) in most of us. The dead parachutist, in Golding's own interpretation, represents History, one war after another, the dreadful gift adults keep presenting to children. Golding's overt intention has some authority, but not perhaps enough to warrant our acceptance of so simplistic a symbol.

Judging *Lord of the Flies* a period piece means that one doubts its long-range survival, if only because it is scarcely a profound vision of evil. Golding's first novel, *Lord of the Flies* does not sustain a critical comparison with his best narratives: *The Inheritors*, *Pincher Martin* (his masterpiece), *Free Fall*, and the much later *Darkness Visible*. All these books rely upon nuance, irony, intelligence, and do not reduce to a trite moral allegory. Golding acknowledged the triteness, yet insisted upon his fable's truth:

> Man is a fallen being. He is gripped by original sin. His nature is sinful and his state perilous. I accept the theology and admit the triteness; but what is trite is true; and a truism can become more than a truism when it is a belief passionately held.

Passion is hardly a standard of measurement in regard to truth. *Lord of the Flies* aspires to be a universal fable, but its appeal to American school-children partly inheres in its curious exoticism. Its characters are implausible because they are humorless; even one ironist among them would explode the book. The Christ-like Simon is particularly unconvincing; Golding does not know how to portray the psychology of a saint. Whether indeed, in his first novel, he knew how to render anyone's psychology is disputable. His boys are indeed British private school boys: regimented, subjected to vicious discipline, and indoctrinated with narrow, restrictive views of human nature. Golding's long career as a teacher at Bishop Wordsworth's School in Salisbury was a kind of extension of his Naval service: a passage from one mode of indoctrination and strict discipline to another. The regression to savagery that marks *Lord of the Flies* is a peculiarly British scholastic phenomenon, and not a universal allegory of moral depravity.

By indicating the severe limitations of Golding's first novel, I do not intend to deny its continued cultural value. Any well-told tale of a reversion to barbarism is a warning against tendencies in many groups that may become violent, and such a warning remains sadly relevant as we approach Millenium. Though in itself a non-event, the year 2000 will arouse some odd expectations among extremists, particularly in the United States, most millenial of nations. Golding's allegorical fable is no *Gulliver's Travels*; the formidable Swiftian irony and savage intellectualism are well beyond Golding's powers. *Literary* value has little sway in *Lord of the Flies*. Ralph, Piggy, Simon, and Jack are ideograms, rather than achieved fictive characters. Compare them to Kipling's Kim, and they are sadly diminished; invoke Huck Finn, and they are reduced to names on a page. *Lord of the Flies* matters, not in or for itself, but because of its popularity in an era that continues to find it a useful admonition.

CLAIRE ROSENFIELD

# "Men of a Smaller Growth": A Psychological Analysis of William Golding's Lord of the Flies

When an author consciously dramatizes Freudian theory—and dramatizes it successfully—only the imaginative re-creation of human behavior rather than the sustaining structure of ideas is apparent. In analyzing William Golding's *Lord of the Flies*, the critic must assume that Golding knows psychological literature and must then attempt to show how an author's knowledge of theory can vitalize his prose and characterization. The plot itself is uncomplicated, so simple, indeed, that one wonders how it so effortlessly absorbs the burden of meaning. During some unexplained man-made holocaust a plane, evacuating a group of children, crashes on the shore of a tropical island. All adults are conveniently killed. The narrative follows the children's gradual return to the amorality of childhood, and it is the very nature of that state of non-innocence which makes them small savages. Or we might make the analogy to the childhood of races and compare the child to the primitive. Denied the sustaining and repressing authority of parents, church, and state, they form a new culture the development of which reflects that of the genuine primitive society, evolving its gods and demons (its myths), its rituals and taboos (its social norms). On the level of pure narrative, the action proceeds from the gradual struggle between Ralph and Jack, the two oldest boys, for precedence. Ralph is the natural leader by virtue of his superior height, his superior strength, his superior beauty. His mild

From *Literature and Psychology* 11:4 (Autumn 1961) © 1961 by the Modern Language Association.

expression proclaims him "no devil." He possesses the symbol of authority, the conch, or sea shell, which the children use to assemble their miniature councils. Golding writes, "The being that had blown . . . [the conch] had sat waiting for them on the platform with the delicate thing balanced on his knees, was set apart." Jack, on the other hand, is described in completely antithetical terms; he is distinguished by his ugliness and his red hair, a traditional demonic attribute. He first appears as the leader of a church choir, which "creature-like" marches in two columns behind him. All members of the choir wear black; "their bodies, form throat to ankle, were hidden by black cloaks." Ralph initially blows the conch to discover how many children have escaped death in the plane crash. As Jack approaches with his choir from the "darkness of the forest," he cannot see Ralph, whose back is to the sun. The former is, symbolically, sun-blinded. These two are very obviously intended to recall God and the Devil, whose confrontation, in the history of Western religions, establishes the moral basis for all actions. But, as Freud reminds us, "metaphysics" becomes "metapsychology"; gods and devils are "nothing other than psychological processes projected into the outer world." If Ralph is a projection of man's good impulses from which we derive the authority figures—whether god, king, or father—who establish the necessity for our valid ethical and social action, then Jack becomes an externalization of the evil instinctual forces of the unconscious. Originally, as in the more primitive religions, gods and devils were one; even Hebraic-Christian tradition makes Satan a fallen angel.

The temptation is to regard the island on which the children are marooned as a kind of Eden, uncorrupted and Eveless. But the actions of the children negate any assumption about childhood innocence. Even though Golding himself momentarily becomes a victim of his Western culture and states that Ralph wept for the "end of innocence," events have simply supported Freud's conclusions that no child is innocent. On a third level, Ralph is every man—or every child—and his body becomes the battleground where reason and instinct struggle, each to assert itself. For to regard Ralph and Jack as Good and Evil is to ignore the role of the child Piggy, who in the child's world of make-believe is the outsider. Piggy's composite description not only manifests his difference from the other boys; it also reminds the reader of the stereotype image of the old man who has more-than-human wisdom: he is fat, inactive because asthmatic, and generally reveals a disinclination for physical labor. Because he is extremely near-sighted, he wears thick glasses—a further mark of his difference. As time passes, the hair of the other boys grows with abandon. "He was the only boy on the island whose hair never seemed to grow. The rest were shock-headed, but Piggy's hair still lay in wisps over his head as though baldness were his natural state, and this imperfect covering would soon go, like the velvet on a young stag's antlers." In these images of age and authority we have a figure reminiscent of the children's past—the father. Moreover, like the father he counsels common sense; he alone leavens with a reasonable gravity the constant exuberance of the others for play or for play at hunting. When they scamper off at every vague whim, he scornfully comments, "Like a pack of kids." Ungrammatically but logically, he tries to allay the "littluns" fear of a "beast." "'Life is scientific, that's what it is. . . . I know there isn't no beast—not with claws and all that, I mean—but I know there isn't no fear, either.'" He has excessive regard for the forms of order: the conch must be held by a child before that child can speak at councils. When the others neglect responsibility, fail to build shelters, swim in the pools or play in the sand or hunt, allow the signal fire on the mountain to go out or to get out of hand and burn up half the island, he seconds Ralph by admonishing the others vigorously and becomes more and more of a spoil-sport who robs play of its illusions, the adult inter-rupting the game. Ralph alone recognizes his superior intelligence but wavers between what he knows to be wise and the group acceptance his egocentricity demands. Finally, Piggy's role—as man's reasoning faculties and as a father—derives some of its complexity from the fact that the fire which the children foster and guard on the mountain in the hope of communicating with the adult world is lighted with his glasses. In mythology, after all, the theft of fire brought civilization—and, hence, repression—to man. As the new community becomes more and more irra-tional, its irrationality is marked by Piggy's progressive blindness. An acci-dent following an argument between Ralph and Jack breaks one of the lenses. When the final breach between the two occurs and Piggy supports Ralph, his remaining lens is stolen in a night raid by Jack. This is a parody of the traditional fire theft, which was to provide light and warmth for mankind. After this event Piggy must be led by Ralph. When he is making his final plea for his glasses—reasoned as always—he is struck on the head by a rock and falls. "Piggy fell forty feet and landed on his back on that square, red rock in the sea. His head opened and stuff came out and turned red. Piggy's arms and legs twitched a bit, like a pig's after it has been killed."

The history of the child Piggy on the island dramatizes in terms of the individual the history of the entire group. When they first assemble to investigate their plight, they treat their island isolation as a temporary phenomenon; they want to play games until they are rescued—until their parents reassert the repressive actions of authority. This microcosm of the great world seems to them to be a fairy land.

> A kind of glamour spread over them and the scene and they
> were conscious of the glamour and made happy by it.
>
> The coral was scribbled in the sea as though a giant had bent
> down to reproduce the shape of the island in a flowing, chalk line
> but tired before he had finished.
>
> "This is real exploring," said Jack. "I'll bet nobody's been here
> before."
>
> Echoes and birds flew, white and pink dust floated, the forest
> further down shook as with the passage of an enraged monster:
> and then the island was still.

They compare this reality to their reading experiences: it is Treasure Island
or Coral Island or like pictures from their travel books. This initial reaction
conforms to the pattern of play which Johan Huizinga establishes in *Homo
Ludens*. In its early stages their play has no cultural or moral function; it is
simply a "stepping out of real life into a temporary sphere of activity." Ironically, the child of *Lord of the Flies* who thinks he is "only pretending" or that
this is "only for fun" does not realize that his play is the beginning of the
formation of a new society which has regressed to a primitive state, with all
its emphasis upon taboo and communal action. What begins by being like
other games in having a distinct "locality and duration" apart from ordinary
life is—or becomes—reality. The spatial separation necessary for the make-
believe of the game is represented first by the island. In this new world the
playground is further narrowed: the gatherings of the children are described
as a circle at several points, a circle from which Piggy is excluded:

> For the moment the boys were a closed circuit of sympathy with
> Piggy outside.
>
> They became a circle of boys round a camp fire and even Ralph
> and Piggy were half-drawn in.

Piggy approximates the spoil-sport who "robs the play of its illusion."
    The games of the beginning have a double function: they, first of all,
reflect the child's attitude toward play as a temporary cessation from the
activities imposed by the adult world; but like the games played before the
formation of civilization, they anticipate the ritual which reveals a developing
society. So the children move from voluntary play to ritual, from "only

pretending" to reality, from representation to identification. The older strictures imposed by parents are soon forgotten—but every now and then a momentary remembrance of past prohibitions causes restraint. One older child hides in order to throw stones at a younger one.

> Yet there was a space round Henry, perhaps six yards in diameter, into which he dare not throw. Here, invisible yet strong, was the taboo of the old life. Round the squatting child was the protection of parents and school and policemen and the law.

Jack hesitates when, searching for meat, he raises his knife to kill his first pig.

> The pause was only long enough for them to understand what an enormity the downward stroke would be. Then the piglet tore loose from the creepers and scurried into the undergrowth. . . .
> "Why didn't you—?"
> They knew very well why he hadn't: because of the enormity of the knife descending and cutting into living flesh; because of the unbearable blood.

The younger children first, then gradually the older ones, like primitives in the childhood of races, begin to people the darkness of night and forest with spirits and demons which had previously appeared only in their dreams or fairy tales. Now there are no comforting mothers to dispel the terrors of the unknown. They externalize these fears into the figure of a "beast." Once the word "beast" is mentioned, the menace of the irrational becomes overt; name and thing become one. At one critical council when the first communal feeling begins to disintegrate, Ralph cries, "'If only they could send us something grown-up . . . a sign or something.'" And a sign does come from the outside. That night, unknown to the children, a plane is shot down and its pilot parachutes dead to earth and is caught in the rocks on the mountain. It requires no more than the darkness of night together with the shadows of the forest vibrating in the signal fire to distort the hanging corpse with its expanding silk 'chute into a demon that must be appeased. Ironically, the fire of communication does touch this object of the grown-up world only to foster superstition. Security in this new situation can be achieved only by establishing new rules.

During the first days the children, led by Jack, play at hunting. But eventually the circle of the playground extends to the circle of the hunted and squealing pig seeking refuge—and it is significant that the first animal slain for food is a nursing sow—which itself anticipates the circle of consecrated ground where the children perform the new rites of the kill.

The first hunt accomplishes its purpose: the blood of the animals is spilled; the meat, used for food. But because Jack and his choir undertake this hunt, they desert the signal fire, which is dictated by the common-sense desire for rescue, and it goes out and a ship passes the island. Later the children reenact the killing with one boy, Maurice, assuming the role of the pig running its frenzied circle. The others chant in unison: "'Kill the pig. Cut her throat. Bash her in.'" At this dramatic representation each child is still aware that this is a display, a performance. He is never "so beside himself that he loses consciousness of ordinary reality." Each time they reenact the same event, however, their behavior becomes more frenzied, more cruel, less like representation than identification. The chant then becomes, "'Kill the beast. Cut his throat. Spill his blood.'" It is as if the first event, the pig's death, is forgotten in the recesses of time; a new myth defines the primal act. Real pig becomes mythical beast.

Jack's ascendency over the group begins when the children's fears distort the natural objects around them: twigs become creepers, shadows become demons. I have already discussed the visual imagery suggesting Jack's demonic function. He serves as a physical manifestation of irrational forces. After an indefinite passage of time, he appears almost dehumanized, his "nose only a few inches from the humid earth." He is "dog-like" and proceeds forward "on all fours" "into the semi-darkness of the undergrowth." His cloak and clothing have been shed. Indeed, except for a "pair of tattered shorts held up by his knife-belt, he was naked." His eyes seemed "bolting and nearly mad." He has lost his ability to communicate with Ralph as on the first day. "He tried to convey the compulsion to track down and kill that was swallowing him up." "They walked along, two continents of experience and feeling, unable to communicate." When Jack first explains to Ralph the necessity to disguise himself from the pigs he wants to hunt, he rubs his face with clay and charcoal. At this point he assumes a mask, begins to dance, is finally freed from all the repressions of his past. "He capered towards Bill, and the mask was a thing on its own, behind which Jack hid, liberated from shame and self-consciousness." At the moment of the dance the mask and Jack are one. The first kill, as I have noted, follows the desertion of the signal fire and the passage of a possible rescue ship. Jack is still revelling in the knowledge that he has "outwitted a living thing, imposed their will upon it, taken away its life like a long and satisfying drink." Already he has begun to obliterate the distinctions between animals and men, as do primitives; already he thinks in terms of the metaphor of a ritual drinking of blood, the efficacy of which depended on the drinker's assumption of his victim's strength and spirit. Ralph and Piggy confront him with his defection of duty.

> The two boys faced each other. There was the brilliant world of
> hunting, tactics, fierce exhilaration, skill; and there was the world
> of longing and baffled common-sense. Jack transferred the knife
> to his left hand and smudged blood over his forehead as he
> pushed down the plastered hair.

Jack's unconscious gesture is a parody of the ritual of initiation in which the
hunter's face is smeared with the blood of his first kill. In the subsequent
struggle one of the lenses of Piggy's spectacles is broken. The dominance of
reason is over; the voice of the old world is stilled. The primary images are
no longer those of the fire and light but those of darkness and blood. The
link between Ralph and Jack "had snapped and fastened elsewhere."

The rest of the group, however, shifts its allegiance to Jack because he
has given them meat rather than something useless like fire. Gradually, they
begin to be described as "shadows" or "masks" or "savages" or "demoniac
figures" and, like Jack, "hunt naked save for paint and a belt." Ralph now uses
Jack's name with the recognition that "a taboo was evolving around that word
too." Name and thing again become one; to use the word is to incite the
bearer. But more significant, the taboo, according to Freud, is "a very primitive prohibition imposed from without (by an authority) and directed against
the strongest desires of man." In this new society it replaces the authority of
the parents. Now every kill becomes a sexual act, is a metaphor for childhood
sexuality.

> The afternoon wore on, hazy and dreadful with damp heat; the
> sow staggered her way ahead of them, bleeding and mad, and the
> hunters followed, wedded to her in lust, excited by the long chase
> and dropped blood. . . . The sow collapsed under them and they
> were heavy and fulfilled upon her.

Every subsequent "need for ritual" fulfills not only the desire for communication and a substitute security to replace that of civilization, but also the
need to liberate both the repressions of the past and those imposed by Ralph.
Indeed, the projection of those impulses that they cannot accept in themselves into a beast is the beginning of a new mythology. The earlier dreams
and nightmares can now be shared as the former subjectivity could not be.

When the imaginary demons become defined by the rotting corpse and
floating 'chute on the mountain which their terror distorts into a beast, Jack
wants to track the creature down. After the next kill, the head of the pig is
placed upon a stake to placate it. Finally one of the children, Simon, after an
epileptic fit, creeps out of the forest at twilight while the others are engaged

in enthusiastic dancing following a hunt. Seized by the rapture of reenactment or perhaps terrorized by fear and night into believing that this little
creature is a beast, they circle Simon, pounce on him, bite and tear his body
to death. He becomes not a substitute for beast, but beast itself; representation become absolute identification, "the mystic repetition of the initial
event." At the moment of Simon's death, nature speaks; a cloud bursts; rain
and wind fill the parachute on the hill and the corpse of the pilot falls or is
dragged among the screaming boys. Both Simon and the dead man, beast
and beast, are washed into the sea and disappear. After this complete resurgence of savagery in accepted ritual, there is only a short interval before
Piggy's remaining lens is stolen, he is intentionally killed as an enemy, and
Ralph, the human being, becomes hunted like beast or pig.

Simon's mythic and psychological role has earlier been suggested.
Undersized, subject to epileptic fits, bright-eyed, and introverted, he
constantly creeps away from the others to meditate among the intricate vines
of the forest. To him, as to the mystic, superior knowledge is given intuitively
which he cannot communicate. When the first report of the beast-pilot
reaches camp, Simon, we are told, can picture only "a human at once heroic
and sick." During the day preceding his death, he walks vaguely away and
stumbles upon the pig's head left in the sand in order the appease the
demonic forces they imagine. Shaman-like, he holds a silent colloquy with it,
a severed head covered with innumerable flies. It is itself the titled Lord of
the Flies, a name applied to the Biblical demon Beelzebub and later used in
Goethe's *Faust, Part I*, to describe Mephistopheles. From it he learns that it
is the Beast, and the Beast cannot be hunted because it is within. Simon feels
the advent of one of his fits and imagines the head expanding, an anticipation
or intuition of the discovery of the pilot's corpse. Suddenly Golding employs
a startling image, "Simon was inside the mouth. He fell down and lost
consciousness." Literally, this image presents the hallucination of a sensitive
child about to lose control of his rational faculties. Metaphorically, it
suggests the ritual quest in which the hero is swallowed by a serpent or
dragon or beast whose belly is the underworld, undergoes a symbolic death
in order to gain the elixir to revitalize his stricken society, and returns with
his knowledge to the timed world as a redeemer. Psychologically, this narrative
pattern is a figure of speech connoting the annihilation of the ego, an internal
journey necessary for self-understanding, a return to the timelessness of the
unconscious. When Simon wakes, he realizes that he must confront the beast
on the mountain because "what else is there to do?" He is relieved of "that
dreadful feeling of the pressure of personality" which had oppressed him
earlier. When he discovers the hanging corpse, he first frees it in compassion
although it is rotting and surrounded by flies, and then staggers unevenly

down to report to the others. Redeemer and scapegoat, he becomes the victim of the group he seeks to enlighten. In death—before he is pulled into the sea—his head is surrounded by flies in an ironic parody of the halo of saints and gods.

Piggy's death, soon to follow Simon's, is foreshadowed when the former proclaims at council that there is no beast. "'What would a beast eat?'" "'Pig.'" "'We eat pig,'" he rationally answers. "'Piggy!'" is the next word. At Piggy's death his body twitches "like a pig's after it has been killed." Not only has his head been smashed, but also the conch, symbol of order, is simultaneously broken. A complex group of metaphors unite to form a total metaphor involving Piggy and the pig, hunted and eaten by the children, and the pig's head which is at once left to appease the beast's hunger and is the beast itself. But the beast is within, and the children are defined by the very objects they seek to destroy.

In these associated images we have the whole idea of a communal and sacrificial feast and a symbolic cannibalism, all of which Freud discussed in *Totem and Taboo*. Here the psychology of the individual contributes the configurations for the development of religion. Indeed, the events of *Lord of the Flies* imaginatively parallel the patterns which Freud detects in primitive mental processes.

Having populated the outside world with demons and spirits which are projections of their instinctual nature, these children—and primitive men—must then unconsciously evolve new forms of worship and laws, which manifest themselves in taboos, the oldest form of social repression. With the exception of the first kill—in which the children still imagine they are playing at hunting—the subsequent deaths assume a ritual form; the pig is eaten communally by all and the head is left for the "beast," whose role consists in sharing the feast. This is much like the "public ceremony" described by Freud in which the sacrifice of an animal provided food for the god and his worshippers. The complex relationships within the novel between the "beast," the pigs which are sacrificed, the children whose asocial impulses are externalized in the beast—this has already been discussed. So we see that, as Freud points out, the "sacrificing community, its god [the 'beast'], and the sacrificial animal are of the same blood," members of a clan. The pig, then, may be regarded as a totem animal, an "ancestor, a tutelary spirit and protector"; it is, in any case, a part of every child. The taboo or prohibition against eating particular parts of the totem animal coincides with the children's failure to eat the head of the pig. It is that portion which is set aside for the "beast." Just as Freud describes the primitive feast, so the children's festive meal is accompanied by a frenzied ritual in which they temporarily release their forbidden impulses and represent the kill. To consume the pig and to reenact the event is not only to assert a "common identity" but also to share a "common responsibility" for the deed. None of the boys is excluded from the feast. The later ritual, in which Simon, as a human substitute identified with the totem, is killed, is in this novel less an unconscious attempt to share the responsibility for the killing of a primal father in prehistoric times, than it is a social act in which the participants celebrate their new society by commemorating their severance from the authority of the civilized state. Because of the juxtaposition of Piggy and pig, the eating of pig at the communal feast might be regarded as the symbolic cannibalism by which the children physically partake of the qualities of the slain and share responsibility for their crime. (It must be remembered that, although Piggy on a symbolic level represents the light of reason and the authority of the father, on the psychological and literal level of the story he shares that bestiality and irrationality which to Golding dominate all men, even the most rational or civilized.)

In the final action, Ralph is outlawed by the children and hunted like an animal. Jack sharpens a stick at both ends so that it will be ready to receive the severed head of the boy as if he were a pig. Jack keeps his society together because it, like the brother horde of Robertson Smith and Freud, "is based on complicity in the common crimes." In his flight Ralph, seeing the grinning skull of a pig, thinks of it as a toy and remembers the early days on the island when all were united in play. In the play world, the world of day, he has become a "spoil-sport" like Piggy; in the world based upon primitive rites and taboos, the night world where fears become demons and sleep is like death, he is the heretic or outcast. This final hunt, after the conch is broken, is the pursuit of the figure representing law and order, the king or the god. Finally, Jack, through misuse of the dead Piggy's glasses, accidentally sets the island on fire. A passing cruiser, seeing the fire, lands to find only a dirty group of sobbing little boys. "'Fun and games,' said the officer. . . . 'What have you been doing? Having a war or something?'"

But are all the meanings of the novel as clear as they seem? To restrict it to an imaginative re-creation of Freud's theory that children are little savages, that no child is innocent whatever Christian theology would have us believe, is to limit its significance for the adult world. To say that the "beasts" we fear are within, that man is essentially irrational—or, to place a moral judgment on the irrational, that man is evil—that, again, is too easy. In this forced isolation of a group of children, Golding is making a statement about the world they have left—a world, we are told, "in ruins." According to the Huizinga's theory of play, war is a game, a contest for prestige which, like the games of primitives or of classical athletes, may be fatal. It, too, has its rules, although the modern concept of total war tends to obscure both its ritualistic and its enobling character. It, too, has its spatial and temporal limitations, as the new rash of "limited" wars makes very clear. More than once the children's acts are compared to those of the outside world. When Jack first blackens his face like a savage, he gives his explanation: "'For hunting. Like in war. You know—dazzle paint. Like things trying to look like something else.'" Appalled by one of the ritual dances, Piggy and Ralph discuss the authority and rationality of the apparently secure world they have left:

> "Grown-ups know things," said Piggy. "They ain't afraid of the dark. They'd meet and have tea and discuss. Then things 'ud be all right—"
> "They wouldn't set fire to the island. Or lose—"
> "They'd build a ship—"
> The three boys stood in the darkness, striving unsuccessfully to convey the majesty of adult life.
> "They wouldn't quarrel—"
> "Or break my specs—"
> "Or talk about a beast—"
> "If only they could get a message to us," cried Ralph desperately. "If only they could send us something grown-up . . . a sign or something."

The sign does come that night, unknown to them, in the form of the parachute and its attached corpse. The pilot is the analogue in the adult world to the ritual killing of the child Simon on the island; he, like Simon, is the victim and scapegoat of his society, which has unleashed its instincts in war. Both he and Simon are associated by a cluster of visual images. Both are identified with beasts by the children, who do see the truth—that all men are bestial—but do not understand it. Both he and Simon attract the flies from the Lord of the Flies, the pig's head symbolic of the demonic; both he and Simon are washed away by a cleansing but not reviving sea. His position on the mountain recalls the Hanged or Sacrificed god of Frazer; here, however, we have a parody of fertility. He is dead proof that Piggy's exaggerated respect for adults is itself irrational. When the officer at the rescue jokingly says, "'What have you been doing? Having a war or something?'" this representative of the grown-up world does not understand that the games of the children, which result in two deaths, are a moral commentary upon the primitive nature of his own culture. The ultimate irrationality is war. Paradoxically, the children not only return to a primitive and infantile morality, but they also degenerate into adults. They prove that, indeed, "children are but men of a smaller growth."

BERNARD F. DICK

# Lord of the Flies *and* The Bacchae

Embedded in the mythic structure of *Lord of the Flies* are discernible motifs from the *Bacchae* which confirm Golding's claim that Euripides was one of his literary influences. Both works are anthropological passion plays in which individuals—children in Golding, adults in Euripides—revert to savagery and murder during a frenzied ritual. Both portray a divided society in which the Dionysan has not been assimilated by way of the Apollonian. In the *Bacchae*, the polarity consists in the followers of Dionysus, and Pentheus who alone opposes the religion. Early in the novel, some of the marooned boys in whom the irrational instinct is paramount separate from the rest to become hunters. Their Dionysan character is subtly underscored by the fact that they were former choristers. The novel centers on the attempt of the hunters first to absorb, then destroy the rational element in much the same way as Pentheus was persuaded by Cadmus and Teiresias to join the new cult, only to reject it and be killed at the hands of the Bacchants. Furthermore, both works have *ex machina* endings. In the *Bacchae*, despite the lacuna after 1329, it is clear from the hypothesis and the final episode that Dionysus appeared to foretell the fortunes of all. A more human epiphany occurs at the end of the novel when a naval officer comes to the rescue and resolves the action in a highly Euripidean manner. But in view of the previous bloodshed, this epiphany is as ironic as the appearance of Dionysus at the end of the *Bacchae*.

From *The Classical World* 57:4:1283 (January 1964). © 1964 by The Classical Association of the Atlantic States.

Specifically, both drama and novel contain three interrelated ritual themes: the cult of a beast-god, a hunt as prefiguration of the death of a scapegoat-figure, and *sparagmos* or dismemberment of the scapegoat.

Euripides depicts a Dionysus who still retains his original characteristics of a beast-deity, the incarnation of animal potency with which his votaries sought communion. Dionysus is both hunter and hunted; consequently, beast-hunt imagery pervades the drama. But more important, the *Bacchae* is the enactment of a ritualistic sacrifice in which the victim is first made to resemble the god before he is dismembered. Thus Pentheus, the scapegoat, is cajoled into wearing the Dionysan attire before going to observe the Bacchants. His death had been prefigured earlier in the dismemberment of the Theban cattle, and when he is finally discovered in the fir-tree, he is literally hunted down and killed.

In *Lord of the Flies,* the obsession with the hunt transforms the hunters into a nameless group that functions conjointly but without personal identity: "the throb and stamp of a single organism." Their choral refrain, *"Kill the beast! Cut his throat! Spill his blood!"* suggests the "hunt, kill, prey" of the Bacchants. The killing of the sow prefigures the death of Simon, the scapegoat, in much the same way as the raid on the cattle foreshadowed that of Pentheus. The pig's head is impaled on a stick (a reminiscence of Pentheus' head on the thyrsus?), and is offered as a trophy to a beast which the children imagine to be lurking on the island. When Simon accidentally interrupts the re-enactment of the pig-hunt, he is mistaken for the beast and brutally killed.

Lastly, both Pentheus and Simon are pitted against elemental forces that are their direct opposites. Pentheus alone sees Dionysus in animal shape, but rooted in a rigid moralism he can neither recognize the god nor understand that his intellectualism must be complemented by irrational yet necessary passions. Only Simon hears the cynical message of the "Lord of the Flies," assuring the child that "everything was a bad business." Confronted with the non-rational, Simon recognizes it, for it is an "ancient, inescapable recognition." But such recognition brings either a loss of innocence or death, and Simon is wantonly destroyed by a surge of anarchy that in Golding's eyes is inevitable in a flawed universe.

BERNARD S. OLDSEY AND STANLEY WEINTRAUB

# *Beelzebub Revisited:* Lord of the Flies

*L*ord of the Flies (1954), Golding's first novel and the one that established
his reputation, is still most widely acclaimed as his major work. Not only has
it captured a large segment of the popular and academic imagination
(having the effect there of replacing J. D. Salinger's *The Catcher in the Rye*),
but it has also attracted the greatest amount of critical attention directed
toward Golding.

To date, that critical attention has proven various, specialized, and
spotty. A remarkable "first novel" on any terms, *Lord of the Flies* has been
praised on literary grounds much less often than as sociological, psychological, or religious tract, as "pure parable," fable, or myth. The terminology of
Frazer and Freud are more often brought to bear upon the novel than the
yardsticks of literary criticism. As literature, however, it has been—even
while praised—called unoriginal and derivative, filled with "gimmickry,"
devoid of characterization, and lacking in logic. Only twice has it been
blasted as insignificant art encased in bad writing.

Certainly *Lord of the Flies* is derivative, in the sense that it falls well
within the main stream of several English literary traditions. It is a "boys'
book," as are *Treasure Island, The Wind in the Willows, High Wind in Jamaica*,
and other books primarily about juvenile characters which transcend juvenile
appeal; it is in the tradition of the survival narrative, along with *Robinson*

From *The Art of William Golding.* © 1965 by Bernard S. Oldsey and Stanley Weintraub.

*Crusoe, The Swiss Family Robinson,* and even Barrie's *Admirable Crichton*; it is in the tradition—best exemplified by Conrad, Cary, and Greene in our century—that examines our culture by transplanting it harshly to an exotic locale where it prospers or withers depending upon its intrinsic value and strength; it is in the long tradition of anti-science writing in England, where authors for centuries have equated scientific progress with dehumanization; and it at least appears to be in the Nonconformist English religious tradition, which assumes mankind's fall from grace.

If all these traditions lead back to one key source of inspiration, it may be no accident. The traditions embodied in *Lord of the Flies* can be discovered in *Gulliver's Travels*—Swift's version of the primeval savagery and greed which civilization only masks in modern man. It seems no coincidence that we also find in Golding a Swiftian obsession with physical ugliness, mean-ness, and nastiness (sometimes bordering on the scatological), and with the sense of how tenuous is the hold of intelligence, reason, and humaneness as a brake upon man's regression into barbarism.

Eventually, of course, Golding must be judged according to his indi-vidual talent rather than tradition or polemical appeal. Other critical visits to his minor devil's island have been accomplished mainly at a distance, through special field glasses. Here we revisit the island armed only with the knowl-edge that Golding is essentially a literary man who uses scene, character, and symbol (not to mention an exceedingly fine style and some admittedly tricky plot methods) to achieve imaginative literary effects.

The scenic qualities of *Lord of the Flies* help make it an imaginative work for the reader as well as the author. Although Golding occasionally provides consolidating detail, he more commonly requires the reader to pull narrative and descriptive elements into focus. For example, he provides no end-paper map or block description of his fictional island. The reader must explore it along with the participants in the story and piece together a usable concept of time and place. What we learn in this way is just enough to keep the work within the realm of fiction, but not enough to remove it from the realm of allegory. *And the essence of Golding's art resides exactly within the area of overlap.*

Fable-like, time and place are vague. The Queen (Elizabeth?) still reigns, and "Reds" are apparently the vague enemy. It is the postcatastrophic near-future, in which nuclear war has laid waste much of the West. ("They're all dead," Piggy thinks. And "civilization," corroborates Golding, is "in ruins.") The fiery crash of the boys' plane upon a tropical island has been the final stage of their evacuation from England. The island seems to lie some-where in the Indian or Pacific Ocean, probably on a line extending from England to Australia, which could well have been the planned terminus of their evacuation. Jack provides the clue for such geographical extrapolation when he speaks of Simon's seizures at "Gib." (Gibraltar) and "Addis" (Addis Ababa), as well as "at matins over the precentor."

Shaped roughly like an outrigged boat, the boys' haven is a tropical island with a coral base. A mile out along one side runs a barrier reef, between which and the island lies a lagoon, on whose inward shore the boys hold their assemblies. At one end of the island there appears to be another, smaller island; but upon close inspection this is found to be attached by a rocky isthmus. Topographically, the island rises from low jungle and orchard land to a mountaintop, or ridge, with few or no trees. By way of food, it provides the boys with bananas, coconuts, an "olive-grey, jelly-like fruit," and wild pig, as well as crab and fish taken from the sea. At midday the island get hot enough to produce mirage effects.

If there were an end-paper map for Golding's island, it would no doubt be marked to indicate these major points of interest: (1) the beach along the lagoon, where Piggy and Ralph find the conch, and where assemblies are held near a natural platform of fallen trees; (2) the mountaintop, from which the island is surveyed, where the signal fire is placed, and where eventually the dead parachutist is trapped by wind and rock; (3) the burned-out quarter mile, where the mulberry-faced boy dies in the first fire; (4) Simon's leafy bower, to which he makes mystic retreats and from which he views the ceremony of impaling the pig's head upon a stake; (5) the orchard, where the fruit is picked and where some of the "littluns" are "taken short," leaving behind their fecal trail; (6) the "castle" at the tail end of the island, rising a hundred feet from the sea, where the first search for the "beast" is made, and where Piggy is killed after Jack has made this bastion his headquarters; and (7) the jungle, with its hanging vines that recall snakes and "beasties," with it pig trails where Jack hunts and where Ralph is finally hunted.

When the details are extracted and given order under an analytical light, Golding's island looks naturalistic in specification. But matters are not at all that clear in the book. The location of the island, for example, is kept deliberately vague: it is sufficiently remote to draw only two ships in a month or so, yet close enough to "civilization" to be the floor above which deadly, and old-fashioned, air battles are fought miles high (the boys' plane itself has been shot down). The nearby air and naval war in progress, with conventional weapons, is somewhat out of keeping with earlier reports of utter catastrophe. Equally incongruous is the smartly attired naval officer and savior of the closing pages, whose jaunty mien is incompatible with catastrophe. Yet he is as important to the machinery of the allegory as the earlier crash, which is equally difficult to explain on rational grounds. During the crash the fuselage of the evacuation plane has apparently broken in two: the forward half (holding pilot and others, including more boys) has been cleanly washed out to sea by a conveniently concomitant storm; and the after-section (which makes a long fiery scar as it cuts through the jungle) tumbles unscathed children onto the island. As incompatible, obscure, askew, and unrealistic as these elements may be, they are no more so than Gulliver's adventures. And Golding's graphically novelistic character and topographic details, both poetic and naturalistic, tend to blur the fabulous qualities of the narrative's use of time and setting in its opening and close. Although it is enough to say that the fabulist must be permitted pegs upon which to hang his fable, it is Golding's richly novelistic elements of the telling that call attention to the subtle dissonance. Paradoxically—yet artistically—this very tension between realistic novel and allegorical fable imparts to *Lord of the Flies* some of its unique power.

Golding's characters, like his setting, represent neither fictional reality nor fabulistic unreality, but, rather, partake of the naturalistic and the allegorical at the same time. As a result, they emerge more full bodied than Kafka's ethereal forms, more subtly shaded than Orwell's animal-farm types, and more comprehensively motivated than Bunyan's religious ciphers. Bit by bit we can piece together fairly solid pictures of the major figures in *Lord of the Flies*. And since a number of commentators have fallen into interpretive error by precipitously trying to state what these characters "mean," perhaps it would be best here to start by trying to state what they "are."

Ralph, the protagonist, is a boy twelve years and a "few months" old. He enters naïvely, turning handsprings of joy upon finding himself in an exciting place free of adult supervision. But his role turns responsible as leadership is thrust upon him—partly because of his size, partly because of his attractive appearance, and partly because of the conch with which, like some miniature Roland, he has blown the first assembly. Ralph is probably the largest boy on the island (built like a boxer, he nevertheless has a "mildness about his mouth and eyes that proclaimed no devil"). But he is not so intellectual and logical as Piggy ("he would never be a very good chess player," Golding assures us), not so intuitively right as Simon, nor even so aggressively able to take advantage of opportunity as Jack. For these reasons there has been some reader tendency to play down Ralph as a rather befuddled Everyman, a straw boy of democracy tossed about by forces he cannot cope with. Yet he should emerge from this rites-of-passage *bildungsroman* with the reader's respect. He is as much a hero as we are allowed: he has courage, he has good intelligence, he is diplomatic (in assuaging Piggy's feelings and dividing authority with Jack), and he elicits perhaps our greatest sympathy (when hounded across the island). Although he tries to live by the rules, Ralph is no monster of goodness. He himself becomes disillusioned with democratic procedure; he unthinkingly gives away Piggy's embarrassing nickname; and, much more importantly, he takes part in Simon's murder! But the true measure of Ralph's character is that he despairs of democracy because of its hollowness ("talk, talk, talk"), and that he apologizes to Piggy for the minor betrayal, and that—while Piggy tries to escape his share of the guilt for Simon's death—Ralph cannot be the hypocrite (this reversal, incidentally, spoils the picture often given of Piggy as superego or conscience). Ralph accepts his share of guilt in the mass action against Simon, just as he accepts leadership and dedication to the idea of seeking rescue. He too, as he confesses, would like to go hunting and swimming, but he builds shelters, tries to keep the island clean (thus combating the flies), and concentrates vainly on keeping a signal fire going. At the novel's end Ralph has emerged from his age of innocence; he sheds tears of experience, after having proven himself a "man" of humanistic faith and action. We can admire his insistence upon individual responsibility—a major Golding preoccupation—upon doing what must be done rather than what one would rather do.

Ralph's antagonist, Jack (the choir leader who becomes the text's Esau), is approximately the same age. He is a tall, thin, bony boy with light blue eyes and indicative red hair; he is quick to anger, prideful, aggressive, physically tough, and courageous. But although he shows traces of the demagogue from the beginning, he must undergo a metamorphosis from a timidity-shielding arrogance to conscienceless cruelty. At first he is even less able to wound a pig than is Ralph, but he is altered much in the manner of the transformation of the twentieth-century dictator from his first tentative stirrings of power lust to eventual bestiality. Although Golding is careful to show little of the devil in Ralph, he nicely depicts Jack as being directly in league with the lord of flies and dung. Jack trails the pigs by their olive-green, smooth, and steaming droppings. In one place we are shown him deep in animalistic regression, casting this way and that until he finds what he wants: "The ground was turned over near the pig-run and there were droppings that steamed. Jack bent down to them as though he loved them." His fate determined, Jack is a compelled being; he is swallowed by the beast—as it were—even before Simon: "He tried to convey the compulsion to track down and kill that was swallowing him up." Jack's Faustian reward is power through perception. He perceives almost intuitively the use of mask, dance, ritual, and propitiation to ward off—and yet encourage simultaneously—fear of the unknown. Propitiation is a recognition not only of the need to pacify but also of something to be pacified. In this instance it is the recognition of evil. "The devil must have his due," we say. Here the "beast" must be mollified, given its due. Jack recognizes this fact, even if he and his group of hunters do not understand it. Politically and anthropologically he is more instinctive than

Ralph. Jack does not symbolize chaos, as sometimes claimed, but, rather, a stronger, more primitive order than Ralph provides.

Jack's chief henchman, Roger, is not so subtly or complexly character-ized, and seems to belong more to Orwellian political fable. Slightly younger and physically weaker, he possesses from the beginning all the sadistic attrib-utes of the demagogue's hangman underling. In his treatment of the sow he proves deserving of his appellation in English slang. Through his intense, furtive, silent qualities, he acts as a sinister foil to Simon. By the end of the novel Golding has revealed Roger; we hardly need to be told that "the hangman's horror clung round him."

Simon is perhaps the most effectively—and certainly the most poignantly—characterized of all. A "skinny, vivid little boy, with a glance coming up from under a hut of straight hair that hung down, black and coarse," he is (at nine or ten) the lonely visionary, the clear-sighted realist, logical, sensitive, and mature beyond his years. We learn that he has a history of epileptic seizures—a dubious endowment sometimes credited to great men of the past, particularly those with a touch of the mystic. We see the unusual grace and sensitivity of his personality crop up here and there as the story unfolds until he becomes the central figure of the "Lord of the Flies" scene—one of Golding's most powerful and poetic. We see Simon's instinc-tive compassion and intelligence as he approaches the rotting corpse of the parachutist, which, imprisoned in the rocks on the hill in flying suit and para-chute harness, is the only palpable "monster" on the island. Although Simon's senses force him to vomit with revulsion, he nevertheless frees it "from the wind's indignity." When he returns to tell his frightened, blood-crazed companions that, in effect, they have nothing to fear but fear itself, his murder becomes the martyrdom of a saint and prophet, a point in human degeneration next to which the wanton killing of Piggy is but an anticlimax. In some of the novel's richest, most sensitive prose, the body of Simon (the boys' "beast" from the jungle) is taken out to sea by the tide, Golding here reaching close to tragic exaltation as Simon is literally transfigured in death:

> . . . The beast lay huddled on the pale beach and the stains spread, inch by inch.
>
> The edge of the lagoon became a streak of phosphores-cence which advanced minutely, as the great wave of the tide flowed. The clear water mirrored the clear sky and the angular bright constellations. The line of phosphorescence bulged about the sand grains and little pebbles; it held them each in a dimple of tension, then suddenly accepted them with an inaudible syllable and moved on.

Along the shoreward edge of the shallows the advancing clearness was full of strange, moonbeam-bodied creatures with fiery eyes. Here and there a larger pebble clung to its own air and was covered with a coat of pearls. The tide swelled in over the rain-pitted sand and smoothed everything with a layer of silver. Now it touched the first of the stains that seeped from the broken body and the creatures made a moving patch of light as they gathered at the edge. The water rose farther and dressed Simon's coarse hair with brightness. The line of his cheek silvered and the turn of his shoulder became sculptured marble. The strange attendant creatures, with their fiery eyes and trailing vapors, busied themselves round his head. The body lifted a fraction of an inch from the sand and a bubble of air escaped from the mouth with a wet plop. Then it turned gently in the water.

Somewhere over the darkened curve of the world the sun and moon were pulling, and the film of water on the earth planet was held, bulging slightly on one side while the solid core turned. The great wave of the tide moved farther along the island and the water lifted. Softly, surrounded by a fringe of inquisitive bright creatures, itself a silver shape beneath the steadfast constellations, Simon's dead body moved out toward the open sea.

With his mysterious touch of greatness Simon comes closest to foreshadowing the kind of hero Golding himself has seen as representing man's greatest need if he is to advance in his humanity—the Saint Augustines, Shakespeares, and Mozarts, "inexplicable, miraculous." Piggy, on the other hand, who, just before his own violent death, clutches at a rationalization for Simon's murder, has all the good and bad attributes of the weaker sort of intellectual. Despised by Jack and protected by Ralph, he is set off from the others by his spectacles, asthma, accent, and very fat, short body. Freudian analysts would have Piggy stand as superego, but he is extremely id-directed toward food: it is Ralph who must try to hold him back from accepting Jack's pig meat, and Ralph who acts as strong conscience in making Piggy accept partial responsibility for Simon's death. Although ranked as one the "biguns," Piggy is physically incapable and emotionally immature. The logic of his mind is insufficient to cope with the human problems of their coral-island situation. But this insight into him is fictionally denied to the Ralphs of this world, who (as on the last page of the novel) weep not for Simon, but for "the true, wise friend called Piggy."

How many children originally landed on the island alive we never learn; however, we do know that there were more than the eighteen boys whose names are actually mentioned in the course of the novel. Census matters are not helped by the first signal fire, for it goes out of control and scatters the boys in fright. Ralph, worried about the littluns, accuses Piggy of dereliction of duty in not making a list of names. Piggy is exaggeratedly indignant: "How could I . . . all by myself? They waited for two minutes, then they fell in sea; they went into the forest; they just scattered everywhere. How was I to know which was which?" But only one child known to any of the survivors has clearly disappeared—a small unnamed boy with a mulberry-marked face. This fact lends little credence to Piggy's tale of decimation.

Of those who remain, at least a dozen of whom are littluns, a significant number come alive through Golding's ability to characterize memorably with a few deft lines. Only two have surnames as well as Christian names: Jack Merridew, already mentioned as Ralph's rival, and the littlun Percival Wemys Madison. Jack at first demands to be called, as at school, "Merridew," the surname his mark of superior age and authority. Percival Wemys Madison ("The Vicarage, Harcourt St. Anthony, Hants, telephone, telephone, tele—") clutches vainly at the civilized incantation, learned by rote— in case he should get lost. And he is. His distant past has so completely receded by the end of the novel that he can get no farther in self-identification than "I'm, "I'm—" for he "sought in his head for an incantation that had faded clean away." We learn little more about him, and hardly need to. Here again, in characterization, Golding's straddling the boundary line between allegory and naturalism demonstrates either the paradoxical power of his weakness as novelist or his ability to make the most of his shortcomings.

Whatever the case, Percival Wemys Madison epitomizes the novel and underlines its theme, in his regression to the point of reduced existence. In fact, most of Golding's characters suggest more than themselves, contributing to critical controversy as well as the total significance of the novel. In the years of exegesis since publication of *Lord of the Flies*, critical analysis has been hardening into dogmatic opinion, much of it allegoristic, as evidenced by such titles as "Allegories of Innocence," "Secret Parables," and "The Fables of William Golding." And even where the titles are not indicative (as with E. L. Epstein's Capricorn edition afterword, and the equally Freudian analysis of Claire Rosenfield), critical literature has generally forced the book into a neat allegorical novel. The temptation is strong, since the novel is evocative and the characters seem to beg for placement within handy categories of meaning—political, sociological, religious, and psychological categories. Yet Golding is a simply complicated writer; and, so much the better for the novel as novel, none of the boxes fits precisely.

Oversimplifying, Frederick Karl writes that "When the boys on the island struggle for supremacy, they re-enact a ritual of the adult world, as much as the college Fellows in Snow's *The Masters* work out the ritual of a power struggle in the larger world." Jack may appear to be the demagogic dictator and Roger his sadistic henchman; Ralph may be a confused democrat, with Piggy his "brain trust"; but the neatness of the political allegory is complicated by the clear importance of the mystical, generalization-defying Simon. Although Simon, who alone among the boys has gone up to the mountaintop and discovered the truth, is sacrificed in a subhuman orgy, those who have seen a religious allegory in the novel find it more in the fall of man from paradise, as the island Eden turns into a fiery hell, and the Satanic Jack into the fallen archangel. But Ralph makes only a tenuous Adam; the sow is a sorry Eve; and Piggy, the sightless sage, has no comfortable place in Christian myth. Further, it is an ironic commentary upon religious interpretations of *Lord of the Flies* that of an island full of choirboys, not one ever resorts—even automatically—to prayer or to appeals to a deity, not even before they begin backsliding. And the Edenic quality of the island paradise is compromised from the beginning, for, although the essentials of life are abundant, so are the essentials of pain, terror, and death: the fruit which makes them ill, the animals which awaken their bloodthirstiness and greed, the cruel war in the air above them, the darkness and the unknown which beget their fears.

As a social allegory of human regression the novel is more easily (perhaps too neatly) explainable as "the way in which, when the civilized restraints which we impose on ourselves are abandoned, the passions of anger, lust and fear wash across the mind, obliterating commonsense and care, and life once again becomes nasty, brutish and short." The island itself is shaped like a boat, and takes on symbolic proportions, not simply in the microcosmic-macrocosmic sense, but as subtle foreshadowing of the regression about to take place among the boys: "It was roughly boat-shaped. . . . The tide was running so that long streaks of foam tailed away from the reef and for a moment they felt that the boat was moving steadily astern." This sternward movement not only conjures up the regressive backsliding away from civilization that constitutes the theme of the novel, but is imagistically associated with Piggy's "ass-mar" and the general note of scatology—as with the littluns being "taken short" in the orchard—which prevails in this book on Beelzebub, lord of the flies *and* dung. Later, when Simon asks the assembly to think of the dirtiest thing imaginable, Jack answers with the monosyllable for excrement. This is not what Simon means at all: he is thinking of the evil in man. But the two concepts merge in Golding's imagination—covertly in *Lord of the Flies* and manifestly in *Free Fall*, which is a literary cloaca, full of that revulsion psychologists try to explain in terms of the proximity and ambiguity of the apertures utilized for birth and excreta.

Some critics who see the allegory of evil as just the surface meaning of the novel have been led into psychological labyrinths, where Jack appears as the Freudian id personified; Ralph the ego; and Piggy the superego, conscience of the grown-up world. But William Wasserstrom has dealt severely with Miss Rosenfield in this kind of interpretation; the experts have fallen out; and, besides, the Freudian *ménage à trois* fails to accommodate the vital Simon. Indeed, the problem in all attempts to explain *Lord of the Flies* as some kind of parable is that the novel is not a parable: it is too long, and lacks the point-by-point parallelism necessary to meet the definition. Nor, in the precise sense, is it a fable, since it deals primarily with human beings, since it does not rely upon folkloristic or fantastic materials, and since it does not provide the convenience of an explicit moral. It *is* allegoristic, rich in variant suggestions, and best taken at the level of suggestive analysis.

This novel has been taken, too, as a straight tale of initiation, with Ralph as hero—an interpretation to which the book's ending is particularly susceptible. Yet there is more to it than Ralph's facing a brutal adult world with a lament for his lost childhood and for the innocence he thinks has been stripped from him. What Ralph dimly fathoms, the naval-officer "rescuer" cannot possibly understand—that the world, in the words of Shaw's Saint Joan, is not yet ready to receive its saints, neither its Simons nor even its Piggys and Ralphs. Whether he means it or not Golding provides a hopeful note, for even at mankind's present stage of development Piggy and Ralph, the latter with shame, relapse only slightly toward the barbarism of their contemporaries (and that of the officer, who is engaged in a no less barbaric war "outside"); while Simon withstands the powerful regressive pressures completely. That these three represent three-quarters of the novel's major characters defeats any explanation of the novel in totally pessimistic terms.

Almost endlessly, the four major characters are thematically suggestive, and are usually identified in the book with certain imagery and talismanic objects: Jack with blood and dung, with the mask of primitive tribalism (imagistically he is in league with the Lord of the Flies); Piggy with pigs' meat (his physical sloth and appetite and eventual sacrifice), with his glasses, which represent intellect and science (though they could hardly coax the sun into making fire); Ralph with the conch and signal fire, with comeliness and the call to duty, with communal hope (all shattered when the conch dwindles in power and is finally shattered, and the signal fire dies out). Again, however, it may be Simon—not so thematically suggestive as the others—who provides the best clues to the un-Swiftian side of Golding's intentions, for we recall not only his mysticism, his intelligence, his fragility, but also his association with the bees and butterflies that hover sweetly and innocently (by comparison with the flies) about the island, and the tragic beauty of his transfiguration. Perhaps it is Simon who best suggests Golding's optimism in the face of his apparent allegory of regression. "The human spirit," writes Golding, "is wider and more complex than the whole of the physical evolutionary system. . . . We shall have . . . to conform more and more closely to categories or go under. But the change in politics, in religion, in art, in literature will come, because it *will* come; because the human spirit is limitless and inexhaustible." Just around the corner, he promises, are the Saint Augustines, Shakespeares, and Mozarts: "Perhaps they are growing up now."

What can be said of *Lord of the Flies* eventually is that, in structure and narrative method, it is Golding's simplest novel. It lacks the ironic mystification of *The Inheritors*, which results from the necessity of working through primitive brains making simple and often erroneous "pictures" of situations. It escapes the often cryptic involvement, the sudden wrench of context, that come from the stream of consciousness and recall methods of *Pincher Martin* and *Free Fall*. But it is not an obvious novel, as sometimes claimed. It shares with his other books an ending technique that constitutes a reversal—a sudden shift of viewpoint. Here the timely arrival of the naval officer acts as no concession to readers demanding a happy ending. What we get instead of "gimmick" or conventional *deus ex machina* is a necessary change of focus: the boys, who have grown almost titanic in their struggle, are suddenly seen again as boys, some merely tots, dirty-nosed and bedraggled. And then a retrospective irony results, since the boys deserve to be thought of as titanic: if they have been fighting our battle, we realize—with both hope and dismay—that mankind is still in something of a prepuberty stage. Thus *Lord of the Flies* ends as no act of hope or charity or even contrition. It is an act of recognition. The tone is peculiarly calm: Golding keeps his distance from his materials; he does not interfere or preach; and the material is made to speak for itself through a simplicity of prose style and a naturalistic-allegorical form. The vision of Golding is through both ends of the telescope.

❊ ❊ ❊

Kenneth Burke has said that any novel is but the expansion of a single sentence, perhaps simply the expansion of a single gesture. In the same way, criticism of any writer is but the expansion of a single sentence definition. We place the author within a *genus* and then describe the *differentia*. We may eventually conclude that his work is *sui generis*, but the defining method helps us to this conclusion. Much the same thing is true if we try to place him by tracing his origins and the influences exerted on his work; and any analysis or evaluation of Golding's fiction must revolve around the compound question of originality and derivation, for although Golding has been called the most original English novelist of the last twenty or thirty years, it is becoming increasingly clear that his originality in prose is much like that of T. S. Eliot's in verse. Golding, in fact, stands as a remarkable example of how the individual talent operates within a strong tradition. Tradition (the English novelistic tradition primarily, but with elements derived from American, French, and Classical sources) leaves its mark on his work, but his work leaves its individual mark, and sometimes excoriatingly, on tradition. What has become apparent is that Golding is a literary counterpuncher. Put another way, *he is a reactionary in the most basic sense of the word.* Reacting strongly to certain disagreeable aspects of life and literature as he sees them, he writes with a revolutionary heat that is contained rather than exploded within his compressed style. Restoration rather than preservation is his aim: he would restore concepts of Belief, Free Will, Individual Responsibility, Sin, Forgiveness (or Atonement, anyway), Vision, and Divine Grace. He would restore principles in an unprincipled world; he would restore belief to a world of willful unbelievers.

From the outset of his career, Golding received critical recognition on the basis of his providing something new, something original (most early commentators put it down to his renovation of parable and fable as literary modes of serious expression). One early reaction to his work was that here at last the Home Counties had succeeded in bringing forth a voice capable of contending with the universal wilderness and the everlasting whirlwind. It might not be the voice of a Dostoevsky or Melville or Conrad or Camus, but certainly it was not the voice of still another angry young man. With each successive novel Golding seemed to be marking an end to all that—the novel of manners, the novel of social commentary—and thus to the great tradition as well. It was as though he were pointing at *Howards End* as a literary cul-de-sac.

Aside from his novels, which did their own attesting, Golding himself lent credence to the idea that he was indeed original, something of an experimenter in the making of modern myths. In a Third Programme radio discussion, for example, he expressed a wish to make each book say something different, and in a different way each time:

> It seems to me that there's really very little point in writing a novel unless you do something that either you suspected you couldn't do, or which you are pretty certain nobody else has tried before. I don't think there's any point in writing two books that are like each other. . . .

> I see, or I bring myself to see, a certain set of circumstances
> in a particular way. If it is the way everybody else sees them, then
> there is no point in writing a book.

This self-portrait of Golding as literary experimenter is fairly accurate, but it needs expansion. In this connection, we should remember that he spent his first years at Oxford as a student of science before he switched emphasis to English literature. And there remains in his literary efforts something of the scientific stance—that of a white-coated experimenter working in the isolation of a laboratory, isolating in turn his literary elements on islands, promontories, and rocks, in closets, asylums, and prison camps. But in doing his experiment Golding inevitably has a finger stuck in someone else's lab book, along with a marginal note indicating what is wrong or at least what remains to be done. If we were allowed to expand Golding's statement about himself, we would have to—on the basis of what proves to be his practice—add this presumptuous comment: "I often see what others have been getting at, and disagree strongly. So I conduct counter-experiments with results that state: 'Not that way, but this.'"

All Golding's novels, products of his peculiar literary temperament and habit, are reactive experiments. The wonder is how habitual a process this has been. Piecemeal, several critics have nicely documented certain influences or stimuli affecting his work. Yet important instances have been left undiscovered, overlooked, underestimated. What remains to be said is that this reactive method of composition has become the *modus operandi*. It provides a key as to what Golding has derived from others and what he has provided that is original. Yet Golding has insisted, "But one book never comes out of another, and *The Coral Island* is not *Lord of the Flies*." And, adamantly, that "*one work does not come from another unless it is stillborn.*" Nevertheless, with Golding the process may be, if he has created counter-experiments which are original fiction, not stillbirth but birth.

The process begins with *Lord of the Flies*, and here the critical documentation has been fairly solid. In separate essays Frank Kermode and Carl Niemeyer make it quite apparent that a strong connection exists between Golding's novel and one published almost exactly a century earlier, R. M. Ballantyne's *The Coral Island* (1857). Golding reworks Ballantyne's basic situation, setting, and narrative episodes. Like Ballantyne in each respect, he isolates a group of English boys on a coral island that seems an earthly paradise, with a plentitude of fruit and coconuts. He introduces pig killings, cannibalistic tendencies, and the question of ghosts. He names three of his major characters Jack, Ralph, and Piggy in honor of Ballantyne's Jack, Ralph, and Peterkin Gay (the last might just as well be called Piggy, because in one instance, when he is off hunting pigs, Jack alludes to him with the phrase "When Greek meets Greek," the implication being, of course, when pig meets pig).

If Golding works closely to Ballantyne's outline, it is mainly to show by contrast to his own findings how inane the nineteenth-century experiment in youthful isolation was. Eventually the contrast shows through strongly. While Ballantyne's characters, for instance, are stout English lads who overcome evil introduced into their worldly paradise by natives and pirates, Golding's characters find evil within themselves and almost go under, until finally extricated by a *deus ex machina*. The officer who is the long arm of that godly machine underscores the difference between Golding's novel and Ballantyne's when he says with Old Boy naïveté: "Jolly good show. Like the Coral Island." Ralph looks at the officer dumbly, uncomprehendingly, and his look measures the distance between generations as well as the distance between the fictional visions of 1857 and 1954.

Knowing about Ballantyne's contribution to *Lord of the Flies* makes for a fuller and richer reading of the novel than might otherwise be obtained. To see how hollow a reading can result when the necessary connection is not made, one need simply read the French version, in which the English naval officer is made to speak for the benefit of an uninitiated audience: "L'officier l'encouragea du menton.—Oui, je comprends. La belle aventure. Les Robinsons . . ." *The Swiss Family Robinson* (and even *Robinson Crusoe*, if it is intended in the pluralization) will not do. (See *Sa Majesté des Mouches*, translated by Lola Tranec, Gallimard, Paris, 1956.) In ironic contrast to *Lord of the Flies*, Golding has written of *The Swiss Family Robinson*, "This is how children live when they are happy. . . . The days are endless and time has no meaning. . . . In the text, as ever, the children take a child's place. There is simply no possibility of juvenile delinquency. The [parental] guiding hand is gentle but adamant. . . ."

As Kermode perceptively declares, the related books of Ballantyne and Golding can be used as documents in the history of ideas, Ballantyne's contribution belonging "inseparably to the period when boys were sent out of Arnoldian schools certified free of Original Sin," ready to keep the Empire shipshape. Golding writes with a vivid sense of paradox, with the eyes of someone who has seen the Empire crumble and witnessed twentieth-century manifestations of Original Sin.

Although it has gone unnoticed or unmentioned in comparisons of Golding and Ballantyne, both authors use similar conclusions involving the technical assistance of the *deus ex machina*. Jack, Ralph, and Peterkin are in the clutches of savages near the conclusion of *Coral Island*; they believe they will never more see home, and await death, only to find their bonds severed, and themselves set free. A "teacher," who stands in the place of the naval officer in *Lord of the Flies*, acquaints them with the miraculous fact that their captor, chief Tararo, "has embraced the Christian religion." This is no less a miracle in its way than the appearance of the naval officer who arrives just in the nick of time to save Golding's Ralph. Religion also appears in *Lord of the Flies* in truncated form: as already mentioned, some of the boys are choir members, but no prayer is ever heard. Religion enters only by way of hindsight and moralistic impingement from the outside, as the reader considers a hidden theme. In *The Coral Island*, as we can see by the quite Christian ending, it plays a central, well-advertised part. Not only are Ballantyne's youths invincible Britons, as they often call themselves, but they have faith, in the usual sense of the word. The Ralph of that group could be speaking for them all when under difficult pressures he remembers his mother's parting homily: "Ralph, my dearest child, always remember in the hour of danger to look to your Lord and Saviour Jesus Christ. He alone is both able and willing to save your body and soul." This is exactly what Golding's children do not do. Golding made clear why in an interview in which he explained his approach to the efficacy of *Coral Island* morality:

> What I'm saying to myself is "don't be such a fool, you remember when you were a boy, a small boy, how you lived on that island with Ralph and Jack and Peterkin." . . . I said to myself finally, "Now you are grown up, you are adult; it's taken you a long time to become adult, but now you've got there you can see that people are not like that." There savagery would not be found in natives on an island. As like as not they would find savages who were kindly and uncomplicated and that the devil would rise out of the intellectual complications of the three white men in the island itself.

Although Golding does not provide easy answers to all the questions he raises in *Lord of the Flies*, it is clear that his religious answer is not Ballantyne's. The real savior in *Lord of the Flies* is not the naval officer, but Simon— and his voice goes unheeded, as once again the crucifixion takes place, this time without redemption or resurrection.

ROBERT C. GORDON

# *Classical Themes in* Lord of the Flies

M̲r. Robert White's article, "Butterfly and Beast in *Lord of the Flies*" is a fascinating revelation of Golding's fresh and original use of classical themes. My comments, based upon my own interest in Golding's use of Homeric and Euripidean elements, are intended to amplify Mr. White's observations and, in just one instance, question what strikes me as a misjudgment of Golding's ending.

If, as T. S. Eliot has suggested, bad writers borrow and good ones steal, Golding is a most versatile thief, and Homer is one of his chief victims. There are times when Golding introduces Homeric imagery almost directly, although this is not his usual practice. An example is the use of the conch, already seen by Peter Green as Homeric. It is Golding's adaptation of the sceptre given to each speaker in turn in Book Two of the *Odyssey* and in Books Two and Eighteen of the *Iliad*. With Golding as with Homer it is a symbol of social order, in both cases of a simple parliamentary type.

Another Homeric image is that of the dead airman. Golding refers to him as a "parody," and once we see him as such the caricature of Zeus becomes clear. Like Zeus he occupies the mountain top, overlooking human conflicts, has a characteristic nodding or bowing gesture, is feared and worshipped, and comes to his seat after a war in "heaven." And if Zeus is really Man, deified and enthroned on Olympus, this possibility, it seems to

From *Modern Fiction Studies* 11:4 (Winter 1965–1966). © 1966 by the Purdue Research Foundation.

me, would add resonance to Mr. White's remark that the corrupt and fallen nature of the airman "emphasizes once again that the object of the boys' dread is, in fact, a dark side of themselves."

Other images and episodes in *Lord of the Flies* suggest characteristic activities of the Homeric warriors, again with a decadent turn. The ritualization of eating in the Homeric combination of feast and sacrifice (a good example is the slaughter of the heifer in Book Three of the *Odyssey*), has its parallels in the killing of the pig by Jack's hunters. There is a degree of ceremony in the slitting of the throat and the offering to the god, although the gratuitously violent and obscene details of the killing process itself make the Homeric episode gracious by comparison. Again, while we may discern in the boys' social arrangements a reflection of the hierarchical structure set forth in Plato's *Republic*, the relationship between Ralph and Jack may also be seen as a grotesque miniature of the Agamemnon-Achilles dispute. The similarities here are arresting. Jack is a callow, brutish diminution of Achilles. He suffers from wounded pride—a feeling that Ralph and others have not sufficiently appreciated his special *arête* of the hunter. His denunciation of Ralph stresses his inactivity and resembles Achilles' denunciation of Agamemnon for living off the efforts of others. And when he finally cuts himself off from the common enterprise symbolized by the conch, Jack's words are a strange, whimpering reminder of Achilles' more lordly *non serviam*: "I'm not going to play any longer. Not with you."

But if certain passages in *Lord of the Flies* suggest Homer, there are still more that suggest Euripides. Some of them are of incidental importance, such as the primitive yells and chants that accompany hunting and fighting. The chant of the vengeful Electra in *Orestes*:

> *Murder!*
> *Butcher!*
> *Kill!*
> Thrust your twin swords home!
> Slash, now slash again!

foreshadows the brutish, imperative yell of Jack's pig-hunters: "Kill the beast! Cut his throat! Spill his blood! Do him in!" Likewise, the Dolon of Euripides' *Rhesus* uses a wolf mask as a disguise and perhaps as a psychological stimulant to his killer instincts: "I shall put a wolfskin upon my back, fitted so that the grinning jaws of the beast are on my head, then, with the forepaws on my hands and the hind feet upon my legs, shall imitate the four-foot tread of the wolf." The disguise establishes a link between warfare and predatory stalking that Jack indicates when he smears his face with clay: "For hunting. Like in the war. You know—dazzle paint."

The true Euripidean note, however, is to be heard, not in such incidental details as these, but in the triumph of unreasoned violence over traditional restraints. Golding's work suggests Euripides because both writers often turn figures associated by tradition with a degree of dignity into creatures wayward and dangerous. Golding's Homeric and classical images are broken and decayed, and his good British boys turn into brutes; similarly Euripides' ancient heroes become thuggish degenerates. For example, Aeschylus' Orestes is violent as he undertakes to avenge his father's death, but he seems a not surprising link in a chain of events others had begun to forge. Euripides' Orestes, however, is violent beyond any conceivable need—gratuitously destructive as he stands among the torches in readiness to butcher Hermione, the innocent daughter of Helen, and burn the palace. And Euripides' treatment of Orestes is matched by his treatment of other traditional figures—Electra, Medea, Heracles, and the gods themselves.

Moreover, the ending of *Orestes* throws light on one of Golding's characteristic, and most controversial, devices—the "gimmick" ending, and here I differ from Mr. White. "The conclusion of *Lord of the Flies*," he writes, "can hardly be dismissed as the use of *deus ex machina*." The naval officer reveals that the "thing which in the embryonic society of the boys we find shocking has been quietly incorporated into our modern society as convention and custom. Any attempt to rid society of evil is clearly impossible." Very true, but the ending is satisfying to the imagination precisely because it most certainly *is* a Euripidean *deus ex machina* drafted into the service of Golding's theme in order to achieve just such ironies as these. *Orestes* provides the prototype. In this play Euripides brings his hero's career of violence to such a point that only butchery can follow; then Apollo enters and makes all right again in one of the most flatly unprepared for uses of *deus ex machina* in the history of the drama. He blandly predicts Orestes' acquittal of his crimes and his eventual marriage to Hermione—"the girl against whose throat your sword now lies." The gasping spectator can only wonder what sort of domestic joy lies ahead for Orestes and his *fiancée*. And our confidence in the god is given little encouragement by his grinning admission concerning Orestes' butcheries: "I compelled him to kill." The rhythm of our responses to such a conclusion is strikingly similar to that of our reactions to Golding's ending when Ralph, driven to the beach of the blazing island and expecting death momentarily, encounters the naval officer. First, relief, almost glandular in its inevitability, then incredulity and suspicion of the author, and finally doubt about the ultimate moral position of the rescuer. The civic Apollo (of all the gods!) proclaims himself the divine agency of death; likewise the British cruiser and the officer are both agents of rescue and reminders that the horrors of the island would not have happened without

the blood lust of the adults. And again, just as we question the future relationship between Orestes and Hermione, so we cannot help wondering how
the boys will reestablish their comradeship.

Apollo's speech at the end of *Orestes* lends relevance to Electra's question in another context: "Where Apollo is ignorant shall men be wise?" The
gods of Euripides' darker plays are ignorant in that they resemble basically
amoral natural forces. As agents of *order* they do not function. Thus
Beelzebub, whom we are justifiably inclined to interpret in Judaeo-Christian
terms, can also be thought of as an image of those wayward and violent
currents in man and nature that Euripides represents in the degeneracy of his
heroes and the moral ambiguity of his gods. In the words of H. D. F. Kitto,
"The servant of Hippolytus . . . thinks what Jason and the chorus think, that
'Gods should be wiser than men.' Perhaps so, but these gods are not. They
exist; as well deny the weather as deny Aphrodite; but they are not reasonable and can make short work of us."

In such a situation Ralph and Piggy, clutching the conch, know the
feeling of back-to-the-wall desperation expressed by Euripides' Tyndareus:

> . . . the law
> that is my concern. There I take my stand,
> defending it with all my heart and strength
> against the brutal and inhuman spirit of murder
> that corrupts our cities and destroys this country.

Golding's adaptation of *deus ex machina* makes it brilliantly clear that
Ralph's rescue will lead him back to a world where law is similarly at bay.
Dionysus the destroyer is king, having deposed Zeus and suborned Apollo
himself.

MARK KINKEAD-WEEKES AND IAN GREGOR

# Lord of the Flies

*Lord of the Flies* has become a compulsory stop on the route of any surveyor of the English novel since the war, an addition to the canon of writings prescribed by school examination boards, the occasion of a volume of critical essays published in the U.S.A., and an award-winning film. Such popular success has eluded the four novels which followed. They have received wide and sometimes generous notice, but it is the earlier work that has guaranteed them their respect. They have achieved virtue by association. Yet Golding's novels are unmistakably all of a piece. Among themselves they reveal a family resemblance, a unity even, that gives the phrase 'a Golding novel' a readily understood meaning. Why does the first occupy so unique a position?

What distinguishes *Lord of the Flies* is its powerful and exciting qualities as narrative, and its appearance of extreme clarity of meaning; the later works are more difficult both to read and to understand. *Lord of the Flies* fulfils most effectively the novelist's basic task of telling a good story. It also meets Conrad's prescription: 'by the power of the written word to make you hear, to make you feel . . . before all, to make you *see*'. It was not surprising that it should have attracted the attention of the film director, providing him with an unwavering narrative drive, and also with an unbroken series of intensely visualized scenes. On the other hand, at every point and with a kind of inevitability that is as impressive as the story itself, we are made aware that

From *William Golding, A Critical Study.* © 1967, 1984 by Mark Kinkead-Weekes and Ian McGregor.

much more than this story is being told; indeed a clearly focused and coherent body of meaning appears to be crystallizing out of every episode. A reader can feel that he possesses this novel in an unusually comprehensive way, and that he could give a lucid, even conceptual account of it. The book has high polish, and seems to present itself for our contemplation as a remarkably complete and solid structure. This of course may not always be regarded as a strength. Many readers may feel the book to be too crystalline, too insistent, too manipulated to be acceptable, but it seems likely that it is this combination of narrative momentum and thematic clarity that explains the popular success, which greater Golding novels have failed to achieve. Whether the art *is* so clear and crystalline, however, is perhaps open to question.

Let us consider the finding of the shell, which provides the title for the opening chapter. We watch the conch, we might say, liberated from ordinariness, grasped, filled with meaning:

> '"What's that?"
>
> 'Ralph had stopped smiling and was pointing into the lagoon. Something creamy lay among the ferny weeds.
>
> '"A stone."
>
> '"No. A shell."
>
> 'Suddenly Piggy was a-bubble with decorous excitement.
>
> '"S'right. It's a shell! I seen one like that before. On someone's back wall. A conch he called it. He used to blow it and then his mum would come. It's ever so valuable—"
>
> 'Near to Ralph's elbow, a palm sapling leaned out over the lagoon. Indeed, the weight was already pulling a lump from the poor soil and soon it would fall. He tore out the stem and began to poke about in the water, while the brilliant fish flicked away on this side and that. Piggy leaned dangerously.
>
> '"Careful! You'll break it—"
>
> '"Shut up."
>
> 'Ralph spoke absently. The shell was interesting and pretty and a worthy plaything: but the vivid phantoms of his day-dream still interposed between him and Piggy, who in this context was an irrelevance. The palm sapling, bending, pushed the shell across the weeds. Ralph used one hand as a fulcrum and pressed down with the other till the shell rose, dripping, and Piggy could make a grab.
>
> 'Now the shell was no longer a thing seen but not to be touched, Ralph too became excited. Piggy babbled:

'"—a conch; ever so expensive. I bet if you wanted to buy one, you'd have to pay pounds and pounds and pounds—he had it on his garden wall and my auntie—"

'Ralph took the shell from Piggy and a little water ran down his arm. In colour the shell was deep cream, touched here and there with fading pink. Between the point, worn away into a little hole, and the pink lips of the mouth, lay eighteen inches of shell with a slight spiral twist and covered with a delicate, embossed pattern. Ralph shook sand out of the deep tube.

'"—moo-ed like a cow," he said. "He had some white stones too, an' a bird cage with a green parrot. He didn't blow the white stones of course, an' he said—"

'Piggy paused for breath and stroked the glistening thing that lay in Ralph's hands.

'"Ralph!"

'Ralph looked up.

'"We can use this to call the others. Have a meeting. They'll come when they hear us—"

'He beamed at Ralph.

'"That was what you meant, didn't you? That's why you got the conch out of the water?"

'Ralph pushed back his fair hair.

'"How did your friend blow the conch?"

'"He kind of spat," said Piggy. "My auntie wouldn't let me blow on account of my asthma. He said you blew from down here." Piggy laid a hand on his jutting abdomen. "You try, Ralph. You'll call the others."

'Doubtfully, Ralph laid the small end of the shell against his mouth and blew. There came a rushing sound from its mouth but nothing more. Ralph wiped the salt water off his lips and tried again, but the shell remained silent.

'"He kind of spat."

'Ralph pursed his lips and squirted air into the shell, which emitted a low, farting noise. This amused both boys so much that Ralph went on squirting for some minutes, between bouts of laughter.

'"He blew from down here."

'Ralph grasped the idea and hit the shell with air from his diaphragm. Immediately the thing sounded. A deep, harsh note boomed under the palms, spread through the intricacies of the forest and echoed back from the pink granite of the mountain.

Clouds of birds rose from the treetops, and something squealed
and ran in the undergrowth.
'Ralph took the shell away from his lips.
'"Gosh!"'

The whole rhythm of this seems one of transformation—the unliving
thing is disentangled and given a new social purpose. It announces man and
summons men together, this 'Sound of the Shell'. As the novel proceeds this
meaning becomes more and more sharply defined. 'We can use this to call
the others. Have a meeting . . .' It is his association with the shell rather than
his size or attractiveness that makes the children choose Ralph as their
leader; and having been established as the symbol of assembly, the conch
becomes identified with its procedure, with democracy and the right to free
speech. It becomes a symbol of immense suggestiveness. Every time a boy
cries 'I've got the conch', he is drawing on the funds of order and democratic
security. We take the point when Jack blows it 'inexpertly', and when he lays
it at his feet in rejection. The conch helps both to trace the trajectory of plot,
and to establish character. Nowhere does Piggy's role seem more economi-
cally and poignantly expressed than when he prepares to confront the Tribe
and its Chief with 'the one thing he hasn't got'. Then the conch in Piggy's
hands becomes no less than the basic challenge to the Tribe to choose
between democracy and anarchy, civilization and savagery. The answer
comes in unequivocal terms: 'The rock struck Piggy a glancing blow from
chin to knee; the conch exploded into a thousand white fragments and ceased
to exist.' The shell, whose sound began as a summons to society, ends as a
murderous explosion on the rocks. It traces out for us the swift tragic
progress of the tale, and condenses its meaning—or so it seems.

But will this kind of reading satisfy, when we stop talking about the
book from a distance and really look at the texture of the writing and the kind
of experience it proffers? What will strike us most immediately is surely that
the episode is far too long and circumstantial for any purely symbolic
purpose. When we investigate the nature of that circumstantiality, what it
reveals is Golding's concern to hold back rather than enourage the concep-
tualizing or interpretative intelligence. The counterpointing of the two boys
shows this very clearly.

It is Piggy who is first excited by the shell, but only as a curio. It is
Ralph's consciousness we live in, and he hardly listens to Piggy. Not one of
the fat boy's sentences is heard to a conclusion. What is important about
Ralph's 'day-dream', moreover, is that intelligence and social memory are
laid asleep, while the physical senses, alone, remain sharply aware. Hence the
description of fulcrum and lever, weight and resistance; the interest in how

the shell is physically disentangled from the weeds. In fact the 'civilizing' intelligence is kept at bay while the actual conch in its strangeness and beauty is made real to the senses. Suddenly Piggy's babble stops, while he too strokes 'the glistening thing that lay in Ralph's hands', wet, reflecting light, strangely beautiful.

The second half of the scene elaborates the contrast. Now Piggy invents the idea of the meeting, giving the shell a social purpose; but again the life of the passage comes from Ralph, and he is only interested, as any schoolboy would be, in finding out how to blow it. Again Piggy moves into unison, the shell is primarily an object of play for both of them, and the simple vulgarity of the farting noises fills them with equal delight. The imagination at work is profoundly physical, and what it seizes is, precisely, the *sound* of the shell. It is made real to us in its context of salt water, brilliant fish, green weed; then in its own strange cream and rose spiral, embossed by an art other than the human; finally in the harsh otherness of the noise which shatters the peace of the island and terrifies bird and beast.

Physical realities come first for Golding and should stay first for his readers. Other meanings are found in and through them, as the man-breath passes through the shell's spiral to emerge as signal. But we must not translate the shell into the signal. What comes out is far from simple; and the human beings will be as taken aback as the animals and for the same reason. If we really look and listen, what we shall see and hear will be the harshness of human self-assertion as well as the signal of human sociability; will be the sound of irresponsibility and childishness as well as of forethought and intelligence; will be the fragility of order as well as the impulse towards it. As the sound penetrates the densest thickets, while clouds of birds fly and 'something squealed and ran in the undergrowth', man-sound prefigures stuck pig and stuck Ralph squealing and running for their life, as well as the assembly and the rules. Golding's symbols are not in fact clear, or wholly articulate, they are always an incarnation of more than can be extracted or translated from them. Even at this early stage, when the fiction seems to offer itself so alluringly for conceptual analysis, it is always richer and more profound than the thesis we may be tempted to substitute for the experience.

It is not a question of rejecting such meanings, so much as developing a delicacy and tact in handling them; a sense of how limited they are in themselves and how far they fall short of accounting for the density of the fiction. We need similar tact with the characters. Even from the finding of the shell, for example, it is easy to see how one could extend Piggy's point of view until he came to stand for something like 'rational humanism'; and many of his physical deficiencies might seem to express Golding's critique of the humanist. We certainly cannot see him as simply a fat boy. Yet he is much more complex than such a formulation could account for, and often inconsistent with it; we would have to mutilate Golding's boy to fit him to so Procrustean a bed. If we respond to what is on the page we shall find in the novel less the pummelling of humanism than the growth in stature, incredibly boyish terms, of the 'true wise friend' who on the last page is almost the tragic hero. Like the other characters Piggy does embody meaning of various kinds, so that we become aware through our imaginative response to the boy of wider horizons and deeper problems beyond him. On the other hand, he is too diminutive to support an acceptable representative significance, just as Jack cannot be Satan or the Power Urge, though he may reveal truths about both to us, and Simon is both less and more than the Saint. Indeed, if we became less eager to confine Golding's creations to a crystalline structure of meaning, we might be rather less worried about the ability of the island and the boys to sustain the weight of a full statement about 'the human condition'. We ought to admit more readily the limitations of the insight Golding can legitimately embody in so select a situation, while at the same time pointing to the fact that his fiction is far richer and more ambiguous, even in *Lord of the Flies*, than it looks. Both too much and too little has been claimed for Golding's first novel. That is why it is often so difficult to be fair to it.

Finally, and on the deepest level, it is now possible to see that there is a sharp irony in the temptation to translate the fiction into an unambiguous emblem: this does worse than simplify, it subverts. It is exactly the tendency to convert and reduce complexity into simplicity which Golding sees as the root of evil. This was not perhaps easy to see when the novel appeared, though it was always there, and there is no missing it now. For in novel after novel Golding has attacked on the same front: the way that 'homo sapiens' makes Neanderthal man the image of his own evil; the way that Christopher Martin and Sammy Mountjoy recreate real people into the shapes of their own need and lust; the set of emblems that must be cleared from Jocelin's mind at the moment of death and replaced by the vivid and complex physical truth of the Spire itself. For Golding, the Evil Tree grows in the human brain, in human consciousness, and emblematic and conceptual reduction are dangerous manifestations of the Fall. So, in *Lord of the Flies*, it is the way in which the children look for an external manifestation of what is really in themselves that releases the sin of Cain. Evil exists, but not as a Beast. There is an analogous truth about the conch. What the Sound of the Shell really is . . . is a sound. Like the whole island, the shell is a unique, physical existence whose being is its meaning. Yet it can reveal man, as the shell shows forth all the implications for good or evil of the human breath that resounds through it. Only it is fatal to forget, as the children and many readers do, that the meaning is in the boys, not the shell. The conch's symbolic meaning depends on the state of the children's minds. Once power becomes more real to Jack than the rules, the conch is meaningless; but when he raids the camp for fire, Piggy thinks he has come for the shell. Though Piggy reaches his greatest stature at the moment of his death, it is also the moment of his greatest blindness, rendered for us at a level far deeper than his lost spectacles. For he holds out as a magic talisman what is, literally, an empty shell. It had a more inclusive sound, and if the boys had been able to understand that sound fully instead of reducing its complexities there would have been no tragedy.

## II

The island gives the children freedom to reveal themselves. We listen with increasing attention to what it is that the Sound of the Shell announces about these human beings. Golding re-occupies R. M. Ballantyne's *Coral Island* and declares its portrayal of those idealized British boys, Jack, Ralph and Peterkin in their tropical paradise, to be a fake, since boys are human beings, and human beings are not like that. Or, rather, he does not 'declare', he shows the falsehood by producing an island and boys that are more convincing than Ballantyne's, and then gradually revealing what the difference implies. The structure and technique of *Lord of the Flies* is one of revelation.

At the beginning the most obvious element of the Shell, its strangeness, its glamour, its beauty, parallels the first reponse to the island itself. Disaster has brought the children there: an atomic explosion, an evacuation by air via Gibraltar and Addis Ababa. Their aircraft has been attacked, probably over the Sunda Sea, and has released its detachable passenger tube to crash-land in the jungle of a convenient island while the plane itself flies off in flames. There is a great storm, the jungle is loud with crashing trees, and the tube, with some children still in it, is dragged out to sea by wind and wave, while the rest scatter into the thickets. It is a terrible experience; but it is not one we share. Indeed, that story has to be pieced together from scattered hints in the boys' conversation. For, once they have slept an exhausted sleep well into the day, the experience has left virtually no scars on their consciousness, though they may have nightmares later. What Ralph is conscious of, and what occupies our delighted attention too, is the *Coral Island* glamour, the unspoilt beauty and excitement of trees, rock and beach. The fact that there are no grown-ups is primarily 'the delight of a realized ambition'. And as Ralph takes in the marvels of the island: the strange green shadows crawling over his body under the coconut palms, the surf breaking on the coral reef across the peacock-blue lagoon, the incredible beach-pool with its ready-made diving ledge, 'here at last was the imagined but never fully realized place leaping into real life'; the perennial boys' dream of which the worlds of

*Coral Island* and *Treasure Island*, and the lake islands of *Swallows and Amazons*, are only shadows.

The first chapter resounds with 'the deep bass strings of delight'. The children gather to the casual summons of the Conch, they elect their leader, draw up laws, divide out function and prerogative; but we ought to be sharply aware of the inappropriateness of this kind of terminology. It is a wonderful game played under perfect conditions in perfect surroundings; and though it acts out memories of grown-up order, it can go on all day with no interference from grown-ups. There are the tensions that there are bound to be in any game, between Ralph and Jack and Piggy, but they are containable because the game is large and splendid enough to have acceptable parts for everyone.

There is not only 'government' but 'exploration'. A specific reminiscence of *Coral Island* occurs as Ralph and Jack, talking over the top of Simon's head, set off to explore their domain, and the aura of glamour is strong.

> 'They turned to each other, laughing excitedly, talking, not listening. The air was bright. Ralph, faced by the task of translating all this into an explanation, stood on his head and fell over.'

There is also something of the fairy-tale: 'The coral was scribbled in the sea as though a giant had bent down to reproduce the shape of the island in a flowing chalk line . . .', but, best of all, there is no giant, no ogre, it all belongs to them.

The 'glamour' is set, however, as it was not in *Coral Island*, against a real jungle, dense, damply hot, scratching. This is not a stroll through a nineteenth-century English wood with different trees. Demonstrably, discomfort and joy authenticate each other:

> 'Here, the roots and stems of creepers were in such tangles that the boys had to thread through them like pliant needles. Their only guide, apart from the brown ground and occasional flashes of light through the foliage, was the tendency of slope: whether this hole, laced as it was with cables of creeper, stood higher than that.
> 
> 'Somehow, they moved up.
> 
> 'Immured in these tangles, at perhaps their most difficult moment, Ralph turned with shining eyes to the others.
> 
> '"Wacco."
> 
> '"Wizard."
> 
> '"Smashing."'

'The cause of their pleasure was not obvious. All three were hot, dirty and exhausted. Ralph was badly scratched. The creepers were as thick as their thighs and left little but tunnels for further penetration. Ralph shouted experimentally and they listened to the muted echoes.

'"This is real exploring," said Jack. "I bet nobody's been here before."'

It is the same with the rock-rolling, which is a specific comment on the scene in *Coral Island* where the boys are taken aback as a huge rock thunders down the mountain side. We are convinced that boys, faced by poised rocks like this, would behave as Golding's do, and there is a realistic sense of mass and force. The boyish argot and happy wrestling, the sweat and dirt and scratches, the shining eyes, all act with one another to make a world that is both solid and boyishly glamorous.

On the other hand, the darker elements we heard in the Sound of the Shell are not forgotten, though they are for the moment submerged. When we look more closely, we can see that the glamour is shot through with more sinister suggestions. Mirages are created for us as one of the physical realities of the South Seas; but we can never be unaware of the deceptiveness of appearances afterwards. The marching choir, and the way Jack treats it, recalls an army world of authority, arrogance and callousness, rather than the holy singing their uniform suggests. Jack's angry blue eyes and his habit of driving his sheath-knife into a tree-trunk hint at a capacity for dangerous violence. Hidden in the games there might also be an irresponsibility which has wider reverberations. When Ralph 'machine-guns' Piggy, or the 'enraged monster' of a rock crashes down 'like a bomb', we are perhaps primarily aware of a kind of 'innocence'. This is obvious in the episode of the piglet, where even Jack cannot kill 'because of the enormity of the knife descending and cutting into living flesh; because of the unbearable blood'. Gun and bomb are only a game, or a schoolboy phrase. But as soon as we replace game and cliché within the context of the situation that brought the children to the island, we may feel less assured; there is certainly blindness, perhaps something worse. The glamour of the 'natural' is also ambiguous. On the one hand there is pleasure in ripping off the clothes that speak of discipline and regimentation at school, the pleasure of nakedness in sun and water. On the other, it needs only a little of Piggy's 'ill-omened talk' about the realities of the situation to make a school shirt 'strangely pleasing' to put on again.

It is however worth pointing out that Golding in his opening chapter is seeking to re-imagine the Coral Island more truly. To imagine fully is, for him, to reveal indications like this existing naturally within the glamour; they are not simply put in like signposts pointing out a fore-ordained road. In retrospect, Ralph's standing on his head can be seen as a warning signal, but it is doubtful if any reader has ever taken it as other than a lifelike movement of joy at the time. It is perfectly ambiguous; that is its success. The diarrhoea might seem to invite allegorical translation—the body of man is no longer fit for Eden—but it is, no less, a realistic comment on the effects of eating nothing but fruit. The snake-clasp speaks of Eden too, but, more than any other detail, it is also eloquent of British schoolboy uniform.

In the first chapter, then, the Coral island glamour is the dominant note in the Sound of the Shell, but there are one or two more sinister undertones if we really listen. The second chapter reverses the over- and undertones of the same concert. Glamour and game are still strongly present in the second Assembly, as rules are made up and Ralph's simple confidence in rescue outweighs Piggy's fear.

> "'This is our island. It's a good island. Until the grown-ups come to fetch us we'll have fun."
> 'Jack held out his hand for the conch.
> "'There's pigs," he said. "There's food; bathing water in that little stream along there—and everything."'

But 'everything' means more than glamour. When the idea of making a fire as a rescue signal takes hold, the coral island element of fun and adventure is still high, and one notices particularly what a sense of community it gives the boys. In this there is irony for the future.

> 'Ralph found himself alone on a limb with Jack and they grinned at each other, sharing this burden. Once more, amid the breeze, the shouting, the slanting sunlight on the high mountain, was shed that glamour, that strange invisible light of friendship, adventure, and content.
> "'Almost too heavy."
> 'Jack grinned back.
> "'Not for the two of us."'

But very soon the harsher sound of the Shell drowns the delight. It is clear that the making of rules may have as much to do with the desire to inflict punishment as the desire for order, for that, too, figures large in boyish games. The profound difference between the second assembly and the first is that the dark side of boys' psychology unmistakably makes its presence felt.

The 'littlun' with the strawberry mark, describing his terrifying night-time vision of a 'snake-thing' or 'beastie', is voicing that part of the child's psyche that is beset with terror of the unknown in himself or his environment. That this is widespread among the children is shown by the intent eyes which fail to respond to Ralphs's reassurances, and by the unexpectedly passionate reaction to his promise of rescue. There is nightmare as well as delight on this island. And finally, with the lighting of the fire, the note of irresponsibility in the Sound of the Shell reaches its full resonance.

We may feel impatient with Piggy's premature middle age: 'I bet it's gone tea-time. . . . What do they think they're going to do on that mountain'; and with the 'martyred expression of a parent who has to keep up with the senseless ebullience of the children'. But if we do, we soon learn the implications of acting 'like a crowd of kids'. We are made aware that innocence which consists largely of ignorance and irresponsibility may be far from harmless. Jack's arrogant chauvinism may find it easy to contrast English boys with savages, as Ballantyne complacently does. But as the fire spreads into the jungle because nobody looks further than keeping 'a clean flag of flame flying', we get a deeper insight.

> 'Small flames stirred at the bole of a tree and crawled away through leaves and brushwood, dividing and increasing. One patch touched a tree trunk and scrambled up like a bright squirrel. . . . The squirrel leapt on the wings of the wind and clung to another standing tree, eating downwards. Beneath the dark canopy of leaves and smoke the fire laid hold on the forest and began to gnaw. . . . The flames, as though they were a kind of wild life, crept as a jaguar creeps on his belly. . . . They flapped at the first of the trees, and the branches grew a brief foliage of fire. The heart of flame leapt nimbly across the gap between the trees and then went swinging and flaring along the whole row of them. Beneath the capering boys a quarter of a mile square of forest was savage with smoke and flame. The separate noises of the fire merged into a drum-roll that seemed to shake the mountain. . . . Startled, Ralph realized that the boys were falling still and silent, feeling the beginnings of awe at the power set free below them. The knowledge and the awe made him savage . . .'

Irresponsibility and ignorance liberate a power that is more and more 'savage', the 'squirrel' turns into a 'jaguar', and that power appeals to something 'savage' in the boys themselves. There were good reasons for bird and beast to be terrified by the harsh sound of the conch as it 'spread through the intricacies of the forest'. And not only bird and beast:

> "'That little 'un—' gasped Piggy—'him with the mark on his face, I don't see him. Where is he now?"
>
> 'The crowd was as silent as death.
>
> "'Him that talked about the snakes. He was down there—"
>
> 'A tree exploded in the fire like a bomb. Tall swathes of creepers rose for a moment into view, agonized, and went down again. The little boys screamed at them.
>
> "'Snakes! Snakes! Look at the snakes!'"

'Like a bomb' isn't such a cliché now, nor is 'silent as death'. And if it is rather over-emphatic for Piggy to look 'into hell', since there is no real evil here, nevertheless we could say that if this was Eden, it has been destroyed; and there has been a 'snake-thing' manifest, not the creepers, but the children's own irresponsibility. The 'drum-roll' of the fire will remind us not only of savage tomtoms, but of the ceremony of execution. What the Sound of the Shell announced was also the coming of Death into the Garden.

As the second chapter focuses on the irresponsibility that had lurked largely undetected in the first, the third proceeds to explore the differences between the boys, present obliquely in the first expedition to the mountain:

> 'Here they paused and examined the bushes round them curiously.
>
> Simon spoke first.
>
> "'Like candles. Candle bushes. Candle buds."
>
> 'The bushes were dark evergreen and aromatic and the many buds were waxen green and folded up against the light. Jack slashed at one with his knife and the scent spilled over them.
>
> "'Candle buds."
>
> "'You couldn't light them," said Ralph, "They just look like candles."
>
> "'Green candles," said Jack contemptuously, "we can't eat them. Come on.'"

Now however we begin to see below mere difference to division and antagonism. Ralph is trying desperately not only to build shelters, but a sense of 'home'; his instincts are to domesticate, to ward off terror by social community, to civilize, to provide against the littluns' nightmares the security of 'home'. Jack on the other hand rediscovers in himself the instincts and compulsions of the hunter that lie buried in every man. On all fours like an animal, he learns to flare his nostrils and assess the air, to cast across the ground for spoor. But the rediscovery is deeper than that, deeper even than 'the compulsion to track down and kill that was swallowing him up'. It is another dimension of awareness:

> 'The silence of the forest was more oppressive than the heat, and at this hour of the day there was not even the whine of insects. Only when Jack himself roused a gaudy bird from a primitive nest of sticks was the silence shattered and echoes set ringing by a harsh cry that seemed to come out of the abyss of ages. Jack himself shrank at this cry with a hiss of indrawn breath; and for a minute became less a hunter than a furtive thing, ape-like among the tangle of trees.'

In the very first paragraph of the book a bird had 'flashed upwards with a witch-like cry'. For Jack, as for human imaginations in all ages, the forest becomes not only a place to hunt in but also a place where one sometimes feels hunted; a place where the human being momentarily locates his intuitions of evil. Jack is in some ways 'reverting to savagery', so that the idea of rescue is hardly real to him any more and pigs matter more than a ship which might take him back to civilization; and so that his eyes sometimes have an 'opaque, mad look' from his compulsion to track and kill. But we are not simply to write this off as evil; he is also acquiring a kind of knowledge that Ralph singularly lacks and would be better for having. Jack understands the littluns and their nightmares, knows that it is not sufficient to proclaim that 'this is a good island'.

But as the difference between the experience of the two boys widens, so understanding becomes more difficult and antagonism mounts. They become 'two continents of experience and feeling, unable to communicate'; and in a later formulation, 'the brilliant world of hunting, tactics, fierce exhilaration, skill . . . the world of longing and baffled commonsense'.

Both of them are worlds apart from Simon, whom they consider faintly crazy. One can see easily enough what Golding meant by calling Simon a 'saint', even a 'Christ-figure'. He acts as peacemaker between Jack and Piggy; he is to be seen suffering the little children to come to him, and getting them fruit where flower and fruit grow on the same tree. Afterwards, by himself in the heart of the forest, he has communion with nature or nature's God, in keeping with the poetic and mystical vein that contrasted so markedly, over the candlebuds, with the visions of the utilitarian and the hunter. What the communion is we do not know, but the place is like a church, as the darkness submerges 'the ways between the trees till they were dim and strange, as the bottom of the sea'.

> 'The candle-buds opened their wide white flowers glimmering under the light that pricked down from the first stars. Their scent spilled out into the air and took possession of the island'.

There is something saintly in Simon; but such labelling accomplishes far less than one might imagine. What brings Simon alive is not good works, or prayer, or faith, or a personal relationship with his creator, and a ten or eleven year old is a slender reed to bear the symbolic weight of saint, let alone of Saviour. This kind of reading will not stand up to examination. What does, demonstrably, bring Simon alive and make the passages where he is by himself among the finest things in the book, is the quality of the imagination that goes into creating his particular sensibility. He is not so much a character, in the sense that the other boys are, as the most inclusive sensibility among the children at this stage.

The presentation of Simon in this chapter is not as symbolic as we think when it starts, and not symbolic at all as it goes on. Those littluns, if we look at them, are 'unintelligible' and 'inscrutable', not paradisal. The flowers and fruit raise the question of Eden, certainly, but they also come direct from *Coral Island*, and represent simple physical fact in the South Seas where many fruit trees bear all the year round. Moreover the enormous fecundity, 'the scent of ripeness and the booming of a million bees at pasture', will strike most readers as excessive for Eden.

This assertive fecundity sets the tone of the scene as it develops. What strikes us with considerable force, as Simon moves through the jungle, is that it is alien to man, and the way that its fecundity is rooted in dissolution. The pale flowers parasitic on the tall trunks are 'unexpected' by the civilized eye; the birds not only 'bright' but 'fantastic'. In the treetops life goes on 'clamorously'; the clearing below is an 'aromatic . . . bowl of heat and light'; the 'rapid' climber 'flaunted' red and yellow blossoms; the butterflies are 'gaudy', the colours 'riotous'. Underfoot the soil is markedly soft, and 'the creepers shivered throughout their lengths when he bumped them'. They are dropped 'like the rigging of foundered ships', and the climber is parasitic on a great tree that has fallen and died. This, clearly enough if we look, is no Eden and never was; there was no death in Eden, no riot or urgency, no creepiness.

Simon is the first child to know, to register fully, what the island and its jungle are like in themselves. The qualities that were present in Ralphs's daydreaming at the finding of the conch, but have subsequently been overlaid by his need to think and lead, are fully realizd in Simon. On the other hand, in solitary communion with nature, he taps Jack's sensitivity to the creepy as well as the beautiful. But he is outside the hunter mentality, the leader mentality, outside even himself. He exists in terms of his sensitivity to what is outside him. This allows him to know comprehensively. He not only registers the heat, the urgency, the riot, the dampness and decay; he also registers the cool and mysterious submergence of the forest in darkness, the pure beauty and fragrance of starlight and nightflower, the peace. Finally he not only registers both, but accepts them equally, as two parts of the same reality. It is these qualities of acceptance and inclusion that give us the 'Simon-ness' of Simon.

In his fourth chapter Golding turns from the 'biguns' to find out whether in the 'passionately emotional and corporate life of the littluns', when they are too small to have 'characters' or different 'points of view', there may be visible a basic showingforth of the human, that will cast light on *all* the children. When Roger and Maurice romp through the 'castle' and 'interesting stones' and the 'complex of marks, tracks, walls, railway lines' of the littluns' domain, filling Percival's eye with sand, we are still in a recognizable moral landscape:

> '. . . Percival began to whimper . . . and Maurice hurried away. In his other life Maurice had received chastisement for filling a younger eye with sand. Now, though there was no parent to let fall a heavy hand, Maurice still felt the unease of wrong-doing. At the back of his mind formed the uncertain outlines of an excuse.'

It is not very reassuring, however, because the suggestion is that 'morality' is a matter of conditioning and memory, not something innate; and if it depends on memory it may well fade as memory does. What about a child too young to have been conditioned, or to remember?

> 'Percival finished his whimper and went on playing, for the tears had washed the sand away. Johnny watched him with china-blue eyes; then began to fling up sand in a shower, and presently Percival was crying again.'

Johnny, almost the tiniest boy on the island, and the first to arrive to the summons of the Conch, was the only one whom the author then described as 'innocent'; but although his babyishness makes him morally innocent still, he is clearly not harmless: 'Johnny was well built, with fair hair and a natural belligerence.' The last words may be suggestive.

Meanwhile, rather older and bigger, Henry busies himself at the water's edge:

'The great Pacific tide was coming in and every few seconds the relatively still water of the lagoon heaved forwards an inch. There were creatures that lived in this last fling of the sea, tiny transparencies that came questing in with the water over the hot, dry sand. With impalpable organs of sense they examined this new field. Perhaps food had appeared where at the last incursion there had been none; bird droppings, insects perhaps, any of the strewn detritus of landward life. Like a myriad of tiny teeth in a saw, the transparencies came scavenging over the beach.

'This was fascinating to Henry. He poked about with a bit of stick, that itself was wave-worn and whitened and a vagrant, and tried to control the motions of the scavengers. He made little runnels that the tide filled and tried to crowd them with creatures. He became absorbed beyond mere happiness as he felt himself exercising control over living things. He talked to them, urging them, ordering them . . .'

There is a comment here both on the 'nature' of the 'myriad of tiny teeth'; and on the 'nature' of the human child whose activity goes beyond food and 'beyond happiness'. The chapter is revealed as a commentary on 'nature' and the 'natural man', Johnny's 'natural belligerence' and Henry's absoption in exercising control are basic elements of human nature.

With Roger these elements develop into something more serious. In him, what we noticed in Johnny and Henry becomes deliberately relished. As he throws stones at Henry he is both enjoying exercising power over him, and flirting pleasurably with the idea of hurting him. Roger is a sadist, that is why he is so forbidding. But his sadism is only an excessive development of what we have seen in Henry and Johnny, revealing itself openly because of the absence of grown-up sanctions. For the moment, he throws to miss:

'Here, invisible yet strong, was the taboo of the old life. Round the squatting child was the protection of parents and school and policemen and the law. Roger's arm was conditioned by a civilization that knew nothing of him and was in ruins.'

But that last sentence shows that the restraint is only a taboo, a social conditioning or superstition, not anything innate. The stone he throws, itself 'a token of preposterous time' which has 'lain on the sands of another shore', speaks of ages which dwarf the waxings and wanings of human civilizations. Moreover, Roger's civilization is in ruins itself because its morality was not sufficient to stop men throwing atom bombs at each other. While he remains conditioned, Roger's incipient sadism is shameful to him: 'a darker shadow crept beneath the swarthiness of his skin'. But we have been made vividly aware, in this chapter on 'The Natural Man', of Roger's connection with Johnny and Henry—who in turn link him with us—and also of the frailty of the conditioning which suppresses that element of basic human nature.

Soon we find out that it is not difficult to invent devices whereby the 'natural' man can be released from shame, and the boys can remember other facets of 'civilization besides its morality. Jack remembers the dazzle-paint with which ships hunting or hunted conceal themselves from their prey; his face-painting starts off as a reversion to civilization, not to savagery. But when it is done,

> 'He looked in astonishment, no longer at himself but at an awesome stranger . . . his sinewy body held up a mask which drew their eyes and appalled them. He began to dance and his laughter became a bloodthirsty snarling . . . the mask was a thing on its own, behind which Jack hid, liberated from shame and self-consciousness.'

Then the last crucial scene in this fourth chapter throws into relief the distance we have travelled. As a ship slowly passes on the horizon, Jack and his hunters let the fire go out while they kill their first pig. But once again there is no 'evil'. Jack is still 'conditioned'. The arm that failed to descend on the piglet before has descended now, but even the painted hunter still twitches at the memory of the blood; and he is still 'charitable in his happiness', wanting to include everyone.

Nevertheless his new knowledge, 'that they had outwitted a living thing, imposed their will on it, taken away its life like a long satisfying drink', provides a last link in the chain. We understand now why the compulsion to kill in Jack has meant so much more than the idea of rescue, and has only disguised itself in the need for meat. Moreover the leader, fresh from this total imposition of his will, cannot brook moral condemnation and humiliation at the hands of Ralph and Piggy. His violence and frustration finally erupt as he attacks Piggy and smashes a lens of his spectacles. Here, if we like, is the birth of evil, since irresponsibility has become viciousness; and a will imposed on an animal has now turned in destructive violence on a fellow human being. Yet we would be mistaken to read in these simple moralistic terms. For, as Ralph asserts his chieftainship, as the newly lit fire builds up like a barrier between him and Jack, as the link which bound him to Jack is broken and refastened to Piggy, we ought to remain aware of both sides. There is no defence of Jack's brutality, or his blindness to what it is that he and his hunters have done. Yet the whole chapter has, surely, given us a human understanding of Jack that Ralph and Piggy lack. If it is an emblematic detail that Piggy now only has one eye, it is also humanly fair. Golding's vision is scrupulous. As Jack throws to Piggy the meat that the fat boy is glad enough to eat, he cannot in his rage express his feelings about the dependence on his courage, his cunning and his self-dedication of those who presume to judge him. It is his fate to look round for understanding and find only respect.

## III

We hear the sound of the Shell again, as Ralph summons a second meeting to try to clarify and set right what has gone wrong. Half way through the novel we get a measure of how far we have come; Ralph, discovering his dirt and realizing how much of his time he spends watching his feet to escape falling, 'smiles jeeringly' as he remembers 'that first enthusiastic exploration as though it were part of a brighter childhood'. He and we have grown up since the *Coral Island* stage. This assembly has to be not fun, but business. Ralph is having to realize what it means to be a leader, to make decisions in a hurry, to think things out step by step. This brings out a new scale of values, whereby he sees how little fatness, asthma, myopia and laziness weigh against Piggy's one great quality—his ability to think. But thinking is complicated by the fact that things look different in different lights, and from different points of view. 'If faces were different when lit from above or below—what was a face? What was anything?'

Ralph produces a workmanlike programme to put things straight: a plan for better sanitation, for keeping the fire going, for never cooking except on the mountain-top. But at a level deeper than any programme can reach, things are breaking up because the children are frightened. So the meeting becomes a testing-ground for Ralph's faith that what is wrong can be cured by talking things over reasonably, and coming to a democratic decision on fear itself, on whether or not there is a 'Beast'.

Jack's experience as hunter tells him that there is no fearsome animal on the island, but it also tells him why the littluns are frightened and have nightmares. They are frightened 'because you're like that'; because it is human nature to be frightened of the world and of life when it is dark and man is by himself. But for Jack, 'fear can't hurt you any more than a dream'. Fear can be lived with, and any Beast can be hunted and killed.

Piggy disagrees about fear. For him, everything can be explained and anything wrong, even in the mind, can be cured. Life is scientific. There is no Beast to fear, and there is no need to fear anything 'unless we get frightened of people'. This rationality, however, is greeted with scorn by those whose experience seems to tell them otherwise. Maurice wonders whether science has, in fact, explored the whole of existence and rendered everything explicable and known. The littlun who claims that the Beast comes from the water, and Maurice's memory of great squids only fleetingly glimpsed by man, are both pointers to a sea that may contain a great unknown.

The worst contempt of the meeting, however, is reserved for Simon, who thinks that there may be a Beast that is not any kind of animal: 'What I mean is . . . maybe it's only us.' He is trying to say that man may fear darkness and solitude because they rob him of the world he builds with this daylight mind, and force him to live with his own interior darkness. Perhaps there is something bestial, something absolutely dirty, not external to man but present deep in himself. But Simon is howled down even more than Piggy; and when the vote comes to be taken Ralph is forced to realize that fear cannot be dispelled by voting.

Worse, with the voicing of these internal fears and darknesses, the world of the Conch has been brought into question. Piggy is not ony scorned, but attacked again by Jack; and this time Jack's rebellion against Ralph also comes out into the open, as well as his growing disrespect for Ralph's concept of order.

> "'The rules!" shouted Ralph, "you're breaking the rules!"
> "'Who cares?"
> 'Ralph summoned his wits.
> "'Because the rules are the only thing we've got!"
> 'But Jack was shouting against him.
> "'Bollocks to the rules! We're strong—we hunt! If there's a beast we'll hunt it down. We'll close in and beat and beat and beat—"
> 'He gave a wild whoop and leapt down to the pale sand. At once the platform was full of noise and excitement, scramblings, screams and laughter. The assembly shredded away. . . . '

Perhaps they only exchange one kind of 'play' for another. But we have a clear hint of what the other game is: what is happening is a re-enactment of the chant and mime of pig-killing that had fleetingly brought them together again on the mountain. But now, with Jack's 'beat and beat and beat', and littluns staggering away howling, it is taking on significance as an expression of their fear and an incantation against it, while the littluns' cries already foreshadow something worse.

Everywhere there is fear, even among the saner, more responsible ones. Ralph no longer dares to blow the Conch in case it should be disobeyed, and all pretence of order be lost in defiance. Piggy, in a telling gloss on what he had said at the meeting, admits to his inner, intuitive fear of Jack. Piggy has a rational mind, but we get a new insight into him; the asthma always appears when he is confronted by something beyond his control and understanding: 'I been in bed so much I done some thinking. I know about people. . . . If you're scared of someone you hate him but you can't stop thinking about him. You kid yourself he's all right really, an' then when you see him again; it's like asthma an' you can't breathe'. Piggy's asthma is an expression of fear, and hate, and how hate may grow from fear and alienation. His sickness tells Piggy truths of human motivation that his rational intelligence, and Ralph's health, are blind to. Jack hates Ralph and Piggy and would hurt both if he could, but Ralph is Piggy's one protection. Simon knows that this is true.

There is fear. In their misery they call to mind the majesty and order of the grown-up world and long for 'a sign or something' from that world; some sort of message that would tell them how to sort things out. But instead:

> 'A thin wail out of the darkness chilled them and set them grab-bing for each other. Then the wail rose, remote and unearthly, and turned to an inarticulate gibbering. Percival Wemys Madison, of the Vicarage, Harcourt St. Anthony, lying in the long grass, was living through circumstances in which the incantation of his address was powerless to help him.'

It may be that other grown-up addresses are as powerless as the vicarage, but the main thing is what has happened to the Sound of the Shell. Man-sound has become a cry of absolute fear—a child lost, alone, in an alien world of nightmare.

## IV

The second half of the novel repeats the structure of the first; not however telling us new things, so much as showing the real depths of what we already know.

There is another battle in the night sky three miles above the island, another 'sudden bright explosion and a corkscrew trail'; but instead of the burning plane with the passenger tube, the body of a single parachutist, riddled with bullets, drifts down to lodge on the mountainside. This, with its immediate ironic response to the children's prayer for a sign from the grown-up world, is obviously the most contrived feature of the novel so far. Given the initial situation, the first five chapters have developed with a fatal inevitability, but this, splendid *coup de théâtre* though it be, betrays the novelist's sleight of hand. Yet it is perhaps no more than a fine flourish of rhetoric, to emphasize what we should already have realized.

This is not a novel about children, demonstrating Golding's belief that, without the discipline of grown-ups, children will degenerate into savages. We could think this only if we had forgotten what had brought the children to the island in the first place; and if we had forgotten, the first function of the parachutist is to remind us. The 'majesty of adult life' is a childish delusion. There is no essential difference between the island-world and the grown-up one. There too, order can be and has been overthrown; morality can be and has been inadequate to prevent wholesale destruction and savagery. The parachutist shows man's inhumanity to man, the record of what human beings have done to one another throughout human history. The children are revealing the same nature as the grown-ups, only perhaps more startlingly because of their age and their special situation. The child world is only a microcosm of the adult world.

But the children are already disposed to objectify their inner darkness and expect a Beast who will be other than themselves; so the parachutist becomes identified as the Beast, sitting on the mountain-top, preventing them from keeping the fire and the rescue-signals going. Only Simon cannot believe in 'a beast with claws that scratched, that sat on a mountain-top, that left no tracks and yet was not fast enough to catch Samneric. However Simon thought of the beast, there rose before his inward sight the picture of a human at once heroic and sick.' But Simon, the dreamer who bashes into a tree because he isn't looking where he's going, cannot be accepted uncritically.

The exploration to find the Beast's lair provides a continually ironic commentary on that first golden day and its *Coral Island* explorers. Instead of the peacock-blue of the calm lagoon, Ralph becomes aware for the first time of the other shore, where no reef offers protection against the endless rise and fall of the sea, those eroding tides that 'soon, in a matter of centuries . . . would make an island of the castle', and manifest a time as preposterous to man as Roger's stone:

> 'Now he saw the landsman's view of the swell and it seemed like
> the breathing of some stupendous creature. Slowly the waters
> sank among the rocks, revealing pink tables of granite, strange

growths of coral, polyp, and weed. Down, down, the waters went, whispering like the wind among the heads of the forest. There was one flat rock there, spread like a table, and the waters sucking down on the four weedy sides made them seem like cliffs. Then the sleeping leviathan breathed out—the waters rose, the weed streamed, and the water boiled over the table rock with a roar. There was no sense of the passage of waves; only this minute-long fall and rise and fall.'

This, while it has the factuality of the conch and the weed, has no allure; its sinister quality is all the more powerful because it is so muted. It will not carry human meaning, the waters obliterate the table rock, it is utterly 'strange' to man. And if Ralph's mind gives it to him as the breathing of a gigantic beast, it is so inconceivable and alien that it is beyond terror.

Moments of resurgent glamour merely underline the irony. When Jack cries out excitedly 'What a place for a fort', or discovers a rock that could be rolled onto the causeway, there is a new sense of the need for protection against enemies that gives the excitement a more sinister undertone. It is with a sickening sense of their childishness that we watch through Ralph's eyes as the children roll a rock into the sea. Only, in the midst of his anger, we can detect the beginning of a diminished sense of civilization in Ralph himself:

> '"Stop it! Stop it!"
> 'His voice struck a silence among them.
> '"Smoke."
> 'A strange thing happened in his head. Something flittered there in front of his mind like a bat's wing, obscuring his idea.
> '"Smoke."
> 'At once the ideas were back, and the anger.
> '"We want smoke. And you go wasting your time. You roll rocks."'

He can no longer convince them of the imperative need for rescue, and has to exert sheer authority against their mutinous grumblings.

If this is the ironic comment on the glamour of chapter one, chapter seven is even darker than chapter two. Ralph becomes vividly aware not only of how dirty and unkempt they have become, but how their standards have fallen so that they accept this situation as normal. Moreover what his eye had already taken in of this 'other side' of the island, now imprints a despair on the understanding:

'Here . . . the view was utterly different. The filmy enchantments of mirage could not endure the cold ocean water and the horizon was hard clipped blue. Ralph wandered down to the rocks. Down here, almost on a level with the sea, you could follow with your eye the ceaseless bulging passage of the deep sea waves. They were miles wide, apparently not breakers or the banked ridges of shallow water. They travelled the length of the island with an air of disregarding it and being set on other business; they were less a progress than a momentous rise and fall of the whole ocean. Now the sea would suck down, making cascades and waterfalls of retreating water, would sink past the rocks and plaster down the seaweed like shining hair: then, pausing, gather and rise with a roar, irresistibly swelling over point and outcrop, climbing the little cliff, sending at last an arm of surf up a gully to end a yard or so from him in fingers of spray.

'Wave after wave, Ralph followed the rise and fall until something of the remoteness of the sea numbed his brain. Then gradually the almost infinite size of this water forced itself on his attention. This was the divider, the barrier. On the other side of the island, swathed at midday with mirage, defended by the shield of the quiet lagoon, one might dream of rescue; but here, faced by the brute obtuseness of the ocean, the miles of division, one was clamped down, one was helpless, one was condemned, one was—'

Simon's quality of sheer faith—'*I just think you'll get back all right*'—brings a momentary lightening of despair. But the remembered cottage on the moors (where 'wildness' was ponies, or the snowy moor seen through a window past a copper kettle; and 'spectre', like the awful picture of the spider in the Magician book, was either not looked at at all, or else safely replaced between the *Boys' Book of Trains* and the *Boys' Book of Ships*) is utterly out of reach and unreal; a flimsy dream.

'Reality' is really wild nature; a charging tusker in the forest. But Ralph's first experience of the hunt is also a revelation of his own darker side; he discovers in himself the excitements, the 'fright and apprehension and pride' the others have known. Moreover, as the boys mime to one another again, their underlying tensions suddenly carry them away, including Ralph. They begin really to hurt Robert, who is acting the boar, and his cries of pain excite them still further. Ralph also feels the 'sudden thick excitement'; and as the chant rises ritually, as Robert screams and struggles, 'Ralph too was fighting to get near, to get a handful of that brown, vulnerable flesh. The desire to squeeze and hurt was overmastering.' The 'game' is becoming dangerous; changing from an imitation of an action, to a ritual of release for fear, hatred, violence. It begins to need a victim to be wholly satisfactory.

Lastly, in this chapter of darker sides, Jack's hatred of Ralph emerges fully. As soon as he ceases to lead and control, Jack turns vicious; and he has clearly begun to hate the boy who bars his leadership. Any possibility of responsible and sane decision on this expedition is sabotaged as Jack insists on turning it into a personal challenge and duel. The next morning, seizing on Ralph's 'insult' to his hunters as excuse, Jack blows the conch and openly challenges Ralph's courage and leadership. When he fails to displace him, Jack splits away to form his own tribe.

What is most immediately remarkable however is the way that the language shows a reversion, not so much to savage, as to schoolboy: 'He isn't a prefect and we don't know anything about him. He just gives orders and expects people to obey for nothing. . . . All right then . . . I'm not going to play any longer. Not with you . . . I'm not going to be part of Ralph's lot—' Jack has never been able to make real to himself the 'democracy' of the conch, or the leadership of anyone else, or the need for responsible thought, or provision for rescue. All that makes sense to him is his own need to control others and impose himself, and hunting, because it is a kind of power asser-tion. The sudden humiliating tears, and the schoolboy language, affect us in very different ways. There is pathos in the realization that this bogey-figure is only a child. There is the equally sudden realization that power obsession is essentially childish when it is stripped of the disguises of the adult world.

What the coming of the 'Beast' has meant is an acceleration of the divi-sions among the children. Chapter eight corresponds with chapter three as an examination of the implications of the division. The hut-builders and home-seekers are now penned to the lagoon and the shoreline. They fear the forest and they no longer have either the view from the mountain or the view from the other side of the island; a limitation of consciousness as well as a limitation of area. Piggy's intellect conceives the daring idea of lighting the fire on the rocks instead of the mountain top; but they cannot disguise the fact that they want it as much for reassurance against the darkness as for rescue, the idea of which is getting steadily more remote. The fruit diet, the conch, and the platform are an insiped contrast to the life of the tribe. With the departure of Jack, Piggy can be fully recognized and given his rightful voice in affairs, but there remains a question mark over the range of his vision. Is it enough to regard Jack as the reason why everything is breaking up?

Jack, for his part, is 'brilliantly happy' now that his leadership is assured. Having renounced communal decision, and having no interest in rescue, the idea of a tribe becomes a satisfying way of life. There is the Beast, but they can keep out of its way and forget it; and if it is a hunter like themselves they can propitiate it with part of the kill. Since a tribe is a power-grouping in a world where strength counts, they believe 'passionately out of the depths of their tormented private lives' that they will dream less as they get nearer to the end of the island where the Fort is sited, and where they can barricade themselves. Hunting is no longer merely a question of getting meat, or even of exercising control or imposing oneself. As the hunters chase the sow through the oppressively hot afternoon, they become 'wedded to her in lust'; as they hurl themselves at her the violence has unmistakably sexual undertones; and finally the sow 'collapsed under them, and they were heavy and fulfilled upon her'. Roger's spear up the pig's anus only shows again a peculiar heightening of an impulse common to all. Having renounced the world of Piggy and Ralph, they begin to reveal what their world of hunting really is. It is only incredible if we think that 'bloodlust' is an empty word; for Golding, in opening out the 'thick excitement' we have already accepted, is vivifying what for him is not a cliché. There is an impulse both in lust and in killing, which seeks the obliteration of the 'other' as the most complete expression of the 'self'. The first killing satisfied Jack's bloodthirstiness 'like a long drink'; now his bloodlust is fulfilled in a killing-wedding.

Meanwhile Simon, as in chapter three, is in his place of contemplation, but this time not only watching the butterflies dance in the almost unbearable heat; he is watching also the place erupt with the squeals and the death-struggles, and watching the disemboweling, the decapitation, the offering of the head to the Beast. Into the quiet place have entered the buzzing flies, the spilled guts, the pool of dried blood, the vile thing on the sharpened stick. What Simon 'sees' is the Lord of the Flies, Baal-Zebub, the Devil. The title of the book tells us we have reached its heart.

Simon is tempted to pretend that nothing important has happened, that the offering was a 'joke', that he has made a 'mistake' in taking it seriously. The temptation is to avoid being thought 'batty' by Ralph and the others. He is then tempted to keep quiet for a different reason. To try to make the others see the truth about what has happened will be very dangerous. But these voices come from inside Simon's own head, and from the very first they only tell him what he already knows. In spite of hallucination, one thing he knows quite clearly is that what he sees is not the Beast, but 'pig's head on a stick'. The worst temptation both for Simon and the reader is to see the encounter as a dialogue with the Devil. The difference is really the difference between Simon's view and Jack's:

"'Fancy thinking the Beast was something you could hunt and

kill!' said the head. For a moment or two the forest and all the other dimly appreciated places echoed with the parody of laughter. 'You knew, didn't you? I'm part of you? Close, close, close! I'm the reason why it's no go? Why things are what they are?'"

To imagine that the evil is in any way in the pig's head; or, more insidiously, that the pig's head symbolizes an evil external to the individual, is in fact to commit the error from which only Simon, in spite of his hallucination, is free. The pig's head is not a symbol of anything abstract or outside the boys, like a Devil; it is, like the parachutist, a solid object with a history that human beings have provided. The hallucination ends with Simon falling into the mouth: he faints into his own emergent consciousness of evil. What is wrong on the island is not Jack, as Ralph and Piggy think, or a Beast or Devil to be propitiated as Jack thinks. What is wrong is that man is inherently evil, as Simon has already maintained; the 'ancient, inescapable recognition' is of something in Ralph and Piggy, and Simon himself, as well as Jack and Roger. This being so, there is reason to fear. Simon has known already an assembly crying out 'savagely' as he tries to tell them of 'mankind's essential illness'. Now the inner voice foretells the cost of trying to tell the truth; warns him not to 'try it on . . . or else . . . we shall do you. See? Jack and Roger and Maurice and Robert and Bill and Piggy and Ralph. Do you. See?' The macabre echo of Ralph's initial promise that they would have 'fun' on the island gains point when we remember what we have already noticed the 'game' of the dance becoming.

At the same time it is important to realize how Golding's imagination guards him against the simple thesis on original sin he is generally credited with. For if there can be little doubt after reading the whole book that the author is inclined to share this view of Simon's, this is by no means necessarily the impression that the scene would leave on an unprepared reader. It carries both mystery and ambiguity. Golding has left it open to a humanist to call Simon's vision sick, or even morbid. Simon himself 'hears' the charge that he is an 'ignorant, silly little boy', a 'poor, misguided child' who thinks he can 'know better' than other people. It is true that he 'hears' these voices as cynical, or with the patronizing testiness of a schoolmaster; but with his point of view he would inevitably do so. This doesn't mean that they are necessarily to be discounted. They might be a wiser and truer valuation. Moreover his peculiarity has been insisted on ever since we first laid eyes on him as he pitched on his face in the sand. If the heat makes him delirious and causes him to faint—he may be a mild epilectic—then where does the delirium start? Only with the pig's head expanding like a balloon, or is that the climax? Or is it that his vision is so frightening that it brings on 'one of his times' as Piggy's fright brings on his asthma? How can we tell for certain what is true vision and what sick hallucination? or which is the product of what?

We cannot of course; any more than men have been sure in real life whether the 'prophets' and 'saints' were sick, or possessed, or crazy; or whether they were saner than everybody else, the only sane ones. What does it mean to say 'the fit of prophecy was upon him'? We may suspect what Golding's own view is—but if we read what is on the page the question is certainly posed. This is not because Golding is evading the issue; but because his primary concern is with the creation of an inclusive account. There are three explanations of what has gone wrong, not one; and they amount to three different readings of the universe.

Piggy and Ralph believe in the essential goodness of people and of the island. If things 'break up'—the implication is that they are naturally whole—then it is the fault of individuals, who deviate because there is something wrong with them. In the adult world Jack would be cured by a psychiatrist or restrained by greater power than his, which would also solve the Beast. Horror and wrong happen, but they are deviations which can be overcome by sanity and responsibility.

Jack thinks that evil and destruction are live forces. In a world of power there are powers at work that are stronger than man. But these powers (Beast, Devil, or God), can be propitiated by ritual, ceremony, sacrifice. And if this view strikes us as 'primitive', we ought to be aware at least that Jack has been open to some kinds of human experience that Ralph and Piggy have not; and moreover that it has not always been the least civilized cultures who have held such views.

Simon's view declares that blaming bad men, and the Devil, is both right and wrong, there is evil, but it is not either outside man or confined to certain men, it is in everyone.

Piggy has one eye; Jack is a savage; Simon is a queer little boy who has fits. There are question-marks over all three views. This is not a *roman à thèse*. We are likely to respond most to Ralph emotionally, since we see so much through his eyes, sharing his feelings and his troubles. What is at stake has however not yet been fully disclosed.

Golding's ninth chapter corresponds to the chapter on Natural Man in the first half: it is the test case for establishing a basic conviction. Both the 'View' and the 'Death' of its title are Simon's; the question is whether they endorse his 'explanation'. It is inevitable that Simon should climb the mountain—'what else is there to do?' He cannot believe in a Beast, but it is established as the Simon-ness of Simon to want to contemplate and understand everything. It is inevitable, too, that we should see behind his slow climb, an age-old symbolism that involves Ararat, Sinai, Calvary, and Parnasses:—

> On a huge hill
> Cragged and steep, Truth stands, and hee that will
> Reach her, about must, and about must goe,
> And what the hill's suddennes resists, winne so.

But once again, the truth is nothing abstract, and it may not be as simple as we think.

Simon contemplates the rotting corpse, the 'mechanics' of its 'parody' of animation, the 'white nasal bones, the teeth, the colours of corruption' and the foul smell, and he is violently sick. The flies in a dark cloud about the head remind us, accurately, of the pig's head; for both record what human beings have done. One is taken up into the other. But then, after the toil of the ascent, and the sickness that expresses and purges the horror of realization, Simon is able to bend down and release the figure from its tangle of lines. These have made it keep drawing attention to itself, in a parody not only of animation, but of death and resurrection again and again. It won't lie down. Simon, because he has understood, can break the pattern and stop the repetition. He can lay to rest the 'history' of man's inhumanity, can be free and can set free. He goes down to the others to tell them that what they have erected into the Beast is 'harmless and horrible'. On a deeper level he has shown that, by recognizing the truth of man's evil, as it is revealed in what men have done, and by purging oneself from it, one can be free to begin again.

The children, already conditioned to expect a Beast external to themselves, are in a state of hysteria. At the feast which Jack has staged to tempt as many as possible to join him, the sense of his own power has given him a newly sinister quality behind his paint. He has ceased to be Jack, he has become the Chief. Personality is overcome by power and he loses his name. He has begun to adopt ritual and oracular speech, he sits throned 'like an idol', waited on by acolytes, and 'power lay in the brown swell of his forearms: authority sat on his shoulder and chattered in his ear like an ape'. All day the heat has been building up static electricity in the atmosphere and the tension of the approaching thunderstorm is palpable. Now the human tension of an approaching showdown between Ralph and Jack stretches the nerves still more. As the lightning begins, and the first raindrops fall, so that 'home' and 'shelter' become meaningful again, it seems for a moment that the balance might swing in Ralph's favour. But Jack begins the dance, and we have seen very clearly how that has been turning into a protective ritual, whereby the children first externalize what they fear and hate, and then 'kill' it. As the lightning scars sky and eyes the hysteria mounts with it, in Ralph and Piggy too, until at its peak of intensity Simon staggers out of the forest into the circle, and is taken for the Beast, whose killing becomes no longer mime but reality. In frantic savagery, a 'desire, thick, urgent, blind' that grows out of the fear but is distinct from it, they 'do him in'. As Piggy and Ralph feared when things began to go wrong, they have become animals who 'leapt on to the beast, screamed, struck, bit, tore. These were no words, and no movements but the tearing of teeth and claws'. The squirrel, the jaguar, the ape, have taken human form.

Meanwhile in the high wind on the mountain-top the figure of the parachutist is lifted, and swept in a great arc across the beach to be carried out to sea, as the screaming boys flee into the darkness of the jungle. Again this is a magnificent *coup de théâtre*, a calculated artifice of rhetoric. But again it merely emphasizes what we should already know. As the parachutist extended the meaning of the pig's head into a wider 'history' of man, so the parachutist has now been subsumed in Simon. The children have done what their fathers have done. The 'sign' is released, not because the children are free in Simon's terms, but because they have made a sign for themselves and need no other.

The death of Simon is the fact on which the whole novel turns and the evidence by which any theory of its significance must be judged. But the first condition it has to meet is whether it can convincingly happen. The answer must be sought in the resources of the novelist, and not in theology. How does Golding convince us that these boys could and would do this terrible thing?

## V

The method of the novel is revelatory as we have seen: the uncovering of an unsuspected depth to something we have already accepted. A backward glance will reveal a cumulative process.

Far back, on the first golden day, Ralph learned Piggy's nickname (and immediately betrayed it, the first betrayal of the novel):

> '"Piggy! Piggy!"
> 'Ralph danced out into the hot air of the beach and then returned as a fighter plane, with wings swept back, and machine-gunned Piggy.
> '"Sch-aa-ow!"
> 'He then dived into the sand at Piggy's feet and lay there laughing.'

It is a 'game', in 'fun', Ralph would no more deliberately kill Piggy than Jack can kill the piglet caught in the creepers, though, when we remember how he comes to be here, we might see in Ralph a dangerous blindness to the realities the game imitates. But, looking back, that 'danced' has a reverberation of unease, as is the 'next time' with which Jack drives his knife into the tree when they have allowed the piglet to escape; for the next time will in fact see both the killing of a pig, and the invention of the chant and the dance which will eventually be the death of Simon. Is this a verbal tick, a 'plant'? Or can we accept that a game may be a game and still reflect attitudes that only want opportunity to fulfil themselves; that there is visible in the nickname itself a conversion of human into beast expressing animus towards a nature disliked and distrusted; and, in the mime of the killing, a putting of that animus into action, permissible and humorous simply because it is recognized as 'only a game'? Ralph has already been trying 'to get rid of Piggy'.

'Next time', the reluctance to kill anything with flesh and blood is overcome, though Jack still twitches. The mimed action of driving the knife, at least, can become real action. But while the kill has been taking place the fire has gone out and the ship has passed, so there is real tension between Ralph and Jack. The knife has just been shifted from Jack's right to his left hand, smudging blood across his forehead, when he 'stuck his fist into Piggy's stomach. Piggy sat down with a grunt—Jack stood over him. His voice was vicious with humiliation.' (We suddenly remember a less vicious voice, but still a fierce one: 'You should stick a pig . . .') And though Piggy doesn't bleed, he is half blinded. Does the animus of the nickname and the 'Sch-aa-ow!' look so far-fetched now, and is this a game?

Not long after this Maurice reduces the tension, and reunites everyone but Ralph, by miming what had actually happened in the killing of the pig. The others sing the chant they made up to keep step by as they carried it back, and to express their triumph:

> 'The twins, still sharing their identical grin, jumped up and ran round each other. Then the rest joined in, making pig-dying noises and shouting.
> '"One for his nob!"
> '"Give him a fourpenny one!"
> 'Then Maurice pretended to be a pig and ran squealing into the centre and the hunters, circling still, pretended to beat him. As they danced, they sang.
> '"*Kill the pig. Cut her throat. Bash her in.*"'

Grin, pretence and dance show that this is still a game. But we have seen how in different, tense circumstances, game can turn into actual violence. The tension has only been reduced, it is still there, and what they are acting is already a reality. The line between game, pretence and reality is becoming much more difficult to draw.

After the assembly's discussion of the Beast, and the break-up in disorder (with Jack's 'If there's a beast we'll hunt it down! We'll close in and beat and beat and beat . . .'), there is dangerous tension again:

> 'The sound of mock hunting, hysterical laughter and real terror came from the beach . . .
>
> '"If you don't blow, we'll soon be animals anyway. I can't see what they're doing, but I can hear."
>
> 'The dispersed figures had come together on the sand and were a dense black mass that revolved. They were chanting something and littluns that had had enough were staggering away howling.'

The dance is becoming a way of fencing off terror, or even of taking it out on a projection of its cause, not merely of reducing it. Although there is no necessary suggestion that the littluns have been beaten, there is ringing in one's ear, both the first suggestion of hysterical animality, and the first cries of terror. The black, revolving mass, like a miniature tornado, is a forbidding phenomenon.

Next time, Ralph is also involved in the experience of hunting, and is caught up into the heady excitement of the mime. The children had been frightened by the boar and, stronger than ever, there is the tension between Jack and Ralph. This time, in the ring, somebody really hurts Robert who is acting the pig; and his cries of pain and frenzied struggle to escape produce a 'sudden, thick excitement' which carries away Ralph too:

> '"Kill him! Kill him."
>
> 'All at once, Robert was screaming and struggling with the strength of frenzy. Jack had him by the hair and was brandishing his knife. Behind him was Roger, fighting to get close. The chant rose ritually, as at the last moment of a dance or a hunt.
>
> '"*Kill the pig! Cut his throat! Kill the pig! Bash him in!*"
>
> 'Ralph too was fighting to get near, to get a handful of that brown vulnerable flesh. The desire to squeeze and hurt was over-mastering.
>
> 'Jack's arm came down; the heaving circle cheered and made

pig-dying noises. Then they lay quiet, panting, listening to Robert's frightened snivels . . .
"'That was a good game.'"

The borderline of game has however clearly been crossed, though in a way which often happens in games ('I got jolly badly hurt at rugger once'). This one has clearly revealed not only the riddance of tension and the acting out of fear and hatred, but the excitement of inflicting pain ('Behind him was Roger, fighting to get close'). And, for the first time, the actor has become the victim. The children feel that they are still not doing it properly, they need a drum, someone dressed up as a pig, no, more.

> "'You need a real pig," said Robert, still caressing his rump, "because you've got to kill him."
> "'Use a littlun," said Jack, and everybody laughed.'

It is said in fun, but we have become uncomfortably aware of the impossibility of positing a secure barrier between 'fun and games' and the darker passions. After this the hunters discover their bloodlust, and Roger the torturer is rewarded by a more satisfying scream than Robert's, but we are disturbingly reminded of Ralph as we see him 'prodding with his spear whenever pigflesh appeared'. We are not likely to be convinced when the 'voice' of the Lord of the Flies tells Simon: 'It was a joke really—why should you bother?'

Finally, in the lightning and thunder, this whole process of revelation reaches a climax. The boys are hysterical with fear of the lightning, with the tension of the 'static', with the conflict between Jack and Ralph at its highest. Clearly and unmistakably, dance and chant have wholly moved over from game or narrative, to a protective ritual: 'Piggy and Ralph, under the threat of the sky, found themselves eager to take a place in this demented, but partly secure society. They were glad to touch the brown backs of the fence that hemmed in the terror and made it governable'. The ritual enacts the hemming in, and then the killing, of their own terrors, all of which are projected in the Beast. So, now, the words of the chant have changed: '*Kill the beast! Cut his throat! Spill his blood!*' The individual loses himself in the mob; the chant 'began to beat like a steady pulse'. 'There was the throb and stamp of a single organism'. Then, out of the screams of terror, rises once again that other desire 'thick, urgent, blind', the desire to 'beat and beat and beat'.

We have learned how each of these scenes revealed something which contained the potentiality of the next. Though it is a terrible shock to inspect the end in one leap from the beginning, or vice versa, there is no leap in the whole progress. Each step is just the same measured advance on the last, and connected with the same inevitability to what went before and what is to come after. Can we point to any discontinuity? Can we, accepting all the other links, refuse our assent to the last? For the achievement has nothing to do with dogma, or the assertion of original sin. Golding does not tell us, he shows us, and that is what makes the book so terrifying, whatever our private beliefs may be. He shows us, at the end of his progress, how 'Roger ceased to be a pig and became a hunter, so that the centre of the ring *yawned emptily*'.

It is impossible not to feel the suspense and menace here; that last phrase crystallizes our whole experience and our own emotions of fear and waiting. We know we are on the brink of tragedy without being able precisely to locate it; we know that blind mouth must close—on something.

So, as chapter three linked Johnny and Henry and Maurice with Roger, and Roger with Jack's 'bloodthirsty snarling', we have now seen all the children as part of a process of becoming which has ended in a second, more terrible death. Whether Simon's view of man be just or not, the prophecy of what the fun and games would lead to has been fulfilled.

Simon's view, however, is not yet complete, even though he is dead, for it has not depended on him only as a character, but on a way of seeing. Golding appeals to no heaven to right the wrong of man and there is no God in his novel; but as the storm gives way to calm and the Pacific tide comes in, Simon's body is beautified, if not beatified, and his kind of vision operates once more, as we take in the fact of its disappearance.

The scene re-orchestrates the earlier one in which Simon's vision was first given to us. The riot and clamour then gave way to peace and beauty; they do so again. After the storm, after even the dripping and running water dies away, the world of tension and violence becomes 'cool, moist and clear'. The residue of the terror, Simon's body, still lies 'huddled' while 'the stains spread inch by inch'. But as night falls, there advances in the great onward flow of the tide, a line of phosphorescence in the 'clear water (which) mirrored the clear sky and the angular, bright constellations'. The essence of Simon's view, *acceptance*, becomes explicitly the mode of the writing.

> 'The line of phosphorescence bulged about the sand grains and little pebbles; it held them each in a dimple of tension, then suddenly accepted them with an inaudible syllable and moved on'.

The broken detritus of man's barbarity is made into something beautiful, like a work of art: as a pebble is decorated with pearls, as the pitted sand is smoothed and inlaid with silver, so:

'The water rose further and dressed Simon's coarse hair with brightness. The line of his cheek silvered, and the turn of his shoulder became sculptured marble.'

But the beauty is not prettified, it co-exists with the alien, even the sinister and the ugly. The acceptance has to include the bubble of Simon's last breath escaping with a 'wet plop', an ugly, final sound. The beautifying creatures are 'strange, moonbeam-bodied . . . with their fiery eyes and trailing vapours.' Indeed, a moment's reflection will tell us more: they are the same 'transparencies' that come in in the daylight scavenging for food like 'myriads of tiny teeth in a saw'.

It was the nature of Simon's view to see things inclusively in both their heroic and their sick aspects, to accept the daylight and the night-time mood. We have to see both tiny teeth and phosphorescent beautification; both the huddled figure, the stains, the wet plop, and the bright hair and sculptured marble; both the riot and clamour of 'day' and the calm, fragrant beauty of 'night'. In the endless processes of the universe, there is the reverse of the terror of the ocean on the 'other side': there is the 'Pacific':

'Somewhere over the darkened curve of the world the sun and moon were pulling; and the film of water on the earth planet was held, bulging slightly on one side while the solid core turned. The great wave of the tide moved further along the island and the water lifted. Softly, surrounded by a fringe of inquisitive bright creatures, itself a silver shape beneath the steadfast constellations, Simon's dead body moved out toward the open sea.'

The studiously scientific description intimates a sense of quiet order; a huge and universal perspective, which yet does not dwarf because it includes everything, accepts Simon as he had accepted it. In a sense we are asked to experience the fact that he has 'got back to where he belonged', to a vision big and inclusive enough to be 'steadfast', to accept and order all. To be true to Golding's book, we must remember the heroism as well as the sickness: not only the Lord of the Flies, the corrupting flesh of the Parachutist, the teeth and claws and huddled body; but also the vision that is given the beautification of this sea-burial.

To the 'world of longing and baffled common-sense' what has happened is shameful and obscene. Ralph struggles, trapped between shame and honesty. Piggy's shrill outrage marks his unwillingness to admit what cannot be hidden. There is attempted excuse: 'It was dark. There was that—

that bloody dance. There was thunder and lightning and rain. We were scared.' But Ralph knows how much more was involved. Piggy's excited 'gesticulating, searching for a formula' is stopped short by a voice in which 'there was loathing, and at the same time a kind of feverish excitement' as well as a note 'low and stricken'. But Piggy will not accept guilt:

> 'Ralph continued to rock to and fro.
> '"It was an accident," said Piggy suddenly, "that's what is was. An accident.' His voice shrilled again. "Coming in the dark—he hadn't no business crawling like that out of the dark. He was batty. He asked for it." He gesticulated widely again. "It was an accident."
> '"You didn't see what they did—"
> '"Look, Ralph. We got to forget this. We can't do no good thinking about it, see?"
> '"I'm frightened. Of us. I want to go home. O God I want to go home."
> '"It was an accident," said Piggy stubbornly, "and that's that."
> 'He touched Ralph's bare shoulder and Ralph shuddered at the human contact. "And look, Ralph," Piggy glanced round quickly, then leaned close—"don't let on we was in that dance."'

It is clear on one level that this amounts to a severe criticism of Piggy— 'We never done nothing, we never seen nothing'—and this attempt to deny their involvement, this last pathetic effort to hang on to the simple view that evil is something done by other people, compares ill with Simon's. But it is pathetic, because no one is fooled: 'Memory of the dance that none of them had attended shook all four boys convulsively.' They have got 'frightened of people' as Piggy had said they should not. All that was complacent about Piggy's point of view in the assembly has been pinpointed. 'We can't do no good thinking about it' is not a statement that inspires.

This however is not a disposal of 'the humanistic view of man', nor, as was obvious after the first assembly, does Piggy merely represent a complacent Humanism. We would even be misreading if we thought that this episode was a weighted demonstration of the superiority of Simon's belief in original sin. For, while it is easy to dispose of what is complacent and narrow in Piggy's view, it is not at all easy to dispose of the view itself; nor is it meant to be. For Piggy has a challenging point. Simon's view, we must remember, was of 'mankind's *essential* illness'. What has happened has proved conclusively that there is evil in all human beings, even in those who try to be rational and civilized. But this does not amount to any proof that the illness is of the *essence* of man. May it not be an 'accident', as one might argue medical illnesses are, produced by special circumstances? That is precisely the question that Piggy poses, and it is a good question for Golding to ask so openly.

Had Simon any business crawling out of the dark like that? Wasn't he batty? From his own point of view even, isn't the 'saint' crazy to believe that people he sees as inherently evil can be so easily converted into the belief that the projection of their inner darkness is 'harmless and horrible'? Doesn't he, on any point of view, allow too little for fear of the dark that he doesn't share? We remember Ralph having to rebuke Simon for terrifying the littluns, in the corresponding chapter in the first section, by moving about in the dark outside the shelters, and he was surely right to do so. That early episode can now be seen to have cast a long shadow. This is a searching psychological question too. If the martyrdom is partly created by the martyr, can he not be truly said to have 'asked for it'? Lastly, if the tragedy happens because of the coming together, at some uniquely dangerous corner, of the special circumstances of hysteria and the special 'case' of the martyr, is it not only the simple truth to speak of accident rather than essence? One is not suggesting that the vision of Simon may not be the more convincing and conclusive; nor that we are not inclined to take the 'impaired vision' of Ralph and Piggy in deeper senses than the physical. But Simon's vision establishes itself, if it does so, by its own imaginative force and the opposing views are given no inconsiderable weight.

On the other hand, both 'longing' and 'common-sense' are clearly shown as more and more vulnerable to the darkness. The longing for rescue is more difficult to keep alive, the flapping curtain in Ralph's brain more pronounced, and the barricades of commonsense can operate only in daylight. Ralph's nightly game of 'supposing' fails to comfort, because the 'wildness' even of Dartmoor and the ponies is no longer securely attractive.

> 'His mind skated to a consideration of a tamed town where savagery could not set foot. What could be safer than the bus centre with its lamps and wheels?
>
> 'All at once, Ralph was dancing round a lamp standard. There was a bus crawling out of the bus station, a strange bus . . .'

The mind releases its secret knowledge that there is no safe barrier between civilization and wild nature. The Conch is becoming emptied of significance, seen as fragile: 'I got the conch' is spoken with hysterical irony by a Ralph who sees no future in what he still pathetically caresses.

For Jack's tribe, on the other hand, the death of Simon is a catalyst. They know the horrors of the island well enough; what they proceed to build up is the full tribal technique for coping with them. They barricade them-selves in the Castle with the huge rock poised over the causeway and sentries posted. This is an extension into daily living of the 'ring'; and the 'stamp of a single organism' is preserved by the absolute authority of the Chief. They know well enough what they have done, but they overcome the knowledge, not by hiding it, but by extending their projection of evil into the Beast. They persuade themselves that the Devil can take different shapes, and be 'killed' in those, but 'How could we—kill—it?' So far they have realized Simon's truth ('Fancy thinking the beast was something you could hunt and kill'); but they still see the Beast as outside them, an evil capricious force that must be placated. The world has fully become a power situation of 'us' and 'not us'. The strong Beast must be propitiated; the tribe makes a surprise attack on 'Ralph's lot' to take what they want. The Chief finally secures his authority when he captures the means of fire in Piggy's glasses. But the 'vicious snarling', hitting, biting, scratching, are now deliberately, not acci-dentally, directed against their fellows.

In this chapter, called *The Shell and the Glasses*, we see that for the tribe the glasses have lost all connection with sight; it is nothing to them that Piggy will be virtually blind and the Conch has no meaning whatsoever, so that the raiders show no interest in it. The release of their inner darkness in the killing of Simon has meant an end of all that the Conch stood for. If the world is one of power, there is nothing for power to be responsible to. Jack does not have to give reasons for beating Wilfred; and this is a revelation to Roger, who receives 'as an illumination . . . the possibilities of irresponsible authority'. The death of Simon precipitates the worst element in the tribe: there is nothing now but power, war against 'outsiders', and a darker threat behind.

The stage is set for a final confrontation, recalling the assembly at the end of the first section. The Conch sounds again, 'the forest re-echoed; and birds lifted, crying, out of the tree-tops, as on that first morning ages ago'; but now 'both ways the beach was deserted'. If the savages will not come to the Conch however, Piggy is determined to take the Conch to them.

"'What can he do more than he has? I'll tell him what's what. You let me carry the conch, Ralph. I'll show him the one thing he hasn't got."

'Piggy paused for a moment and peered round at the dim figures. The shape of the old assembly, trodden in the grass, listened to him.

"'I'm going to him with this conch in my hands. I'm going to hold it out. Look, I'm goin' to say, you're stronger than I am and you haven't got asthma. You can see, I'm goin' to say, and with both eyes. But I don't ask for my glasses back, not as a favour. I don't ask you to be a sport, I'll say, not because you're strong, but because what's right's right. Give me my glasses, I'm going to say—you got to!"

'Piggy ended, flushed and trembling. He pushed the conch quickly into Ralph's hands as though in a hurry to be rid of it, and wiped the tears from his eyes. The green light was gentle about them, and the conch lay at Ralph's feet, fragile and white. A single drop of water that had escaped Piggy's fingers now flashed on the delicate curve like a star.'

The words are brave, but the mode of their reception is already established in the irony of the different salt water that has become the element of the 'fragile' white shell. And, though Ralph dimly 'remembered something that Simon had said to him once, by the rocks', Simon's fate has hardly made his faith reassuring. Nevertheless Piggy is given real stature at this moment, the stature of tragedy.

On the causeway before the castle, we hear the Sound of the Shell for the last time as there is a final hopeless attempt to summon back into the painted savages the consciousness of the British schoolboy. But the language of reminder has lost its meaning, because the standards it appeals to are gone. The 'silvery, unreal laughter' from the height is an insufferable element, dissolving the appeal to civilized value before it can have any effect: '"If he hasn't got them he can't see. You aren't playing the game—" The tribe of painted savages giggled and Ralph's mind faltered.' The idea of rescue has quite vanished, and the protest of the twins against their imprisonment only underlines the helplessness, the lack of language, of their cries 'out of the heart of civilization': 'Oh I say!'; '—honestly!'

There is only denunciation, and the language can only be ironic. When Ralph shouts 'You're a beast, and a swine, and a bloody bloody thief', it is only our ears that take in the literal meaning, and even to us it is clear that it is really only an invitation to battle, for moral values have no validity here.

Piggy stops the battle by holding up the Conch . . . for the last time we see the emblem at work. 'The booing sagged a little, then came up to strength. "I got the Conch".' But it is only a momentary memory, and when they do listen to Piggy, it is as a clown. While he speaks, there sounds through the air the faint 'Zup!' of the stones that Roger is dropping from the height, where his hand rests on the lever of the great rock, feeling how 'some source of power began to pulse' in his body. From his height the boys

are not even human: 'Ralph was a shock of hair, and Piggy a bag of fat.'
Then comes the final challenge:

> "'I got this to say. You're acting like a crowd of kids."
>
> 'The booing rose and died again as Piggy lifted the white,
> magic shell.
>
> "'Which is better—to be a pack of painted niggers like you
> are, or to be sensible like Ralph is?"
>
> 'A great clamour rose among the savages. Piggy shouted again.
>
> "'Which is better—to have rules and agree, or to hunt and
> kill?"
>
> 'Again the clamour and again—"Zup!"
>
> 'Ralph shouted against the noise.
>
> "'Which is better, law and rescue, or hunting and breaking
> things up?"
>
> 'Now Jack was yelling too and Ralph could no longer make
> himself heard. Jack had backed right up against the tribe and they
> were a solid mass of menace that bristled with spears. The inten-
> tion of a charge was forming among them; they were working up
> to it and the neck would be swept clear. Ralph stood facing them,
> a little to one side, his spear ready. By him stood Piggy still
> holding out the talisman, the fragile, shining beauty of the shell.
> The storm of sound beat at them, an incantation of hatred. High
> overhead, Roger, with a sense of delirious abandonment, leaned
> all his weight on the lever . . .
>
> '. . . The rock struck Piggy a glancing blow from chin to knee:
> the conch exploded into a thousand white fragments and ceased
> to exist. Piggy, saying nothing, with no time for even a grunt,
> travelled through the air sideways from the rock, turning over as
> he went. The rock bounded twice and was lost in the forest.
> Piggy fell forty feet and landed on his back across that square, red
> rock in the sea. His head opened and stuff came out and turned
> red. Piggy's arms and legs twitched a bit, like a pig's after it has
> been killed. Then the sea breathed again in a long, slow sigh, the
> water boiled white, and pink, over the rock; and when it went,
> sucking back again, the body of Piggy was gone.'

The boy has now literally been seen and killed like a pig; the implications of
this nickname fully brought out; what they hated about him turned into 'red
stuff' welling out of an 'opened' head. The 'table' Ralph saw has become a
place of sacrifice. 'Viciously, with full intention', Jack hurls his spear at Ralph

to kill, while 'anonymous devil faces swarmed across the neck', and another
human Pig 'obeying an instinct he did not know he possessed' swerves in his
flight, and goes crashing through foliage to be hidden in the forest. 'Something', the words echo from far back, 'squealed and ran in the undergrowth'.
We hear a familiar sound, but this time it is human, and what the Sound of
the Shell has become is 'a great noise as of sea-gulls': the harsh sound not of
the conch, but of the hunters screaming hatred and bloodlust.

The hunt is called off, for the moment. But there advances on Sam and
Eric, finally liberated from all control, almost brushing Jack aside because of
the 'nameless, unmentionable authority' that surrounds the Executioner and
Torturer, the figure of Roger: 'The yelling ceased, and Sam and Eric lay
looking up in quiet terror.' There is silence, but we know, although we do not
hear it yet, that we are listening for something. Gulls' scream and hunters'
cry, and the high scream of a victim in pain, these are only postponed,
suspended—for a moment.


## VI


Alone and terrified, Ralph goes on trying to believe that 'they're not as
bad as that. It was an accident'; but he knows better. There is no further
reliance on their 'common sense, their daylight sanity'; and there is that 'unde-
finable connection between himself and Jack; who therefore will never let him
alone; never'. Jack can never be free from the Ralph-in-him till Ralph is dead.
There can be no end to this game. It is the nightmare of 'play' that must go on
and on past nightfall, with no rules, no 'Sir' or Mummy or Daddy to call a halt.

> 'Might it not be possible to walk boldly into the fort, say—"I've
> got pax," laugh lightly and sleep among the others? Pretend they
> were still boys, schoolboys who had said "Sir, yes, Sir"—and
> worn caps? Daylight might have answered yes; but darkness and
> the horrors of death said no. Lying there in the darkness he knew
> he was an outcast.
> ""'Cos I had some sense."'

But this echo of Piggy poses once more the question of whether the reason
for what has happened does not lie a good deal deeper. Ralph suddenly finds
himself in the clearing, where a 'pig's skull grinned at him from the top of a
stick':

> 'He walked slowly into the middle of the clearing and looked

steadily at the skull that gleamed as white as ever the conch had done and seemed to jeer at him cynically. An inquisitive ant was busy in one of the eye sockets but otherwise the thing was lifeless.

'Or was it?

'Little prickles of sensation ran up and down his back. He stood, the skull about on a level with his face, and held up his hair with two hands. The teeth grinned, the empty sockets seemed to hold his gaze masterfully and without effort.

'What was it?

'The skull regarded Ralph like one who knows all the answers and won't tell. A sick fear and rage swept him. Fiercely he hit out at the filthy thing in front of him that bobbed like a toy and came back, still grinning into his face, so that he lashed and cried out in loathing. Then he was licking his bruised knuckles and looking at the bare stick, while the skull lay in two pieces, its grin now six feet across. He wrenched the quivering stick from the crack and held it as a spear between him and the white pieces. Then he backed away, keeping his face to the skull that lay grinning at the sky.'

Again, Golding himself is silent. We are asked to measure and judge the contrast for ourselves; the skull doesn't, in fact, hold 'answers'. There is the white conch, and the white skull; Ralph's and Piggy's 'meaning', and Simon's. There is the view that accepts the evil and takes it to himself; there is the 'sick fear and rage', the hitting out that expresses the loathing and rejection of something utterly alien. 'What was it?' It is for us, finally, to say.

The next day the inevitable hunt begins. Great rocks, 'big as a car, a tank' are sent crashing down like bombs in a full-scale war. This is not game, not defence, not even the work of a single sadist, but military strategy. We notice again the familiar opening-out technique spreading from that first delighted dispatch of the 'enraged monster' into the jungle. The forest is set on fire again, but deliberately this time, the smoke is not for rescue, and the drum-roll heralds an execution quite literally. Worse, it heralds a propitiatory sacrifice to a new Lord, not Beelzebub, but Moloch; for though Ralph does not recognize the meaning of the stick sharpened at both ends, we do. Ralph's head will replace the pig's. And Ralph is becoming an animal, launching himself snarling, knowing the experience of being hunted, desperate, with no time to think, and dreading always the flapping curtain in the mind which might black out the sense of danger and make him mindless. Finally he does become Pig. His last thought of rescue, the hopeless memory of Simon's groundless faith, is replaced by a 'scream of fright and anger and desperation. His legs straightened, the screams became continuous and foaming. He shot forward, burst the thicket, was in the open, screaming, snarling, bloody.' There is the cry of the hunters, the roar of the fire, the 'desperate ululation' advancing 'like a jagged fringe of menace', the narrowing pig-run to the beach past the blazing shelters, then certain and horrible death:

> 'Then he was down, rolling over and over in the warm sand, crouching with arm up to ward off, trying to cry for mercy.
> 'He staggered to his feet, tensed for more terrors, and looked up at a huge peaked cap . . . He saw white drill, epaulettes, a revolver, a row of gilt buttons down the front of a uniform.
> 'A naval officer stood on the sand, looking down at Ralph . . .'

There is probably no remark about his work that Golding regrets more than referring to this ending as a 'gimmick'. For though there is device, there is no suggestion of trickery. The murder of Ralph takes place in the imagination as surely as if Golding had written FINIS under the word 'mercy'. But what happens is like turning on the lights in the theatre before the curtains close, and then letting the cast suddenly step outside the action that had mesmerized us. We are forced to distance the completed experience, and measure how far we have travelled. For that measurement Golding needed Ralph's eyes.

The change of perspectives justifies itself as a challenge to us in the midst of shock. Suddenly we see 'a semicircle of little boys, their bodies streaked with clay, sharp sticks in their hands'; some tiny tots 'brown, with the distended bellies of small savages'; a 'little scarecrow' who 'needed a bath, a haircut, a nose-wipe, and a good deal of ointment'; and another 'little boy who wore the remains of a black cap on his red hair and who carried the remains of a pair of spectacles at his waist'. Is that all?

There could have been no more dramatic way of bringing home to us how much more there is, than thus forcing us to measure the gap that separates what the officer sees from what we ourselves know, through seeing with the eyes of Ralph. To our horror, the officer's language reveals the kind of attitudes to children and coral islands that we might very well have started with; each word is filled with corrosive irony: 'Fun and games . . . Having a war or something? . . . I should have thought that a pack of British boys—you're all British aren't you—would have been able to put up a better show than that . . . Like the Coral Island.' We measure the implications of that 'pack' against the Jack who had voiced just such a confidence in the British at the second meeting. 'We've got to have rules and obey them. After all, we're not savages: We're English; and the English are best at everything. So we've got to do the right things.'

But the novel has gone beyond being a critique of *Coral Island*; and there is much more involved than our better knowledge of what children are like. For the measure of the officer's inadequacy is not only that he doesn't know what children are like, but that he doesn't know what adults are like. For as our eyes take in the uniform, the revolver and sub-machine gun, the 'trim cruiser' on which the eyes that are embarrassed by the children prefer to rest, we know the significance of uniforms and weapons as the officer does not. 'Having a war or something' . . . in thinking of himself as not only superior to, but even other than the children, it is the man that is the child.

It is Ralph who is 'grown-up', but he shows his adulthood by weeping. Golding needs him not only to see, but to register the proper response in pain and grief.

> 'Ralph looked at him dumbly. For a moment he had a fleeting picture of the strange glamour that had once invested the beaches. But the island was scorched up like dead wood— Simon was dead—and Jack had . . . The tears began to flow and sobs shook him. He gave himself up to them now for the first time on the island; great, shuddering spasms of grief that seemed to wrench his whole body. His voice rose under the black smoke before the burning wreckage of the island; and infected by that emotion, the other little boys began to shake and sob too. And in the middle of them, with filthy body, matted hair, and unwiped nose, Ralph wept for the end of innocence, the darkness of man's heart, and the fall through the air of the true, wise friend called Piggy'.

This is the truest of all the sounds; in the sense that it shows the human response to all the others that Golding wishes to leave in our ears.

It is however a *response*, not an answer. What Ralph weeps for is the failure of Piggy's idea of a rational world, Piggy's friendship, Piggy's intelligence. We might ask whether there has not been a truer 'innocence', a greater 'wisdom', a more loving 'kindness', a better attitude to 'darkness' and the 'fall'. If Ralph weeps for Piggy, may it be because he only knows one degree better than the officer? Ought we to be weeping . . . for Simon? But, though we may ask such questions, the novel will give us no dogmatic answer. Golding's fiction has been too complex and many-sided to be reducible to a thesis and a conclusion. *Lord of the Flies* is finer art than the polish and clarity of its surface. Even in his first novel, it is not explanation and conclusion, but imaginative impact which is finally memorable.

LEIGHTON HODSON

# *The Metaphor of Darkness:* Lord of the Flies

Making people understand their own humanity, which Golding sees as the basic quality in a writer, can be narrowed down to mean, in his case, making people become self-aware and honest with themselves about the condition they find themselves in, and the kind of life they lead. The characters he creates and the presentation of their behaviour and motives are aids to the understanding of the darkness that lies in the heart of man. For Golding the dark places are very real, as "The Ladder and the Tree" shows, and all his work seems to be a coming-to-terms with them. He is determined they shall be understood; salvation and sanity seem to lie in the complete and honest understanding of the evil that resides in us.

The novels not only demonstrate this but also convey Golding's urgent feeling about his point of view. The boys isolated on the island in *Lord of the Flies* discover their true natures but also illustrate both the depravity and the nobility in human nature. The new men in *The Inheritors* show unflatteringly how the human race must make its way. Pincher Martin is tortured until he comes to the full realisation of the wickedness of his past. Sammy in *Free Fall* sets out explicitly in search of his true self but what he uncovers is mainly unpleasant. Father Jocelin in *The Spire*, in delirium on his deathbed, recognises his foul spiritual pride and all the shady sexual motives hidden behind his vision of being architect for God's glory. The total effect is not gloom but

From *William Golding*. © 1969 by Leighton Hodson.

a serenity of understanding that looks at the human condition frankly and admits and resolves the contradictions we are all aware of and torn between: life is both a fine thing and a corrupt thing, both sunny and dark. Golding describes the presence of these two elements in his outlook on life in "The Ladder and the Tree," quoted above, together with the idea that a "meddling intellect" inevitably destroys innocence.

In the novels the idea of darkness becomes very complex in its terms of reference. It becomes particular faults of character, especially selfishness and greed. It becomes the urge to use other people, to exploit them, an urge none can escape, as with the new men triumphing over the apemen or Sammy using Beatrice Ifor. It becomes the urge to power and violence, notably with certain of the boys in *Lord of the Flies* where, in its crudest form, it is superstition and explains the setting-up of the pig's head on a stick. It can be blinding vanity as it is for Jocelin. More than anything it is the split between body and soul.

There is, in the novels, a steady progression from the first oblique statements about this split between body and soul to a more explicitly intellectual discussion of the problem. The ending of *The Spire* comes nearest to the resolution of it. To take the novels in sequence: the groups in *Lord of the Flies* and in *The Inheritors* act out a drama in which the reader is left to draw his own conclusions. In *Pincher Martin*, the drama of a single individual, the author is more explicit and leads us firmly to the interpretation he wants. We are taken down into the cellars of Pincher's mind—this is Golding's own image—and shown what he must face there: the knowledge that life is not appetite alone:

> Well of darkness. Down, pad, down. Coffin ends crushed in the wall. Under the churchyard back through the death door to meet the master.

We are shown how Pincher is forced to admit what, in the imagined fullness of his life, he has been running away from.

The idea of avoiding the final answer, of spiritual cowardice, is applied also to Sammy Mountjoy in *Free Fall*. Where Pincher Martin found himself floundering in the sea and was obliged only *in extremis* to question his behaviour in life, Sammy on the other hand begins with apparent honesty and the best will in the world to analyse his existence from as far back as he can go. He seems to be an improvement on Pincher Martin in that he is not blind to his shortcomings and, in a sense, wants to atone for them. But when it comes to the crisis he balks the issue and runs away. After having examined his life he sees the way to join up body and soul. He sees his selfishness at the end of the novel in perspective but no bridge (the image Golding uses) between the physical and spiritual worlds.

Father Jocelin in *The Spire* goes one step further. Without the benefit of Sammy's analytical powers he is forced by circumstances to admit that all along his true motives have been mixed. He combines the elemental quality the author put into Pincher with the honest intentions of the analytical Sammy and reveals to us a creature who, in fever on his deathbed, sweats out the truth about himself and the position of man in the world. We are committed in various ways to consuming each other and there is no one to guide us. We are alone. For we see and understand everything in terms of our self-centered bodies. Jocelin sees through this trap but his revelation of the isolation of man is only a wisp of thought, unexpressed in formal terms, drifting through his mind:

> . . . he saw all people naked, creatures of light brown parchment, which bound in their pipes or struts. He saw them pace or prance in sheets of woven stuff, with the skins of dead animals under their feet and he began to struggle and gasp to leave this vision behind him in words that never reached the air.
> *How proud their hope of hell is. There is no innocent work. God knows where God may be.*

When Jocelin dies the priest gives him absolution but he has already found his own absolution in his private thoughts, without need of any sacrament. He seems to be the fullest realisation of Golding's ideal of man who finally comes to terms with the "cellarage," the word Golding uses to describe what Jocelin, throughout his life, has been wearing his body out in avoiding. Golding implies that this is the furthest one can go in self-knowledge. But by bringing this self-knowledge to Jocelin on his death-bed he further implies that its practical application in the ordinary run of existence is too difficult.

In *Lord of the Flies* Golding immediately comes to terms in a masterly way with his main preoccupation: the problem of evil. He shows how evil is dormant in human nature and how the world may appear a sunny place when in fact the corruption of darkness can arise from man himself and cast shadows over it. We learn that the boys are sole survivors of an aircrash which occurs when they are being evacuated to the southern hemisphere during some future catastrophic war. The island they find themselves on could be a happy playground and, at the very beginning of the book, Ralph in sheer delight at being on a real coral island stands on his head and looks at Piggy through his legs. But this is only the point of departure that

Golding's book shares with R. M. Ballantyne's *The Coral Island* (1858), the avowed original for his thoughts on the theme of innocence and experience. Thereafter the gap of divergence grows ever wider. His view of the Ballantyne situation he considers to be ironic, not in the bad sense "but in almost a compassionate sense," and he goes on to explain:

> You see, really, I'm getting at myself in this. What I'm saying to myself is "don't be such a fool, you remember when you were a boy . . . you lived on that island with Ralph and Jack and Peterkin . . . Now you are grown up, you are adult; it's taken you a long time to become adult, but now you've got there you can see that people are not like that; they would not behave like that if they were God-fearing English gentlemen and they went to an island like that." Their savagery would not be found in natives on an island. As like as not they would find savages who were kindly and uncomplicated and that the devil would rise out of the intellectual complications of the three white men on the island itself.

He objects to *Lord of the Flies* being thought of as a black mass version of Ballantyne and sees it as a realistic view of the situation.

In Ballantyne's book Ralph Rover, Jack Martin, and Peterkin Gay are three "jolly young tars" for whom being shipwrecked is so jolly for the world is kind. Ralph, the narrator, frequently refers to "the great and kind Creator of this beautiful world." They are all considerate towards one another and exist in harmony: "There was indeed no note of discord whatever in the symphony we played together on that sweet Coral Island . . . (we were) tuned to the same key, namely that of Love! Yes, we loved one another with much fervency." There is no sense of irony; a severe storm does not cause any feeling of insecurity. They return home under a clear sky to find their cat cosily sleeping and waiting for them. Violence exists on Ballantyne's Coral Island but it comes from outside with the arrival of the cannibals and the pirates (who kill the cat). The problem of evil is touched on. Ralph recognises "the strange mixture of good and evil that exists not only in the material earth but in our own natures." However, the effects of storms and the experience of the cannibals lead him to reflect that "the works of God are wonderful and His ways past finding out." All fits into a frame of benevolent planning. The latter part of Ballantyne's story, especially the conversion of the savages to Christianity, ends happily with the boys bound for home "leaving far behind us the beautiful bright green coral islands of the Pacific Ocean." The impression the reader is left with is that it was all very curious and interesting, even the self-slaughtering cannibals, and also a very edifying and jolly adventure.

In Golding's story the possibility of discord soon makes its appearance. A group has already gathered around Ralph in an attempt to establish an assembly, with their newly found conch as symbol of order, when Jack and the choir come trudging over the beach. The beginnings of the degeneration of his society lie in Jack's natural arrogance:

> The boy (Jack) came close and peered down at Ralph, screwing up his face as he did so. What he saw of the fair-haired boy with the creamy shell on his knees did not seem to satisfy him . . .
>
> "I ought to be chief," said Jack with simple arrogance, "because I'm chapter chorister and head boy. I can sing C sharp."

They do not really trust each other. Jack is given second place as chief of the hunting choir, but it is not long before the rankling of this failure causes a split and leads to Jack being chief on his own terms. The position then becomes Ralph, Piggy, and Simon versus Jack and the choir-hunters. Among the boys divided into the good and decent (Ralph-Piggy) and those who succumb to evil (Jack and his followers) Golding has placed a particular creation of his own: the visionary Simon.

He is the prototype of Golding's ideal of man given fuller realisation in Jocelin in *The Spire*. The man Golding admires is the one who will look darkness in the face and, with great human courage, come to terms with the ignoble within us which is potentially destructive of our humanity. Simon, a quiet, withdrawn, skinny boy with a tendency to epilepsy, likes to wander off on his own in order to be alone. His usual haunt is a carefully enclosed glade. It is one of the ironies of the book that this "holy" place is the very spot where Jack and his hunters bring the head of the pig, impale it, and revere it. This pig's head, rotting on its stick, is the Lord of the Flies, Beelzebub, Evil, the Dark. Simon looks at it hard. He is seeing the symbol of the evil Golding describes as being in us. It is only the outward form of those forces that work in Jack and the hunters turning them into murderers. The pig's head is described as a "Gift for the Darkness," but a gift cannot drive the darkness away and hunting the Beast and killing it are an illusion. The evil is inside people and ineradicable. As Simon looks at the pig's head he learns this:

> "Fancy thinking the Beast was something you could hunt and kill!" said the head. For a moment or two the forest and all the

other dimly appreciated places echoed with the parody of laughter. "You knew, didn't you? I'm part of you? Close, close, close! I'm the reason why it's no go? Why things are what they are?" . . . Simon's head wobbled. His eyes were half-closed as though he were imitating the obscene thing on the stick. He knew that one of his times was coming on. The Lord of the Flies was expanding like a balloon . . .

Simon found he was looking into a vast mouth. There was blackness within, a blackness that spread . . .

Simon was inside the mouth. He fell down and lost consciousness.

This moment, in the heart of the book, shows Golding's art at its finest. The incident and Simon's fit are described on a naturalistic level but at the same time the reader is aware of the author's symbolic intention working through—an intention all the richer in its force for its obliqueness. When Simon imagines he has fainted into the mouth of the Beast the author is getting over his point that the pig's head is only an external device for referring to the evil that is within people. Simon's awareness of it is not of something outside himself but a recognition that it is potentially within all people whether they are good or bad, hence the associating of it with himself physically, his acceptance of it, as he faints into the Beast's jaws.

The characters, in fact, are not conveniently divided up into "goodies" and "baddies," though Jack and Simon do lie towards the extremes. Both Ralph for all his decency and Piggy for all his commonsense are involved in murder, and both are willing to accept the meat of the hunters in spite of their principles. It is the complexity of human nature that accommodates the possibilities of both good and evil and this is reflected in Simon's own private thoughts on the nature of the Beast:

> However Simon thought of the Beast, there rose before his inward sight the picture of a human at once heroic and sick.

Night time on the island and the children's night fears have prompted irrational feelings and silly talk of a monster. But this is only a side-issue compared with the real evil developing in some members of the group. It is given to Simon, wandering perplexed after his interview with the pig's head, to discover the real cause for the talk of a supernatural monster inhabiting the island. It is he who discovers that the cause of their fears is the pathetic rotting corpse of a parachutist that has drifted down from an overhead battle. He looks with noble compassion on this figure caught among the rocks:

The tangle of lines showed him the mechanics of this parody; he examined the white nasal bones, the teeth, the colours of corruption. He saw how pitilessly the layers of rubber and canvas held together the poor body that should be rotting away. Then the wind blew again and the figure lifted, bowed, and breathed foully at him. Simon knelt on all fours and was sick till his stomach was empty. Then he took the lines in his hands; he freed them from the rocks and the figure from the wind's indignity.

Having faced Evil he can face the Dark and has, in doing so, discovered the truth—both the literal truth that the monster does not exist and the deeper truth that the boys have nothing to fear but themselves. But for Golding's ideal of man, the full knowledge of life, of the truth, cannot survive in the full reality of ordinary existence. Pincher Martin and Sammy Mountjoy are brought to the verge of self-knowledge and no further. Those who cross the boundary must die, as Simon must and Jocelin must. It is Simon's tragic fate, and another irony of the book, that this bringer of enlightening news is killed in the frenzied dance in praise of the hunt, in praise of the Beast, conducted by Jack and all the boys on the shore. Unlike Father Jocelin Simon is innocent, preserving still that innocence that Sammy in *Free Fall* goes in search of. The particular quality of Simon is to be "a lover of mankind, a visionary, who reaches commonsense attitudes not by reason but by intuition" and to be "a Christ-figure in my fable" as Golding himself states. He calls Simon a saint and sees him going away to his glade like the child Vianney, the future Curé d'Ars. Any difficulty in understanding Simon exists only for the sophisticated; the illiterate find it easy to understand Simon voluntarily embracing the Beast, giving the news to "the ordinary bestial man on the beach" and being killed for it. It is for this reason that the removal of Simon's body by the tide is described in terms that are magical and naturalistic at the same time, so that he is naturally and not at all picturesquely re-absorbed and embraced by the material world. This recalls how his own quality of intuitive understanding had been one of all-embracing completeness:

The water rose further and dressed Simon's coarse hair with brightness. The line of his cheek silvered and the turn of his shoulder became sculptured marble. The strange, attendant creatures, with their fiery eyes and trailing vapours, busied themselves round his head. The body lifted a fraction of an inch from the sand and a bubble of air escaped from the mouth with a wet plop. Then it turned gently in the water.

Somewhere over the darkened curve of the world the sun and moon were pulling; and the film of water on the earth planet was held, bulging slightly on one side while the solid core turned. The great wave of the tide moved further along the island and the water lifted. Softly, surrounded by a fringe of inquisitive bright creatures, itself a silver shape beneath the steadfast constellations, Simon's dead body moved out towards the open sea.

There is more violence: a littlun killed by accident in a fire on the Island, the obscene hunting of Ralph, and the killing of Piggy. To read the description of the death of Piggy immediately after that of Simon is very revealing for the interpretation the reader feels obliged, through the stylistic devices, to place on the book. Piggy, holding the conch in his hands, is struck a glancing blow from a deliberately aimed boulder, and he and the symbol of order are shattered. He falls onto a platform of rock in the sea and the waves simply wash the body away. The description is brief, matter-of-fact; Piggy is a piece of flotsam and the sea does not dignify his departure as it does Simon's. Golding manages to deepen his meaning of what the boys' attitudes represent by providing them, in their common ends, with descriptions that correspond to the limited practical intelligence in the case of Piggy—dry in tone—and the intuitive depth of understanding in the case of Simon—eloquent and transfiguring. It is obvious that Golding favours, and would wish the reader to favour, the rarer qualities of Simon, described by one commentator as "the one character that the book clearly endorses" and whose qualities are "those that the novel itself expresses and promotes in its readers."

On the other hand another commentator has attempted to outline a case against Simon even to the extent of making the unwarranted assumption that the author should have cut him out in an early draft. The objection is based on a misunderstanding of the text. It seems that we should not accept Simon bringing the news about the dead airman because his discovery that the Beast is rationally explicable would invalidate his symbolic value and would be out of character in a mystic. This ignores the fact that Simon's message is twofold since in bringing the boys the news that the Beast does not exist outside them he is also bearing witness to the grimmer truth that it exists within. The real hero, according to this view, is Piggy who reaches the same conclusion as Simon that there is nothing to fear unless it is other people, and he loses his life in facing up to Jack. Simon on this score then becomes a pretentious enrichment of the symbolism of the book and the irony that Piggy is honourable but limited is lost.

This kind of approach which tends not to allow the text to speak for itself is typical of some of the considerable criticism *Lord of the Flies* has received in its short career. Some commentators have felt obliged to label the characters with points of view that they are alleged to stand for and thereafter unwittingly falsify Golding's fictional creation to fit into their favoured thesis—that he is a pessimist, maybe, or an optimist or a Freudian. This has happened particularly in the case of this novel and has not been left without comment by the author.

It is tempting, for instance, to cast the boys in roles that correspond to different facets of personality in the Freudian manner, so that one is *ego* another *id* and so on. This kind of approach has been fully put by Claire Rosenfield for whom Ralph is God, Jack the Devil, Piggy a father-figure, Simon a victim in primitive sacrifice, and Piggy again, in his death, a case of symbolic cannibalism. Almost any illustration from Freud, particularly from his *Totem and Taboo*, can be made plausible by picking out of *Lord of the Flies* those elements that suit the thesis. Very soon the author's own voice is drowned. Thus Claire Rosenfield can categorically claim that "events have simply supported Freud's conclusions that no child is innocent": but this ignores the central position given to Simon and to the author's attempts to assert that he was the exception among the boys. She also claims that in Golding's view bestiality and irrationality dominate "all men, even the most rational and civilised." But again Simon, Golding's unique creation, does not fit here. When she does attempt to fit Simon into the Freudian view she is forced to simplify and so falsify. For her, Simon at his death "becomes not a substitute for beast, but beast itself." Golding has, in another connexion, explained this quite simply: Simon during the dance "*doesn't* become the beast, he becomes the beast *in other people's opinions*." She is too hasty in claiming that Golding is consciously dramatising Freudian theory and a similar position taken by William Wasserstrom who sees Ralph as *ego*, Piggy as *super-ego*, and Jack as *id* is equally unhelpful. Golding, even allowing for exaggeration, denies this approach quite flatly:

> And to think I've never read Freud in my life. Someone wrote a terribly erudite article showing that Ralph was an *id* and Piggy an *ego*. Or was it the other way round? I was quite impressed, but the whole thing was simply untrue. I suppose I'm doing the same thing as Freud did—investigating this complex phenomenon called man. Perhaps our results are similar, but there is no influence.

There has been, on the other hand, a tendency towards a political interpretation with the roles redistributed. Ralph is "*l'homme moyen sensuel* but even more clearly the 'liberal' politician who has found he can talk fluently and enjoys the applause of the crowd." In this way Piggy's commonsense and his position as outsider among the other middle-class boys underline social attitudes so that he appears as a democrat and intellectual in opposition to the "officer class," with its automatic assumption of leadership. Samneric represent the nonentities of good will most of us became when faced with crises and Jack, with Roger, his henchman, like a potential concentration camp guard, becomes a Hitler. But once again the character who cannot be fully fitted into this scheme of things is Simon who simply cannot be described as representing integrity. And if the political fable should have such importance one might well ask why absolute power corrupts only Jack when Ralph is just as vulnerable in his position of authority.

The force of the book is such that behind these views is the assumption of a meaning in actuality far more important than the fiction itself, a feeling that there is a message to decipher and once deciphered the book can be ignored. The main difficulty with *Lord of the Flies* has been, from the outset, deciding its form; a similar problem arises for the other novels. Sure enough there is meaning in it beyond the fiction itself; there is allegory in it somewhere but the reader should not forget that the themes and characters first emerged into his consciousness as part of a work of imagination and that to discuss them out of that context is only a convention it would be wrong to forget.

Whatever label is finally decided on it is certainly a work that presents a challenge to the reader who at the end must question his attitudes to the book; to pass over it as an entertainment is impossible. There is the feeling that if it is an allegory then what is the author trying to convince us of? Though to some the allegory is sombre but realistic to others it appears as a falsely black and impossible view of man. This alleged negative meaning of the work has occasioned some of the unwillingness to admit its literary worth.

One of the main disputes has centred round the question, should one go for Golding or Salinger, *Lord of the Flies* or *The Catcher in the Rye?* This has been particularly an American interest because of the rivalry and popularity of these two works among American students. There is also an element of the modish in it but more generally what is at stake is the opposition between the pictures of youth and society that these two works give—Salinger's with his Holden Caulfield, innocent until corrupted by society which is phoney through and through, and Golding's with his boys potentially evil at the outset. The dispute depends upon oversimplifying and omitting subtleties. As we have seen, Golding's emphasis is on potential evil and, for his elect like Simon, even the absence of evil. His picture, in fact, is realistic since even the decent Ralph likes to hunt and but for his respect for the rules which he says are "all we've got" could be a hunter too. It is details of this kind which give the book its fine quality as a composition that have got lost in the argument over whether Golding is presenting us with an optimistic or a pessimistic view of life. F. E. Kearns has placed *The Catcher in the Rye* in the tradition of the innate goodness of man until corrupted by society and *Lord of the Flies* in the tradition of the insuperable depravity of human nature which makes all human effort at justice or order futile, hoping to prove that Golding's book is one of unrelieved pessimism. He stresses that even if Ralph is saved he is saved, in the person of the naval officer, by a sophisticated form of the violence he is running from. Ralph must return to a world at war, which in turn shows that whatever free will exists it is doomed to be ineffectual. He is able to quote Golding's own comment on the saving of Ralph: "And who will rescue the adult and his cruiser?" but misses the irony of the ending. This effectively transfers the action from the island back to life at large but also makes the reader automatically apply the story he has read to adult life where its obliquely stated truths are meant to have their full impact. F. E. Kearns does not see that Golding is not, in underlining the inevitability of evil, approving it. What he approves is the contrary of evil, but shut his eyes to the existence of evil he will not, as his Simon does not. In his determination to be human and tolerant and not succumb to evil or man's dark side Golding is compassionate and realistic. Man's nobility is to stare the Beast in the face rather than pretend it does not exist. Ralph weeps "for the end of innocence, the darkness of man's heart, and the fall through the air of the true, wise friend called Piggy." He has travelled a long sobering journey from the moment of high spirits when he stood on his head. He does not weep for Simon or even know, as the reader does, of his vision of their life. The "saint" has been completely ineffectual, to Ralph, from the practical point of view: but he is not meant to be for the reader who returns with Ralph, to our normal world of dissensions and war. The message, if it has to be insisted upon, does not fit easily into the categories: pessimistic or optimistic. It is not that man is either good or evil but simply that he is capable of becoming, and needs to become, self-aware. Golding is stating our problems, reminding us of them or even making us reexperience them, but it is too much to expect him to solve them. Criticism which goes straight for the message presupposes that the author is offering solutions when in fact he is only offering an imaginative experience.

The return to normality at the end of *Lord of the Flies* where, because of the power of the book and especially of the description of the hunt, every reader expects Ralph to be annihilated constitutes the celebrated "gimmick" ending. The term is Golding's own, but it has unfortunately been taken up without the qualifications he appended to it and, instead of meaning a legitimate contrivance, has been interpreted mostly in the sense of a trick or even a let-down. He has explained that in *Lord of the Flies*, *The Inheritors*, and *Pincher Martin* it was essential as an aid to putting over what he wanted to say:

> ... I have a view which you haven't got and I would like you to see this from my point of view. Therefore, I must first put it so graphically in my way of thinking that you identify yourself with it, and then at the end I'm going to put you where you are, looking at it from outside.

Each case of this deliberate change of viewpoint must be taken on its merits but in *Lord of the Flies*, at least, it is difficult to agree with James Gindin who has objected to the use of the gimmick because it "palliates the force and the unity of the original metaphor." When he writes: "If the adult world rescues the boys are the depravity and brutality of human nature so complete?" he is simply forgetting the irony of a rescuer who is also a hunter but doesn't know it.

Golding expects his reader to be very careful; it is strange therefore that he has so often been accused both of being too explicit and too obscure. He is clearly committed to writing in such a style that he can entrap the reader into seeing everything his way and only at the end allow him to escape so that he can reconsider it from his own point of view, outside the tale. This explains the extremely close direction of events so that compared with most novels action and character-development seem to lack the free give and take of ordinary life. This special conditioning is a mark of all Golding's work and where it has been thought that the moral intentions have become too obvious some readers have felt that the freedom of the novel-form has been sacrificed to allegorical statements. Some of the first comments on *Lord of the Flies* made much of this while conceding its excellent quality and the author's great skill. Walter Allen found that the burden on the children was "too unnaturally heavy for it to be possible to draw conclusions" from the book. Douglas Hewitt, however, saw the weaknesses in the tendency to be too explicit; the pig's head scene in particular was too pat to be plausible. Margaret Walters, likewise, attacks the stress placed on Simon as being obtrusive and obvious though on the whole she considers Golding succeeds in uniting the idea, character, and situation, particularly by his ironic references throughout to the world of adults. The main charge, however, is clearly that Golding has omitted—in a way unbecoming in a novelist—the complexities of ordinary life.

Such objections seem inevitable to any kind of allegorical fiction. But how far can they be taken in this case? The author himself accepts the term fable to describe *Lord of the Flies* but is fully aware that the novelist ought not to preach overtly. He has also distinguished "myth" and "fable" bringing out the deliberate contrivance necessary to the latter:

> . . . what I would regard as a tremendous compliment to myself would be if someone would substitute the word "myth" for "fable" because I think a myth is a much profounder and more significant thing than a fable. I do feel fable as being an invented thing on the surface whereas myth is something which comes out from the roots of things in the ancient sense of being the key to existence, the whole meaning of life, and experience as a whole.

Legitimate contrivance is necessary to any kind of fiction and instances of contrivance must be measured against the imaginative force of their context before being condemned. No sensible critic of *Lord of the Flies* has ever denied its great brilliance and power and yet it has been summed up by Walter Allen as "a considerable confidence-trick." His view tends to take the fable too literally:

> . . . the behaviour of the children is taken, as many of Golding's admirers seem to take it, as paradigmatic of general human behaviour in the absense of restraint. There can be no conceivable parallel at all, as would be plain if Golding had lowered the age-range of his boys from roughly five years old to twelve to, say, from one to seven.

Objections of this kind can easily prompt others equally irrelevant: such as, why are there no girls? why no talk of sex? etc. But the fabulist deliberately contrives to concentrate his story and his characters so that they have the force of images which create, if successful, the inescapable feeling, not that what happens is plausible, so much as convincing in its essence. This is the poetic quality of Golding's fiction, successful in *Lord of the Flies* by its overwhelming sense of the potential evil and potential good in man, suggested basically by the image of child as potential adult.

His novel is sufficiently naturalistic for his purpose and has been described as "naturalistic-allegorical." Though to hunt pedantically for symbols and parallels would be to destroy pleasure in the book, nevertheless any reader comes upon the rich texture with delight in its interlocking design where every incident or description upon reflexion illuminates something else. There is a particular pleasure in the sense of nothing wasted. It's the literary approach that yields most from the text without forcing. In broad outline there is a progression from innocence and fun to the sobering effect of grim experience, conveyed by the images of Ralph playful at the beginning and hard-pressed and weeping at the end. Other images interlock: his discovery of the island grows less lovely as things deteriorate; the odour of decay pervades life from the diarrhoea of the littluns happily eating the fruit to Jack hunting the pigs by following their steaming droppings; the association of the Beast, evil, excrement, and blood is both overpowering and purposeful. There is in general a progression from light to dark.

*Lord of the Flies* was a triumph for Golding but also a test-case. He has survived principally through the poetic conviction of his composition. Critical attitudes and ideas arise when the book is finished; during the reading one is eager to know what happened next, to feel what nerve will be unerringly touched on next rather than to assess what all these complexities add up to. Because of the moralistic intention in his work Golding has been too easily pushed into the role of explainer when he is only being what one expects the novelist to be—a describer.

HOWARD S. BABB

# Lord of the Flies

William Golding has himself supplied a starting point for discussion of *Lord of the Flies*, his first novel—published originally in 1954—and still his most popular work: "The theme is an attempt to trace the defects of society back to the defects of human nature. The moral is that the shape of a society must depend on the ethical nature of the individual and not on any political system. . . . The whole book is symbolic in nature. . . ." These sentences about the book's purpose and its method do in fact indicate the main lines along which commentary on the novel has proceeded. Much of it is concerned with Golding's meaning, the commentators moving out from his statement of the theme to explore the different levels on which the story may be interpreted. Clearly Golding's words themselves here provide some warrant for reading the story variously, with their references to society, individual man, ethics, and politics. As for Golding's method, which has come in for its own share of attention, there is some difference of critical opinion, his books being called fables, allegories, symbolic structures, or even romances. But the critics agree that his method, however one defines it, is radically conditioned by meaning: that the entire fictional structure—in all its details, some would say—is created with a view to its significance. Such a method, in its devotion to meaning, runs the risk of oversimplifying the texture of the virtual life that we commonly assume it is the job of fiction to render. The

From *The Novels of William Golding*. © 1970 by The Ohio State University Press.

method would seem to pose a threat, also, to the story as a story, perhaps subjecting it to the imperatives of meaning rather than of narrative power.

Certainly the spareness of the controlling narrative in most of Golding's books and the significance generated by so many local details tempt one to talk about meaning, and I shall be talking about it throughout the chapter. But in their concern to tie down his method, Golding's critics have passed over his artistry in narrative, though acknowledging the impact of his stories. Thus I want first to bring out the narrative structures in *Lord of the Flies*. After that, I shall take up the characters in the novel, who develop according to much the same principle as the narrative itself. Finally, I shall isolate a particular scene in order to suggest how the method of the novel is realized in its language.

As our cue to reviewing *Lord of the Flies* in its main outline, we may take Golding's statement that the book deals in part with "the defects of society." For the group of boys who find themselves on an uninhabited island—as the result of a plane crash during their evacuation from England in an atomic war—try to create a society for themselves, but experience its disintegration. The society begins to come into being when Ralph blows the conch he has discovered, the children collecting on the beach. But already there is a hint of irresponsibility in the pleasure the young ones feel at the notion of "something purposeful being done"—by others (Ralph is sounding the conch, and Piggy gathering names)—a pleasure underscored by the action of one who starts sucking his thumb. At the first assembly, the group exercises what Golding terms the "toy of voting" to elect Ralph chief, attracted to him not by any "good reason" but by his possession of the conch. When, after the island has been explored, Ralph guides the second assembly toward determining to light a signal fire for facilitating rescue, the group bolts off after Jack—Ralph's defeated rival for the position of chief, the leader of the choirboys designated by Jack himself as this society's "hunters"—and kindles a blaze that burns up part of the island, moves the children to delight and "awe at the power" they have "set free," and causes the first death on the island.

Society's attempt to build shelters proves as ineffective as its effort to keep a signal fire going. Only Ralph and Simon are still on the job when Golding first shows us this world at work, the other children having drifted off to doing whatever they enjoy, with Jack devoting himself to mastering a technique for hunting pigs. The split between Jack and Ralph, discernible when they met initially, starts to emerge as a split between different organizing principles of society (among other things) when Ralph complains that Jack hunts because he likes to, "You want to hunt," while implying that he himself builds from a sense of duty. If the pleasures of some older children reveal their irresponsibility and latent cruelty—in one scene, Roger and Maurice kick over the sandcastles of the "littluns," Roger then throwing stones to frighten a child on the shore—Golding insists that the same qualities inhere in the "littluns" themselves, one of whom keeps throwing sand at his crying playmate, while another basks in the joy of "exercising control over [the] living things" at the waterline and "ordering them." Appropriately enough, the first killing of a pig, which both gratifies Jack's dark pleasure in hunting and marks the initial success of the children in having "imposed their will" on "a living thing," costs society a chance to be rescued, for the hunters have abandoned the signal fire as a ship passes the island—and Jack smashes one lens of Piggy's glasses, the instrument of the society for lighting its signal fire, when he is rebuked for the hunters' irresponsibility.

The assembly that ensues, called by Ralph in part for the purpose of "deciding on the fear" which afflicts the children, dissolves into a confused dance when the children testify that they are indeed haunted. And soon their fear is embodied in the dead airman—civilization's ironic response to Ralph's wish for some stabilizing "sign" from the world of grownups—who parachutes to the island to become "the beast" in the eyes of this society. The expedition that Ralph organizes in the service of the group to discover whether the reported beast really exists, an expedition led at many moments by Jack, is itself sidetracked for a time into a hunt and dance, Ralph participating in both. Once the presence of the beast is validated—once society has thus enthroned its evil—Jack openly challenges Ralph for the position of chief in an assembly which Jack himself has called, departing to found a society of hunters himself when the group fails to support him formally.

Behaving with typical inconsequence, the children nevertheless desert one after another to Jack, whose society shows itself committed to fun and feasting, to power and its ceremonies, to hunting pigs and sacrificing to the beast—to the pleasures and terrors of savagery. The first assembly of this new group translates itself into the ritual dance eventuating in the murder of Simon, a dance in which even Ralph, Piggy, and the few still loyal to the former society take part. The split between the two societies brings on war, Jack's particular raid to bear off the last lens of Piggy's glasses leaving the remnants of the rational society fighting savagely with each other in the darkness. When these four children present themselves to Jack's group the next day, intent on holding an assembly and securing the return of the spectacles, Ralph quickly gets embroiled in a fight with Jack—who cannot stand to be named a "thief," thus to have his society publicly accused of formalizing evil. So it is Piggy who must juxtapose finally the values of the two societies that the island has known: "Which is better—to have rules and agree, or to hunt and kill"; "Which is better, law and rescue, or hunting and breaking things up." He is answered by the rock that smashes him to death. Jack's group, which at last includes everyone except Ralph, sets it sights on killing the lone outsider and offering his head as a sacrifice, while Ralph himself is transformed into a beast in his efforts to avoid the pursuit and the fire, which, lighted to drive him from his hiding place, threatens to engulf the island. Although Ralph and the others are shocked into regaining some sense of themselves as children by the sudden appearance, at the novel's close, of a naval officer from a cruiser that has sighted the smoke of the conflagration, Golding forbids us to imagine that civilized values have indeed been effectively restored, for the adult world is thoroughly engaged in its own war.

One rather minor indication of Golding's narrative skill is the number of ways in which his primarily expository first chapter yet anticipates the story to come. On our introduction to Ralph and Piggy, for instance, it is Ralph who strips off his clothes almost immediately, reverting more readily than does Piggy to the natural state that ultimately characterizes all the survivors on the island. Piggy is the more conscious of the adult world and of those who might have died in the plane crash—the past from which the two step forth—whereas Ralph is absorbed in daydreaming about the pleasures now lying before him of life without adults (in ironic contrast to his daydreams, as the island's society later breaks down, about the adult world that he has left behind). Similarly, Piggy announces the necessity of listing the children's names and holding a meeting, viewing the conch as a means to call all together, while Ralph simply surrenders himself to the "violent pleasure" of blowing it. Details such as these imply what proves to be the truth: that Ralph, despite all the affection and respect that he later develops for Piggy, is at bottom much more like the other children. In this first chapter itself he is allowed to betray to the others the nickname that Piggy has begged him to keep secret; and, in a telling image, when Ralph initially learns the nickname, he "danced out into the hot air of the beach and then returned as a fighter-plane, with wings swept back, and machine-gunned Piggy." None of this should be taken to mean, of course, that Ralph stands already beyond the pale of civilization. When Piggy fearfully observes, in a statement that does indeed predict what happens to him and almost happens to Ralph, "We may stay here till we die," Ralph feels "the heat . . . increase till it became a threatening weight," trots off quickly to round up his clothes, and finds that "To put on a grey shirt once more was strangely pleasing." In a somewhat different narrative vein, the exploration of the island by Ralph, Jack, and Simon described towards the end of Chapter 1 contains the first instance of a rock being pried over a cliff by the children, an expression here of their sheer delight in exploring, though this fun also interrupts their mission. By the close of the expedition, a faintly religious air already clings to Simon through his repeated mention of candles to describe some bushes which they pass, and Jack has encountered his first pig, though he cannot yet bring himself to strike it.

In outlining the progressive degeneration of the children and noting several of the details in the first chapter that reappear in some fashion further on, I have wanted to point towards Golding's fundamental narrative method. The principle is common enough: the recurrence of some event, situation, or fact in slightly varying form, the variations so managed that the sequence generates an ever-increasing emotional intensity. The effect of an inexorable progress towards and inevitable conclusion may remind us of the gradually accumulating pressure in a novel like *Clarissa*, though Richardson works by subjecting us to a series of alternatives: when the given set is exhausted, one possibility having come to dominate the other, the dominant possibility itself divides into new alternatives. In *Lord of the Flies*, with its strictly linear plot structure, Golding's narrative power derives not only from the carefully graded variations in any particular sequence, but from the number of these sequences that move in parallel, as it were, towards a single destination. His precise control over both gradation and parallels would seem to me indirect evidence, incidentally, of the substantial amount of fiction Golding wrote before creating *Lord of the Flies*.

The variety of parallel sequences that help to structure the novel, each of them revealing some kind of regression from innocence to savagery, can be illustrated fairly briefly. Two major points of reference are the huge fires near the beginning and at the end of the narrative: the first, an attempt to promote rescue which in fact causes a death; the second, a means of promoting death which brings about a rescue of sorts. In the first part of the story, the fires that the children light are normally associated with rescue, while in the second half they are linked with cooking the killed pigs and feasting. The final conflagration, of course, not only dramatizes the literal cruelty of the children in hunting down Ralph but implies as well that the world which began as Eden has become Hell. Golding centers another sequence on the dropping of rocks: Ralph, Jack, and Simon, as we have already seen, experience a communal joy when they first send a boulder crashing down; Roger throws stones to frighten a littlun, but with an arm still "conditioned by . . . civilization"; the group seeking to discover whether a beast really exists diverts itself by toppling a rock into the sea until called back to its duty by Ralph; Roger pries loose the rock that kills Piggy; finally, Jack's group drives Ralph from a thicket by heaving boulders over a cliff that smash the hiding place. Similarly, the first fight among the children is a mock affair, a testimony to the sheer joy of Ralph, Jack, and Simon in exploring: ". . . Ralph expressed the intensity of his emotion by pretending to knock

Simon down; and soon they were a happy, heaving pile in the under-dusk." But this sequence proceeds through the arguments of varying intensity between Ralph and Jack; to Jack's first raid for fire after his own society has begun to take shape; to the twins—still members of the more civilized group—fighting each other in their sleep; to Jack's second raid, this one for Piggy's glasses rather than burning branches, which results in Ralph and the twins fighting with each other rather than with their enemies; to the fight between Ralph and Jack at the time of Piggy's death; to the total war that Jack's society makes on Ralph just prior to the novel's close. The repeated dances constitute still another motif: it is initiated by Jack's capering about when he first succeeds in fashioning a hunting mask; the motif evolves through the ritual dances that domesticate ever greater cruelty and culminate in the murder of Simon; by the end of the story, the dance has become a habitual ceremony of Jack's group. Finally, the actual deaths on the island and Ralph's potential death, all so artfully spaced by Golding through the book, make up a crucially important sequence. The boy with the birthmark dies accidentally, though as a result of the island society's irresponsible indulgence in the pleasure of kindling the signal fire that gets out of hand. Simon is beaten to death by the children acting as a group, but the killing is far from deliberate, for they are caught up in a frenzied dance to ward off the terrors of a storm. The killing of Piggy is the act of an individual, one who surrenders himself to the pleasure of destroying: ". . . Roger, with a sense of delirious abandonment, leaned all his weight on the lever." The nature of Roger's deed is underlined by Jack's attempt, as chief, to take the act to himself—"I meant that"—and by his immediate hurling of a spear at Ralph "with full intention," though Roger does in fact achieve an authority rivalling Jack's through the killing of Piggy. In the final hunt for Ralph, all the children know exactly what they are doing, the whole society devoting itself to murder and human sacrifice.

The fact that all these sequences move in a single direction helps to explain, I think, the effects of clarity and simplicity that the narrative produces on a first reading. Certainly the fact contributes to the pace. The story rushes forward, with the few interruptions—such as Ralph's memories of his former life or the brief glances back to the children's first days on the island—serving less as breathing spaces for the reader than agonizing dramatic reminders of how far events have gone. But at the risk of laboring Golding's narrative method, I want to treat one last motif, the matter of the "beast," for it will show us how relentless a power can be developed through a sequence of meticulously graded variations, and the motif is also central to the novel's meaning.

The beast first appears as the "snake-thing" reported to an assembly by the boy with the birthmark, who imagines it as moving about in the dark—

though this "beastie" achieves, properly enough, a kind of public definition further on when the children scream, on seeing creepers burn up in the fire that rages out of control and has killed the boy, "Snakes! Snakes! Look at the snakes!" On the earlier announcement of the "snake-thing," however, Ralph denies the claim flatly, while Jack, with appropriate illogic, already accommodates the irrational, saying in one breath, "There isn't a snake-thing," and in the next, "we'll look for the snake too." When the topic crops up again during a lull in the building of the shelters, with only Simon having the courage to verbalize what Ralph and Jack do not wish to—the fear of the littluns that "the beastie or the snake-thing" is "real"—Ralph betrays uneasiness, yet remains "incredulous," whereas Jack testifies that he knows how the younger children feel and that he has experienced a sense of "being hunted" by a beast, not when "getting" the "fruit" on which the civilization still feeds, significantly, but when he is on his own, hunting to kill pigs. So far the beast has been associated with this society's fear, irrationality, and dark pleasure in wielding power—precisely the qualities that inhere, of course, in its first killing of a pig with the attendant neglect of the signal fire. It comes as no surprise that the ensuing assembly, called by Ralph in some hope of "deciding on the fear" and then settling the matter of the beast, reveals instead how pervasive the terror is. Ralph admits to his own fears, though terming them "nonsense"; Jack declares that all the children must "put up with being frightened" even if "there is no beast"; Piggy, in keeping with his rational attitudes, denies both beast and fear, but immediately qualifies his denial—"Unless we get frightened of people"—in words that to some extent anticipate Simon's; Simon hazards that there may be a beast, but that "it's only us"; when a voice proposes that Simon means "some sort of ghost," the children vote in overwhelming numbers that they believe in ghosts, and the assembly breaks up with Jack whooping, "If there's a beast, we'll hunt it down! We'll close in and beat and beat and beat." The vast majority of them having thus endorsed their irresponsibility, the children are prepared to take the dead airman who drops to the island as the beast itself.

During the children's search over the island to verify the presence of the beast, Ralph may still at bottom doubt its existence. But in the hunt that interrupts the search, he offers the opinion that the pig he has struck may be the beast, and worse, from the point of view of maintaining order, though he well knows that they should wait until daylight to conclude the search, he yields to Jack's challenge that they climb the mountain in the darkness, with the result that they cannot see the beast to be a dead man. Society's fears now translated into a substantial form, it follows naturally that Jack should break away to found a group of his own on everything that the beast represents. Indeed, the beast is enshrined as the dominant principle of Jack's society when the hunters sacrifice to it the head of a slaughtered pig. This is the head referred to by Golding as "the Lord of the Flies" (i.e., Beelzebub), the head that says, when Simon confronts it, "I'm the Beast," "I'm part of you," the reason "Why things are what they are," and thus declares man's allegiance to cruelty, irrationality, and fear. When Simon returns from the mountain to tell the children the truth about the dead airman, they regard him as the beast, but Golding's language converts the children themselves into a beast as they kill Simon: ". . . the crowd . . . screamed, struck, bit, tore. There were no words, and no movements but the tearing of teeth and claws." Since society has thus taken evil to itself, the beast in which it earlier objectified its terrors—the body of the airman—may appropriately disappear from the island.

The beast becomes a permanent institution when Jack, asked by his own group whether it did not die with Simon, replies, "No! How could we—kill—it," his words in part refusing to acknowledge the actual killing, but also making of the beast an indestructible living presence. The raid for Piggy's glasses is so narrated by Golding that Jack's hunters are again identified as a beast. But even more significant, by the end of the novel Ralph, the sole survivor of civilized society, has turned into a beast himself. He may scream at Jack "You're a beast" when they fight just prior to Piggy's death. But on his subsequent flight from the hunters, he obeys "an instinct that he did not know he possessed," keeps wishing for "a time to think" that he can never seize on, and at last emerges from a thicket with "screams" that "became continuous and foaming. He shot forward . . . was in the open, screaming, snarling, bloody. . . . He forgot his wounds . . . and became fear." In accordance with an apparently inexorable logic, the novel has rendered a civilization deteriorating step by step until it lies in ruins.

What I have said so far about the plot will have made clear the impossibility of talking about the narrative structure apart from meaning in *Lord of the Flies*, and I hope to have suggested as well the varieties of meanings—social, psychological, religious—that obtain simultaneously in the story. These multiple meanings can also be traced, of course, in the main characters of the book. But before treating the characters separately, I had better state that—the opinion of many critics to the contrary—Golding seems to me for the most part successful in preventing his figures from becoming simplified allegorical types, and extraordinarily successful in sustaining the representation of the children as children. With regard to the first point, I suspect that we may be unduly influenced by the sort of statements that Golding makes from time to time, as omniscient author, which comment explicitly on the significance of a character: ". . . there was a mildness" about

Ralph "that proclaimed no devil"; as Jack and Ralph face each other, "There was the brilliant world of hunting, tactics, fierce exhilaration, skill; and there was the world of longing and baffled common-sense"; "Simon became inarticulate in his effort to express mankind's essential illness"; "Samneric protested out of the heart of civilization." But such statements should not obscure the fact that, in their behavior, the children normally reveal contradictory impulses which complicate them as individuals: Piggy, for example, is eminently rational yet very frightened; and Ralph, though trying to cling to civilized forms and common sense, feels the pull of the anarchic and the pleasure of emotional release. As for the childishness of the characters, Golding strikes me as having taken great pains to incorporate in the run of terrifying events a series of passages which keep insisting precisely that the children are indeed children. One might cite Piggy's speech when he wants to accompany Ralph on the first expedition over the island, or Ralph's assertion of his leadership and rebuke to Jack by forcing Jack to build the signal fire in a different spot, of the wonderfully true-to-life scene in which Jack leaves the assembly because he is not voted chief. But the example I shall quote appears near the end of the story, when Jack and Ralph are about to fight and Piggy is about to be killed:

> With ludicrous care he embraced the rock, pressing himself to it above the sucking sea. The sniggering of the savages became a loud derisive jeer.
> Jack shouted above the noise.
> "You go away, Ralph. You keep to your end. This is my end and my tribe. You leave me alone."

Despite the encompassing terror here, the words of Jack—with their petulant emphasis on "my" and "me"—might be heard on any playground.

In terms of what the characters signify, one of the sharpest juxtapositions in *Lord of the Flies* pits Jack against Piggy, the two presented as instinctively antagonistic from the start. Although Jack turns out to be the leading force in destroying the society established originally on the island, he stands forth at first as an advocate of civilized values, inquiring for the adult in charge when he appears on the beach with his choir and later declaring to an assembly: "After all, we're not savages. We're English; and the English are best at everything. So we've got to do the right things. Through these opening pages too, of course, Jack betrays his delight in sheer power—by bullying the choir—and his incipient cruelty: "We'll have rules. . . . Lots of rules! Then when anyone breaks 'em—" Soon he realizes himself in hunting. Through this activity, Golding associates him with the abandoning of civilized restraints, "Jack hid [behind his hunting mask], liberated from shame and self-consciousness"; with, as opposed to the rational, the primitively—even bestially—instinctive, as in "He . . . breathed in gently with flared nostrils, assessing the current of warm air for information. The forest and he were very still," or in "there were droppings that steamed. Jack bent down to them as though he loved them"; with the spilling of pig's blood, which Jack may at first try to clean from his hands, but which he finally uses to initiate another hunter. In the assembly for "deciding on the fear," Jack repudiates the organizing principle of Ralph's society—"Why should choosing make any difference?"—and utters his commitment to power, "Bollocks to the rules! We're strong—we hunt." This is the sort of power on which Jack's society proves later to be based, a power manifested in the ceremonial obeisance to himself that Jack requires of his tribe, and expressed in another way through those sacrifices by which the tribe creates its beast, thus sanctifying the forces of irrationality and fear that reign in the children themselves. Jack, we remember, has acknowledged his fear much earlier in the story, even though questioning the existence of a beast. And on that search for the beast which brings the boys to the mountain, Jack challenges Ralph to climb with him to the top in order to assert his own powers, his own capacity to lead—not in order to serve society, certainly not in order to outface the beast. Once the beast materializes in the body of the airman, the triumph of Jack and all he represents is virtually assured.

Whereas Jack lawlessly thrusts aside the restraints of civilization, makes a principle of fear, and relentlessly pursues power, Piggy is devoted to the orderly processes of civilization, constantly brings to bear what rationality he can muster, and proves woefully weak. Even for Ralph's society he is an outsider, a comic butt because of his fatness, asthma, and dependence on spectacles—a figure already faintly discredited by his trips to the bushes when "taken short" in the opening pages of the novel. If we are to imagine him as vaguely Promethean because be provides the means by which society kindles its fires and later has "the intellectual daring to suggest moving the [signal] fire from the mountain," Piggy nevertheless reveals the limitations of mere rationality. He may stand out against the assembly in denying the existence of ghosts, but he thinks Simon "cracked" for intending to search out the beast. And when confronted by the fact of his own participation—compelled by his terror—in the murder of Simon, he tries to evade his responsibility, first by explaining what has happened as "an accident" and then by clutching at the only straw left for the rationalist, "We got to forget this." Although in this matter Piggy is less willing than Ralph to acknowledge his guilt, in the affairs of society Piggy becomes Ralph's guide, calling him back again and again to the thread of some argument about signal fires or rescue which Ralph has lost under pressure. It is appropriate that Piggy should want finally to demand his glasses from Jack on the grounds simply that "what's right's right," and that Ralph should want Piggy to carry the conch during this last stand of reason—as appropriate as it is that, with the death of Piggy, rationality should disappear from the island.

The most striking fact about Ralph is his inch-by-inch regression—so much slower than Jack's—to savagery. To be sure, he keeps striving to preserve a civilized order, learns to value Piggy's brains and to like him as a person, is even represented as growing intellectually to some extent ("With a convulsion of the mind, Ralph discovered dirt and decay"), and shows himself readier than Piggy to admit his share in Simon's death. But Ralph's weakness is marked by his lapses in logic (in contrast to Piggy's physical disabilities), lapses often accompanied by the sense of emotional release that so exhilarates the irresponsible among the children. Ralph's failures in reasoning are dramatized by those recurrent sentences that trail off in "because—"; and, towards the end of the novel, Piggy must supply him with the logical connective itself, for Ralph can only grasp the imme-diate necessity:

> "I said 'smoke!' We've got to have smoke."
> There was silence. . . . At last Piggy spoke, kindly.
> "'Course we have. 'Cos the smoke's a signal and we can't be rescued if we don't have smoke."
> "I knew that!" shouted Ralph. . . . "Are you suggesting—?"

Despite his affection for Piggy, Ralph betrays again and again his funda-mental emotional kinship with the others: when he must force himself to look "away from the splendid, awful sight" of the first destructive fire; when he attempts to repress his memory of the first death on the island; when, in one of the ritual dances, he is "carried away by a sudden thick excitement" to strike at Robert with a spear and struggles "to get a handful of that brown, vulnerable flesh" because "The desire to squeeze and hurt was over-mastering"; or when he joins with the other children in laughing at Piggy, who has been burned by a chunk of roast pig, "Immediately, Ralph and the crowd of boys were united and relieved by a storm of laughter." The knowl-edge by which Ralph acts at the end of the book, when he is becoming an animal himself, is quite explicitly instinct, the reverse of Piggy's rationality: "He argued unconvincingly that they would let him alone. . . . But then the fatal unreasoning knowledge came to him again. The . . . deaths of Piggy and Simon lay over the island like a vapor. These painted savages would go further and further." And when he comes at last upon the pig's head on a stick, the Lord of the Flies whom Simon has faced and gone beyond, Ralph can only hit out at the skull, which—in a significant phrase—"bobbed like a toy and came back," and "Then he backed away, keeping his face to the skull that lay grinning at the sky."

Simon is as much an outsider as Piggy, but for different reasons. Although he too has his weaknesses—his liability to fits and his inarticulateness in public—he constantly reveals a kindness that no other child possesses, and he is gifted with suprarational insight. A saint, Golding has called him, and Simon's charity declares itself in his comforting of Ralph, his offering of food to Piggy, or his getting fruit for the littluns. Predictably enough, he is regarded as "batty" by the rest of the children, in part because the more-than-logical truth about man which he intuits does not lend itself to sheerly logical statements: after confusingly proposing to the assembly that the beast may be "only us," he tries again with an analogy—"What's the dirtiest thing there is?"—which is morally valid, but which is turned by Jack into a dirty joke that overjoys Simon's uncomprehending listeners. Nevertheless, Simon holds fast to his intuition: "However Simon thought of the beast, there rose before his inward sight the picture of a human at once heroic and sick." Alone among the boys, he insists that the beast must be faced, accepts—in the scenes with the pig's head, to one of which I shall return shortly—the fact that evil resides in the hearts of all men, and climbs the mountain to discover the truth about the beast, the truth that the others enact in killing Simon.

In spite of all my references so far to the meaning of events and characters in *Lord of the Flies*, I have aimed at illuminating the power of the story as a narrative and at indicating the lifelikeness of the children. I turn at last to a single scene which evidences both these qualities, but which will show us as well how Golding's style creates a magnificently substantial world in which the symbolic values emerge almost of themselves—which will illustrate, in short, the essential method of the novel. It is the scene of Simon's first encounter with the pig's head that Jack and his group have left as an offering to the beast. The passage moves toward a climax of its own in its symbolic statement, so realistically rendered, that Simon will himself become a sacrificial victim. And the passage moves toward the first appearance of the phrase "Lord of the Flies," which identifies the Devil with society's reification of its own fears through its sacrificing to them. What is remarkable, however, is the sustained naturalism of the scene, despite its symbolic implications. The Lord of the Flies remains a literal pig's head on a stick (it does not speak aloud until the second encounter, a fact perhaps suggesting that it becomes more defined as a force, a person, to Simon only after he has recognized that he himself must be sacrificed); and Simon remains a child, one subject to fits and badly frightened of the object in front of him.

Simon stayed where he was, a small brown image, concealed by the leaves. Even if he shut his eyes the sow's head still remained like an after-image. The half-shut eyes were dim with the infinite cynicism of adult life. They assured Simon that everything was a bad business.

"I know that."

Simon discovered that he had spoken aloud. He opened his eyes quickly and there was the head grinning amusedly in the strange daylight, ignoring the flies, the spilled guts, even ignoring the indignity of being spiked on a stick.

He looked away, licking his dry lips.

A gift for the beast. Might not the beast come for it? The head, he thought, appeared to agree with him. Run away, said the head silently, go back to the others. It was a joke really—why should you bother? You were just wrong, that's all. A little headache, something you ate, perhaps. Go back, child, said the head silently.

Simon looked up, feeling the weight of his wet hair, and gazed at the sky. Up there, for once, were clouds, great bulging towers that sprouted away over the island, grey and cream and copper-colored. The clouds were sitting on the land; they squeezed, produced moment by moment this close, tormenting heat. Even the butterflies deserted the open space where the obscene thing grinned and dripped. Simon lowered his head, carefully keeping his eyes shut, then sheltered them with his hand. There were no shadows under the trees but everywhere a pearly stillness, so that what was real seemed illusive and without definition. The pile of guts was a black blob of flies that buzzed like a saw. After a while these flies found Simon. Gorged, they alighted by his runnels of sweat and drank. They tickled under his nostrils and played leap-frog on his thighs. They were black and iridescent green and without number; and in front of Simon, the Lord of the Flies hung on his stick and grinned. At last Simon gave up and looked back; saw the white teeth and dim eyes, the blood—and his gaze was held by that ancient, inescapable recognition. In Simon's right temple, a pulse began to beat on the brain.

The visual richness of this writing and the precise diction are self-evident. But it is worth noting, first, how carefully Golding handles the scene so that we may read it as the plausible experience of a terrified boy. Thus Simon keeps striving to shut out the sight of the head, and in the next to last paragraph, for all the insight he reveals elsewhere in the story, he momentarily imagines the beast as actual in the same way that the other children do when he wonders whether it may not "come" to take its "gift." All the things that the head utters so "silently" represent, of course, the thoughts of Simon: earlier in the novel he has expressed the idea that evil is in man, though in the present context the sound of his own voice unsettles him when he declares, "I know that"; and what the head says of a "joke," a "headache," and "something you ate" are Simon's rational attempts to excuse himself from going up the mountain. Even the phrases about "the head grinning amusedly" and "ignoring the flies," though we later come to view them as something more, seem at first reading the kind of odd perception normal enough to a boy under stress. And the interior dialogue is followed immediately by our return to a physically actualized Simon, "feeling the weight of his wet hair," and to the circumstantial description of the world around him.

But we should also notice how delicately Golding roots the symbolic values in physical details, thus preparing us from the start of the passage for the explosion of symbolic meaning at its close. If the phrase "small brown image" provides a faintly religious air for Simon, the subsequent "after-image" underplays the suggestion by recalling our minds to some extent to optics. The "daylight" is "strange" primarily because of the relentless sun and the pressure Simon feels, but the setting is appropriate for the metamorphosis of the pig's head into the Devil. The fact that the head grins and ignores the flies, though a vision proper to a frightened child, is also a covert statement about the head as the "Lord of the Flies." Simon may look up for God's help, but what he looks at is simply "the sky." If the "butterflies" are to suggest souls that avoid the Devil, they have nevertheless been literal presences in the clearing before this point in the novel. The only statement that may ring slightly false in the passage (and I am not sure that it does) is "what was real seemed illusive and without definition." This must come from the omniscient narrator, for Simon's eyes are closed, and it sounds a little like a hint to the reader to be on the alert for what is morally "real," that is, for the symbolic equations that emerge clearly by the end of the passage. But even this statement, abstractly though Golding phrases it, accords well enough in its literal sense with the "strange daylight" mentioned earlier, and he actualizes the claim in the next sentence, where the "pile of guts" (the "real") is transformed into "a black blob of flies that buzzed like a saw." The climax of the scene, though fraught with symbolic significance, is brilliantly rendered in almost purely naturalistic terms. The flies move from the pig to Simon, this fact of itself identifying Simon as the next sacrifice (the tickling and playing of the flies harmonize wonderfully with the "fun" that the Lord of the Flies later preaches). Only after this identification has been made is the head referred to as "the Lord of the Flies," though the surrounding details insist that we keep viewing it as a pig's head on a stick. And when Simon finally looks at the head, what he sees are simply the details that he has seen before, though we are made to understand all this as Simon's acknowledgment that an evil principle has been enthroned in man and that he himself—such is the force of the climactic placing of "blood"—must die. The passage as a whole, then, is superbly poised between realism and symbolism, and this is the mode of the entire novel, whose statement about man is anchored in the substantial world of the island and children.

The degree to which Golding engages us in that world—partly through its substantiality, partly through the momentum of his narrative, but especially through his management of point of view—seems to me to differentiate *Lord of the Flies* radically from such a novel as Richard Hughes's *A High Wind in Jamaica*, with which Golding's story has frequently been compared. Certainly both books present unorthodox views of children (though even an admirer of Hughes may feel at moments a certain coyness in his account which is utterly alien to the tone of *Lord of the Flies*). But Hughes systematically uses his position as omniscient narrator to keep us at a distance from his fictional world, writing bits of travelogue and essays on children, presenting potentially distressing incidents in a manner—sometime mock-heroic—that cultivates our disengagement, sustaining everywhere an adult perspective that keeps us emotionally detached. Thus his story affects us finally as an extreme version of a fable: as rather a statement about children than the rendering of a world that compels our assent to its actuality. In *Lord of the Flies*, the sorts of explicit commentary that I have now and then quoted may make us periodically aware of an omniscient narrator, yet they scarcely qualify our absorption in the events of the novel.

And it is our very absorption in the run of the story, I suspect, that explains why many readers are unsettled by the ending of *Lord of the Flies*—in which the naval officer suddenly appears on the island to take charge of the children—or indeed by the endings of Golding's next three novels. For at the close of each he does of course dislocate us by altering in one fashion or another the perspective through which we have viewed the characters during most of the books, sometimes by introducing new characters. The main objection to such endings would seem to be that the unexpected shift threatens or fractures the illusion of reality generated by the foregoing narrative, and, since that illusion is so powerful in most of Golding's writing, the shift may feel especially disconcerting. But Dr. Johnson, for one, taught us long ago in his "Preface to Shakespeare" that the reality represented in literature is an illusion, and thus that it is naïve of us to imagine a work plausible only when it confines itself to one fixed set of circumstances: concerning the unity of place, for instance, Johnson remarks, "an action must be in some place; but the different actions that complete a story may be in places very remote from each other; and where is the absurdity of allowing that space to represent first *Athens*, and then *Sicily*, which was always known to be neither *Sicily* nor *Athens*, but a modern theatre?" While some readers may continue to regard Golding's conclusions as narrative misfortunes, it should at least be clear that his endings work in various ways to expand and bring home the meanings of the stories. In *Lord of the Flies*, to mention only the case at hand, the adult world adumbrated at the close is carrying on a war of its own, does not differ fundamentally from the children's world to which we have already been exposed, and so reinforces the claim about man dramatized throughout the book in the behavior of the children.

The implications of that claim are perhaps debatable, some readers interpreting the novel as determinedly pessimistic and others finding in it some rays of hope. Certainly the civilization created by Golding disintegrates in the course of the story. And if we take the children separately as representing certain qualities within any individual, the book becomes hardly less somber. For Piggy shows us that rationality alone will not sustain us; Ralph, that good intentions, a capacity for leadership, and a commitment to social order will not suffice to prevent a reversion to savagery under pressure; and Jack, that the fears, cruelty, and lust for power which inhabit every one of us can gain dominance all too easily. But Simon seeks to confront his fears and comes to accept the evil that inheres in him as well as in the other children, though he pays with his life for what he discovers. By thus struggling against and yet recognizing his limitations as a person, Simon engages in that perennial human task which is the source of man's defeats as of his triumphs— whether one regards man from the Christian perspective suggested by certain details in the novel or from a preeminently secular perspective.

JEANNE DELBAERE-GARANT

# *Rhythm and Expansion in* Lord of the Flies

Water and rocks, ebb and flow, angles and circles, microcosm and macrocosm, reason and intuition, good and evil, flies and butterflies: rhythm beats in *Lord of the Flies*, sometimes loud, sometimes with "an undertone less perceptible than the susurration of the blood," but always with the regularity of waves against the reef. This continual back-and-forth motion, the rhythm of life, is complemented by a rhythmic use of gradation suggesting the constant progress of evil. The killing of pigs and the throwing of rocks, two important activities of the boys on the island, provide a metaphorical structure for the illustration of the author's theme.

In the description of the setting is a basic opposition between sea and island, liquidity and hardness, flux and fixity, roundness and angularity. The "circular horizon of water" contains the "square motif of the landscape." This pattern, however, is not closed upon itself. It expands upwards, outwards, inwards in a never-ceasing reproduction. Sea and sky, islands and stars answer each other: the sky mirrors itself in the water together with the "angular bright constellations." At a mile's distance from the island and parallel to it lies a coral reef, against which waves break so that the beach is duplicated in the sea, "as though a giant had bent down to reproduce the shape of the island in a flowing, chalk line but tired before he had finished." Finally, there is a reminder of the water motif in the island, a reminder of the

From *William Golding: Some Critical Considerations*. © 1978 by The University Press of Kentucky.

rock motif in the sea. As in the yin and yang of the Chinese, there is a black patch in the white surface and a white patch in the black, a piece of squareness in the liquid element and a pool in the island: "There, where the island petered out in water, was another island; a rock, almost detached, standing like a fort, facing them across the green." Likewise "Some act of God—a typhoon perhaps—had banked sand inside the lagoon so that there was a long, deep pool in the beach," a pool which is only invaded by the sea at high tide.

There is rhythm also in the abrupt succession of night and day and even in the configuration of the island itself. The boys, having come with their rhythmic changes set to the time of the clock and of their European tradition, must now adapt to the physical cycles of their new abode: "The first rhythm that they became used to was the slow swing from dawn to quick dusk." Time is no longer measured by the clock but by the regular movement of sunlight from the horizontal at dawn to the perpendicular at noon and back to the horizontal in the evening. On the island the sandy beach is interrupted by the "square motif" of the mountain: "The most usual feature of the rock was a pink cliff surmounted by a skewed block; and that again surmounted, and that again, till the pinkness became a stack of balanced rock projecting through the looped fantasy of the forest creepers." As this rhythmical alternation of vertical and horizontal planes measures the tropical day and underlies the structure of the island, so contrastive and repetitive patterns govern the structure of the novel, which is built on a contrapuntal balance of opposites and on repetitions, echoes, parallels, which blend and culminate in the last chapter.

The action starts smoothly. The first chapter consists of an alternation of pictures and scenes according to whether Golding describes the place or presents the characters. From the beginning we are aware of correspondences: a bird's cry on the first page is answered by Piggy's voice, and the noise emitted by Ralph's blowing of the conch is echoed by the mountain. Even the fundamental patterns of the geophysical world will be unconsciously imitated by the boys in their activities: the contrast between the circular horizon of the sea and the angular shape of the island is reproduced in the circles and triangles into which they fall when they come together. When they hold meetings the boys form a triangle which eventually deteriorates into a sketchy and empty shape. When they hunt, Jack's choir-boys form a circle around the pig, and this pattern becomes neater as the boys revert to savagery. On the evening of Simon's death the circling movement has become so regular that it begins "to beat like a steady pulse." The conch, reconciling roundness and angularity, the irrational and the rational, in its "slight spiral twist" is a symbol of wholeness. The boys do not know this but take it as a talisman and feel that it is precious and rare.

The basic opposition between sea and reef corresponds to a contrast between the two groups of boys. Ralph's group—the democratic one—is characterized from the start by its heterogeneity, Jack's—the authoritarian one—by its organization. The boys of the first group come one by one, adding individual face to individual face: "There were badges, mottoes even, stripes of colour in stockings and pullovers. Their heads clustered above the trunks in the green shade; heads brown, fair, black, chestnut, sandy, mouse-colored; heads muttering, whispering, heads full of eyes." The choirboys, however, are first perceived as "something dark," a creature whose blackness interrupts the clear sand as the square motif of the mountain interrupts the beach. The geometrical elements suggest strict organization: "The creature was a party of boys, marching approximately in step *in two parallel lines* and dressed in strangely eccentric clothing. Shorts, shirts, and different garments they carried in their hands: but each boy wore *a square black cap* with a silver badge in it. Their bodies, from throat to ankle, were hidden by black cloaks which bore *a long silver cross*" (italics mine).

As a rock stands detached amid the water and a pool stretches on the island, a boy is singled out on each side: Simon and Piggy do not really belong to their groups. They are first noticed because of physical particularity which sets them apart and is commented on by the other boys: Simon because of his fainting fits, Piggy because of his obesity. They are outsiders: Piggy is laughed at and rejected; Simon goes off to meditate in the jungle. These two boys play a more important part in the novel than Ralph and Jack, who are most often set against each other. Indeed, in their opposition and complementariness Piggy and Simon epitomize all that exists in the universe: Simon is the passive element; like the candle-buds in his shelter opening their white flowers to meet the night air, he is always open, ready to let the world enter his soul and fill it. Piggy's protruding belly is the image of his affirmation, of his determination to change the world instead of accepting it. He is the rational mind opposed to intuition and insight. The two boys die significant deaths: Piggy's skull breaks into pieces against the rock which stands apart at the other end of the island, a symbol of himself keeping forever outside the triangle of the other boys' meetings or the circle of their ritual dances. Simon's body is lifted gently by the tide that fills the pool—an empty receptacle like himself—and takes him away to the open sea. The event manifests a larger rhythm into which it is integrated: "Somewhere over the darkened curve of the world the sun and moon were pulling; and the film of water on the earth planet was held, bulging slightly on one side while the solid core turned. The great wave of the tide moved further along the island and the water lifted. Softly, surrounded by a fringe of inquisitive bright creatures, itself a silver shape beneath the steadfast constellations, Simon's dead body moved out towards the open sea."

By introducing correspondences between setting and characters Golding intimates that the same law governs the geophysical world and the world of man. Human nature is an aspect of nature at large. Man is neither worse nor better than nature: the same evil principle permeates and harms both. Before the boys came to the island "some unknown force" had split the rocks and given the place its present aspect. When the boys scramble up these rocks they notice a scar across the landscape, probably made by the fuselage of their plane when it crashed. They smash a deep hole in the canopy of the forest by dislodging a boulder in order to reach the top of the mountain. The place is wounded successively by "some unknown force," by the civilized world of grown-ups, and by the boys themselves. At the end of the novel Ralph, with his bruised flesh and a "swollen and bloody scar where the spear had hit him" is identified with the island. The metaphorical scar of the first chapter was real after all.

In chapter 4 Golding concentrates on this rhythm of life in which each living creature is the victim of a force larger than itself. The littluns are on the beach, building castles in the sand. Two bigger boys, Roger and Maurice, look for a while at the castles and start kicking them over. The littluns do not protest any more than a grown-up would if his town had been suddenly destroyed by a typhoon. One of them, Henry, leaves the place and goes to the edge of the water. There his attention is caught by little organisms which come scavenging over the beach, and he starts poking about *"with a bit of stick that itself was wave-worn and whitened and a vagrant"* (italics mine). He is fascinated because he can exercise control over these tiny transparencies which, though embryonic, are endowed with life. Absorbed in his play he fails to notice Roger, who has remained near the scattered castles and observes him with the same attention as the littlun observes the scavengers. Suddenly a breeze shakes a palm tree sixty feet above Roger's head and nuts fall like stones about him. Roger is not touched but looks "from the nuts to Henry and back again": "The sub-soil beneath the palm tree was a raised beach; and generations of palms had worked loose in this *the stones that had lain on the sands of another shore.* Roger stooped, picked up a stone, aimed, and threw it at Henry—threw it to miss. The stone, *that token of preposterous time,* bounced five yards to Henry's right and fell in the water" (italics mine). Man and nature are in turns victims and victimizers. It is this confused new knowledge that Jack brings back from the hunt: you "feel as if you're not hunting, but—being hunted; as if something's behind you all the time in the jungle." The same blind force moves Henry's hand when he destroys the work of the scavengers on the beach, Maurice's when he scatters the sandcastles, Roger's when he throws stones at Henry, the wind's when it looses nuts around Roger, and the afternoon sun's when it "emptied down invisible arrows" on

Henry's head. The fact that the stick is wave-worn and that the stones have lain on the sands of another shore situates the whole process in a larger perspective not limited in time or space.

To remind us of this general rhythm, of which the action of *Lord of the Flies* is only a miniature manifestation, Golding selected his material with care and reduced the episodes of the book to two types of opposite activities developing inversely. On the positive, rational side are expeditions and assemblies; on the negative, irrational side, throwing rocks and killing pigs. Keeping the fire is not for the boys a regular activity since they soon neglect it. A symbol of man's reason and intelligence (there could be no fire without Piggy's glasses), the fire can be either positive or negative according to how it is used. Meant as a signal fire for passing ships or planes it becomes, through misuse, a wild beast with a life of its own which invades the whole place, kills the little boy with the mulberry-colored birthmark, and threatens to destroy them all. What happens by accident in the second chapter is done deliberately at the end by the boys turned savages.

Each of the three expeditions on the island is made by a three-boy party: successively, Ralph, Jack, Simon; Ralph, Jack, Roger; Jack, Maurice, Roger. Jack, the red-haired devil figure, is present in each. The first aims at exploring the place to make sure it is an island. The worlds of common sense (Ralph wants to draw a map of the island), of action (Jack wants to kill a pig), and of imagination (Simon sees candle-buds among the bushes) are united in the joy of common discovery and experience. About the middle of the book a second group of boys decides to climb the mountain to look for the beast. Ralph and Jack remember their first exploration, and "consciousness of the bad times in between came to them both." Ralph senses the rising antagonism between himself and Jack. Roger now replaces Simon; hatred replaces love. The third expedition takes place after Jack has formed his own group and has decided to steal Piggy's glasses to light their own fire. The forces of evil (Roger, Maurice) gradually replace love and common sense (Simon, Ralph). The constructive aim degenerates into robbery and destruction. At the end Ralph is alone against an expedition made by savages and conducted against himself.

The first assembly gathers in the afternoon following the first expedition. Ralph sits on a fallen trunk with the choir boys on his right, the larger boys on his left, and the littluns in front. He finds he can speak fluently and has the self-confidence of a real chief. The question about the snake-thing asked by the boy with the mulberry-colored birthmark casts a gloom over the general optimism and is a premonition of evil. The second meeting is described at length. It occurs after the fire has gone out. Ralph is in a grim mood and, looking at the other boys with new eyes, he begins to adjust his views and to fall into a mood of speculation foreign to him ("If faces were different when lit from above or below—what was a face? What was anything?"). The third assembly is called by Jack after the second expedition. Jack tells the others that Ralph ran away when he saw the beast and that they should now choose him, Jack, as chief. As nobody answers he goes off by himself, leaving order and reason behind. Ralph is vaguely aware of the situation but seems powerless to change anything: it is as though the great force that split the rocks was now splitting their group; the sky, "as if in sympathy with the great changes among them," is different and the air is stifling. Piggy blows the conch after the third expedition, when his glasses have been stolen. But the beach is deserted and only "the shape of the old assembly, trodden in the grass" answers the call. Ralph can no longer find words, cannot think properly, and Piggy must help him remember what to say.

Those meetings indicate the gradual deterioration of the civilized element, as Ralph's confident talk turns into a lamentable stuttering and the neat geometrical pattern of the first assembly wears off into a sketchy triangle before becoming a mere shape emptied of people. The meetings are in direct connection with the explorations, which are presented directly and then commented upon in the assemblies, so that the same event is seen from two different angles. Besides, each new meeting accretes new meaning by being charged, in Ralph's mind, with memories of the previous ones, which gradually awaken him to the consciousness of something he did not know before. He becomes more and more silent, conscious of the increasing evil but unable to stop it.

With the throwing of rocks and the killing of pigs the movement is first confused and only gradually asserts itself as the boys lose control of the rational in themselves. The memory of punishment received for throwing sand in a younger boy's eyes holds back Maurice's hand on the beach. The interdictions from his former life keep Roger from throwing stones at Henry: "There was a space round Henry, perhaps six yards in diameter, into which he dare not throw. Here, invisible yet strong, was the taboo of the old life. Round the squatting child was the protection of parents and school and policemen and the law. Roger's arm was conditioned by a civilization that . . . was in ruins." When Jack raises his hand to kill his first pig, "There came a pause, a hiatus, the pig continued to scream and the creepers to jerk, and the blade continued to flash at the end of a bony arm. The pause was only long enough for them to understand what an enormity the downward stroke would be." At the end of the novel the same boys, Maurice, Roger, and Jack, have become real forces of evil, intoxicated with their own power and impatient to exercise it.

Indeed, the throwing of rocks begins with Roger's first stone in the sea, which is a perfect diagram of Golding's technique to depict the progress of evil. The same act recurs with an amplification similar to that of waves spreading in larger and larger circles around a stone thrown in the water. When he kills Piggy, Roger makes the same gesture as when he threw stones at Henry. Only the stone has become a "monstrous red thing" and Roger a murderer. Yet at the beginning the boys mean no harm. If they roll a rock through the forest, it is because it bars their progress; they join efforts to move it and are happy when they succeed:

> "Heave!"
> Sway back and forth, catch the rhythm.
> "Heave!" . . .
> The great rock loitered, poised on one toe, decided not to return, moved through the air, fell, struck, turned over, leapt droning through the air and smashed a deep hole in the canopy of the forest. . . .
> "Wacco!"
> "Like a bomb!"

After that, the way to the top is easy. Although this is only a first step in deterioration, the boys' exclamations point to the future and a further expansion of evil which, like the rock, will gather pace as it tumbles down. From the start the boys are aware of their power ("Eyes shining, mouths open, triumphant, they savoured the right of domination") and look with exhilaration at the platform beneath with "insect-like figures moving near it." The second throwing of rocks takes place in chapter 6 when the hunters decide to look for the beast. The antagonism between the chiefs makes them think of war and see the pink bastion as a fort. Jack suggests that a palm trunk might be shoved as a lever under the last broken rock so that it can be launched more easily at an imaginary invader. Meanwhile the hunters are heaving and pushing rocks for fun. Under them the grass is "dotted with heads."

Once they have imagined a weapon, the hunters are not satisfied until they use it against a real enemy. They do so as soon as the opportunity offers: Roger, leaning all his weight on the lever, lifts the big rock and propels it at Piggy. A change of perspective takes place at the end, when the throwing of rocks is seen from the point of view of one of the insectlike figures. Because he is now one of them, Ralph knows that nothing will stop the tumbling monster. He can make out the familiar "Heave! Heave! Heave!" as the hunters try to catch the rhythm, and he knows that the rock, "half as big as a cottage, big as a car, a tank" is aimed at him.

There is the same tidelike amplification in the killing of pigs. After he has overcome his repulsion, Jack thrusts his knife into the living flesh of his victim. The reader does not witness the scene directly; it is related by the hunters when they come back from the forest. Ralph is waiting for them, furious and helpless on the ashes of the signal fire which they have let go out. They are so excited they fail to notice his anger and speak all at once:

> "We got in a circle—"
> "We crept up—"
> "The pig squealed—"

Again, as after the throwing of the first rock, there is perfect harmony between the boys who have been caught in the same rhythm ("so then the circle could close in and beat and beat—"), who have shared the same experience and are now rich with the same knowledge and memories. But the world of Jack ("of hunting, tactics, fierce exhilaration, skill") and the world of Ralph ("of longing and baffled common sense") part here. Envious and resentful, Ralph watches them while Maurice acts the pig and runs squealing to the center of the circle made by the hunters who mimic the killing and dance around him.

The mock hunt is repeated in chapter 7. The hunters have just missed a boar and console themselves by organizing a game in which Robert enacts the pig while other boys dance and chant around him. As in the second throwing of rocks, the hunters are disappointed because it is just a game: the desire to spill blood possesses them, and they see this as only a surrogate for the real thing. Once more Jack is the instigator of evil when he suggests that a boy might be used as a substitute for the pig:

> "You want a pig," said Roger, "like in a real hunt."
> "Or someone to pretend," said Jack. "You could get someone to dress up as a pig and then he could act—you know, pretend to knock me over and all that—"
> "You want a real pig," said Robert, still caressing his rump. . . .
> "Use a littlun," said Jack, and everybody laughed.

Again what Jack conceives in imagination and presents as a joke will become reality. When they hunt the third time (the reader now witnesses the scene directly), the game turns into murder. It begins with the killing of a sow surrounded by her young piglets. The hunters pursue her to the open space where Simon, concealed by the leaves, has retired to meditate. The violence of the hunt contrasts with the fragile beauty of the butterflies which, as usual, occupy the center of Simon's clearing. Jack orders Roger to

"Sharpen a stick at both ends" so that they can impale the sow's head and leave it as an offering to the beast. It is some time before the butterflies desert the open space and are replaced by flies that alight on the sow's dripping head and Simon's sweating face. Identification with the sacrificial victim fore-shadows his fate. After the hunt the boys' excitement is increased by the stifling heat and the menace of an approaching storm, and they fall back on their ritual dances to protect themselves: "Some of the littluns started a ring on their own; and the complementary circles went round and round as though repetition would achieve safety of itself." Even Ralph and Piggy, "under the threat of the sky, found themselves eager to take a place in this demented but partly secure society." The tension grows, the need to kill becomes urgent, and when Simon comes out of the forest to tell them that the beast is a dead parachutist he is assaulted and slain.

In the last chapter, everything is seen from Ralph's point of view. He hears the chant that accompanies the killing of a pig and is told by the twins that Roger has "sharpened a stick at both ends." It takes him some time to make sense of this enigmatic sentence, which the reader immediately under-stands; he then remembers that the hunters needed such a stick to impale the sow's head and that they now want another for his own.

The throwing of stones and the killing of pigs develop in similar ways: both pursuits are initiated out of necessity, repeated for fun, turned against a human being (significantly, Piggy and Simon, who represent the two poles of the human mind) and finally against Ralph, who has become the center of consciousness and learns to decipher, now that he is its victim, the darkness of the human heart. The change of perspective takes place at the beginning of the last chapter, when the action—which had been up to then observed from the outside—is seen entirely through the eyes of the main character. In *Pincher Martin* Golding drops the external presentation of the action alto-gether and writes a whole novel on what takes place inside the mind of a character, leaving it to the reader to reassemble disconnected pieces of the jigsaw. Here we are both outside and inside, witnessing the hunt and sharing the thoughts of the hunted. This gives the novel an apparent simplicity, which is misleading. Because its surface offers no real resistance many critics have tended to ignore the complexity of *Lord of the Flies*, though this novel is no less subtle than *The Inheritors* or *Pincher Martin*.

After making clear, through a rhythmical balance of opposites recalling the waves of the ocean, that all things, animate and inanimate, are governed by the same law, that evil does not spare man any more than it does nature, that each living creature is in turn hunter and hunted, Golding shows, through a series of repetitions expanding like the movement of the tides, that there is no stopping evil. When he shifts the focus of the novel in the last chapter, he anticipates a device used later in *The Inheritors* and *Pincher Martin*. In the last chapter of *The Inheritors* there is a switch in point of view; the action is no longer seen through the eyes of Lok but through those of a new man. In *Pincher Martin* the sudden intrusion of the naval officer—a duplicate of the one that rescues the boys—gives a twist to the novel and generalizes its effect. These gimmicks are combined in Golding's first novel: after focusing on Ralph to present the action through the boy's consciousness, the author focuses on infinity and universalizes his theme. Not only is this contraction-expansion in keeping with the movement of the novel, but the metaphorical structure itself is borrowed from the two main activities through which the progress of evil has been illustrated.

The killing of the pigs provides Golding with his first metaphor: all the concentric circles of the novel now close in on Ralph—identified with the pig and the place—in a climactic high tide of evil that threatens to engulf him and the island alike. He has become the prey of the evil force which he had so far observed from the outside: he is the boar tracked by the hunters and considers the possibility of bursting the line; he is Piggy menaced by the great block above his head; he is Simon used as a sacrificial victim by the savages; he is the littlun who perished in the fire at the beginning of the story ("There was another noise to attend to now—a deep grumbling noise, as though the forest itself were angry with him. . . . He knew he had heard it before somewhere, but had no time to remember.") Finally he is the island itself, "scorched up like dead wood." And then, when the scar is no longer a metaphor but is felt in his own bruised flesh, he weeps for the end of innocence.

This contraction is immediately followed by an expansion when the officer appears. His "fun and games" echoes Ralph's words at the beginning of the novel and suggests, like the white beach line reproducing the contour of the island in the sea, a further duplication of the whole story. This time it is the throwing of stones that provides Golding with his metaphor: the movement is no longer centripetal but expands from the center outwards, from the world of the children to the world of the grown-ups, from the island to the world at large. The island is a microcosmic stone thrown in the middle of the ocean with waves of evil radiating around it in larger and larger circles. The events witnessed in *Lord of the Flies* do not end when the book does. If Roger's first stone leads to his murderous gesture, there is no reason why the rock thrown at Piggy should not also lead to the bomb launched against an enemy's country and ultimately to the atomic bomb that will destroy mankind. At this stage not only Ralph but the reader himself is aware that once the process has started there is no stopping the enraged monster.

ARNOLD JOHNSTON

# Lord of the Flies: *Fable, Myth, and Fiction*

*L*ord of the Flies deals, ostensibly, with a group of English schoolboys who, in the process of being evacuated by airplane from the dangers of a nuclear war, find themselves alone on a tropical island after their plane crashes. The boys, ranging in age from about six to thirteen, are faced with the problem of survival on the uninhabited island while attempting to attract the attention of passing ships and planes.

The problem of physical existence solves itself—the island is rich in fruit and game and the climate is favorable. The real problem that arises among the boys involves their own inner nature, and emerges most directly from a clash between those who wish to keep a fire burning on the island's mountain to attract rescuers and those who wish to hunt and indulge in what at first seems to be the natural inclination of children toward unrestrained play. The conflict begins in apparent childish innocence, and reaches its climax in acts of shocking brutality that carry far-reaching implications of guilt.

Golding has summed up the theme of *Lord of the Flies* as follows:

The theme is an attempt to trace the defects of society back to the defects of human nature. The moral is that the shape of society must depend on the ethical nature of the individual and

From *Earth and Darkness: The Novels of William Golding*. © 1980 by The Curators of the University of Missouri.

not on any political system however apparently logical or respectable. The whole book is symbolic in nature.

As I have mentioned, Golding feels that evil arises from man's essential being, and he attempts to demonstrate his thesis in this self-consciously symbolic work which shows civilization totally unable to contend with man's apparently natural and voracious propensity for savagery. A systematic probing into the question of man's inherent good or evil is, without doubt, one of Golding's major concerns; and in the course of this study I shall attempt to show that his apparent preoccupation with the problems of survival (*Lord of the Flies, The Inheritors, Pincher Martin*) is an important key to understanding both his philosophy and his techniques.

*Lord of the Flies* falls into that hardy genre of accounts of shipwreck and survival on tropical islands: *Robinson Crusoe, The Swiss Family Robinson, The Coral Island,* and so forth. Golding particularly wishes the reader to associate his novel with Ballantyne's *The Coral Island.* The two main characters in both books are named Ralph and Jack, and the relationship between the names of Ballantyne's Peterkin and Golding's Simon needs little elaboration. Then, too, there are two direct references to *The Coral Island* in Golding's book, one near the beginning—

> "It's like in a book."
> At once there was a clamour.
> "Treasure Island—"
> "Swallows and Amazons—"
> "Coral Island—"

and one near the end—

> The officer nodded helpfully.
> "I know. Jolly good show. Like the Coral Island."

Frank Kermode and Carl Niemeyer, in separate essays, discuss at some length Golding's use of *The Coral Island* as an ironic parallel to his own novel, pointing out the difference between Golding's vision of human nature and what Niemeyer calls the "cheerful unrealities" of Ballantyne. And Golding himself, in the interview with Kermode, had this to say of his book's connection with *The Coral Island*:

> What I'm saying to myself is, "Don't be such a fool, you remember when you were a boy, a small boy, how you lived on that island

with Ralph and Jack and Peterkin. . . . Now that you are grown up, . . . you can see people are not like that; they would not behave like that if they were God-fearing English gentlemen, and they went to an island like that." Their savagery would not be found in natives on an island. As like as not they would find savages who were kindly and uncomplicated and that the devil would rise out of the intellectual complications of the three white men on the island itself.

Golding's remark about kindly, uncomplicated savages stacks the anthropological cards a bit heavily against civilized man, and ignores a number of basic facts about primitive cultures. Of course, *Lord of the Flies* doesn't allow the reader any "real" savages with whom to compare the boys, as Golding's artistic sense evidently told him to avoid confusing the central human issue with such anthropological quibbles. However, the aforementioned remark does underline Golding's moralistic bias, and points toward a more serious charge that might be leveled against the novel: that his authorial presence is often overly obtrusive, either in didactic interpositions or, more seriously, in unconvincing manipulation of his characters.

In this connection Lionel Trilling says that Golding succeeds in persuading the reader that the boys' actions result from the fact that they "are not finally under the control of previous social habit or convention," but adds that he "should not have credited this quite so readily of American boys who would not . . . have been so quick to forget their social and moral pasts." For my part, I am unable to see why Mr. Trilling is unwilling to carry his pertinent critical comment to its logical conclusion, without involving himself in speculations about the relative acculturation processes in Britain and the United States. Had he pursued his doubts to an expression of dissatisfaction with the credibility of the boys, he would have been on firmer ground, since there are several points at which Golding's manipulations of narrative and dialogue do ring false.

Two interrelated but discernibly distinct threads are evident in *Lord of the Flies*. One is the actual narrative, detailing meticulously the boys' descent into savagery; the other is the gradually developed symbol of the "Beast" that is first suggested by the wholly natural night fears of the "littluns" and that eventually becomes the object of worship by the boys-turned-savages. The Beast is an externalization of the inner darkness in the children's (man's) nature, and its ascendency is steady, inexorable, as is the path to savagery, increasing in intensity with each new regression on the part of the boys. But despite his often brilliant handling of this apposite motivating symbol of the book, it is especially during scenes involving the Beast that Golding becomes particularly intrusive.

At one point, for instance, when the assembled boys are discussing the problem of the Beast, Piggy (the pragmatic rationalist) explains: "'Course there isn't a beast in the forest. How could there be? What would a beast eat?'" And the answer, supplied by the chorus of boys, is "'Pig!'"— to which the unmistakable voice of Golding (by way of reminding the reader just what his symbol represents) can be heard to add, "'We eat pig.'" And a few pages later Simon, the convulsion-afflicted mystic, says of the Beast: "'What I mean is . . . maybe it's only us.'" This rather subtle interpretation of human nature from a small boy demonstrates further that Golding is so intent on his moral message that he will not hesitate to make the youngsters dance to his tune.

This assembly scene is central to the novel's development in that it marks the last point at which "civilized" rules and procedures can be said to dominate the boys' words and actions. Grounds for the breakdown of the rules are furnished by dissent among the representatives of order (Ralph, Piggy, and Simon), as Piggy, with his unimaginative rationalist's intelligence, answers Simon's observation with a resounding "'Nuts!'" Even among the "civilized," communication is lacking, and when Jack—leader of the forces of disorder— shouts "'Bollocks to the rules!'" chaos and darkness are ushered in.

However, Golding cannot let the matter of the Beast rest here, and after the assembly has dispersed, Ralph, shaken, turns to Piggy and asks, "'Are there ghosts, Piggy? Or Beasts?'" And here the ventriloquist's lips can be seen to move, as Piggy answers: "'Course there aren't. . . . 'Cos things wouldn't make sense. Houses an' streets, an'—TV—they wouldn't work.'" Although beautifully camouflaged in boyish diction, the implication that a boy of about ten can reason that the existence of supernatural phenomena challenges the validity of natural law is simply too much to swallow.

A major objectification of man's inner Beast appears in the shape of a pig's head on a stick that Jack and his "hunters" leave as an offering for the Beast. Unknown to the hunters, Simon has been nearby during the killing of the pig, having hidden himself in some bushes at the onset of one of his fits. He is then left alone with the head, thus setting the scene for the most self-consciously symbolic incident in the book. At this point the significance of the book's title becomes evident, as the head, swarming with flies, enters into an imaginary conversation with Simon, a conversation in which Golding, speaking through this grotesque agent, removes any doubts that might still have lingered in the reader's mind with respect to the novel's theme or the source of the evil described therein:

> The Lord of the Flies spoke in the voice of a schoolmaster.
> "This has gone quite far enough. My poor, misguided child,

do you think you know better than I do?"

There was a pause.

"I'm warning you. I'm going to get waxy. D'you see. You're not wanted. Understand? We are going to have fun on this island! So don't try it on, my poor misguided boy, or else—"

Simon found that he was looking into a vast mouth. There was blackness within, a blackness that spread.

"—Or else," said the Lord of the Flies, "we shall do you. See? Jack and Roger and Maurice and Robert and Bill and Piggy and Ralph. Do you. See?"

The above scene, which places perhaps the greatest strain on the reader's credulity, may be defended as the book's clearest indication that human guilt is pervasive, including even the "good" characters, Ralph and Piggy. However, by comparing this strained encounter between Simon and the head with the scenes immediately preceding and following it, one may see that Golding makes his point there just as clearly and much more effectively.

The killing of the pig by Jack's hunters is a case in point. The pig-hunting of former days has been relatively innocent, but to fully dramatize the deep inner evil that takes possession of the boys after they accept the Beast as their god, Golding depicts more than a mere killing. Conjuring up the most shocking imagery he could use to show the degeneration of these preadolescents, he describes the slaughter of a mother sow in terms of a sexual assault. How better to portray the children's loss of innocence (since children are no strangers to killing) than by picturing them as perpetrators of an Oedipal violation?

> ... the sow staggered her way ahead of them, bleeding and mad, and the hunters followed, wedded to her in lust, excited by the long chase and the dropped blood. . . .
>
> Here, struck down by the heat, the sow fell and the hunters hurled themselves at her. This dreadful eruption from an unknown world made her frantic; she squealed and bucked and the air was full of sweat and noise and blood and terror. Roger ran round the heap, prodding with his spear wherever pigflesh appeared. Jack was on top of the sow, stabbing downward with his knife. Roger found a lodgment for his spear and began to push till he was leaning with his whole weight. The spear moved forward inch by inch and the terrified squealing became a high-pitched scream. Then Jack found the throat and the hot blood

spouted over his hands. The sow collapsed under them and they
were heavy and fulfilled upon her.

The vividness of this scene makes it both a powerfully realistic component of
the essential story and a major contribution to the novel's symbolic scheme.
The episode involving Simon and the head, however—especially the
"conversation"—is difficult to view in other than symbolic terms, marking it
as another nagging flaw in a book that—whatever its thematic concerns—
seems committed from the outset to creating believable boys on a believable
island. Actually, the mere physical presence of the pig's head, the Lord of the
Flies, would have served well without the didactic pronouncements, since
"lord of the flies" is a translation of the Hebrew *Ba'al zevuv* (Beelzebub in
Greek), implying quite effectively that the head is representative of man's
"inner devil."

In any event, the most successful symbolic portrayal of the Beast as man
appears earlier in the novel in the form of a dead airman whose parachute
carries him in the night to the top of the mountain, where, tangled in the
complication of strings, he becomes lodged in a sitting position, the upper half
of his body alternately rising and falling as the breeze tightens and slackens the
lines. Sam and Eric, the twins, are horrified by this grisly figure when they
come to tend the fire, and when a subsequent expedition (headed by Ralph and
Jack, but notably excluding Simon and Piggy) climbs the mountain to confirm
the twins' garbled report, the following powerful passage shows the Beast
impressed forever on the minds and hearts of the boys:

Behind them the sliver of moon had drawn clear of the horizon.
Before them, something like a great ape was sitting asleep with
its head between its knees. Then the wind roared in the forest,
there was confusion in the darkness and the creature lifted its
head, holding toward them the ruin of a face.

This is the experience that accelerates the deterioration of civilized procedures, bringing confusion to the final assembly and committing Jack fully—
in a parody of his initial appearance as leader of the choir, or perhaps an
oblique commentary on the ritualistic mind—to high priesthood in the dark
new religion. And it is to determine the truth of this experience and the
nature of the so-called Beast from Air that Simon, after his ghastly interview
with the head, courageously ascends the mountain, where he frees the wasted
body "from the wind's indignity."

Simon, whom Golding has called quite explicitly a "Christ-figure,"
comes down from the mountain to carry the truth to the others, but—still

weak from his recent attack—he stumbles instead into a ritual reenactment of the pig-killing and is killed by the frenzied and fear-maddened boys, who ironically mistake him for the Beast. And here Golding's sweeping indictment of humanity becomes most nearly complete, for Ralph and Piggy, lured by the prospect of food, have temporarily joined with the hunters and take part, albeit unwittingly, in the murder of Simon. And here, too, at the moment of Simon's death, in the midst of a storm that thunders within as well as around them, the boys are visited by the spectre of human history, embodied in the form of the dead airman. Dislodged from atop the mountain and carried again into the air by the winds, the grotesque figure of the decaying parachutist plummets to the sands, scattering the terror-stricken boys, and sweeps far out to sea. The beach is left desolate save for the small broken body of Simon, which follows the parachutist into the sea:

> Along the shoreward edge of the shallows the advancing clearness was full of strange, moonbeam-bodied creatures with fiery eyes. Here and there a larger pebble clung to its own air and was covered with a coat of pearls. The tide swelled in and over the rain-pitted sand and smoothed everything with a layer of silver. Now it touched the first of the stains that seeped from the broken body and the creatures made a moving patch of light as they gathered at the edge. The water rose farther and dressed Simon's coarse hair with brightness. The line of his cheek silvered and the turn of his shoulder became sculptured marble. The strange attendant creatures, with their fiery eyes and trailing vapors, busied themselves round his head. The body lifted a fraction of an inch from the sand and a bubble of air escaped from the mouth with a wet plop. Then it turned gently in the water.
>
> Somewhere over the darkened curve of the world the sun and moon were pulling, and the film of water on the earth planet was held, bulging slightly on one side while the solid core turned. The great wave of the tide moved farther along the island and the water lifted. Softly, surrounded by a fringe of inquisitive bright creatures, itself a silver shape beneath the steadfast constellations, Simon's dead body moved out toward the open sea.

The amount and kind of description devoted to Simon's death is ample indication of his saintly role even without Golding's identification of him as a Christ-figure.

All of the obvious parallels to Christ are there—from Gethsemane to Golgotha—and one may easily identify Simon's story with that of many a martyred mystic. But why are they there? Why is Simon there? Is Golding merely speaking with the voice of moral and religious orthodoxy? As his subsequent novels have shown, Golding is not to be labeled so easily. But in those novels one sees a consistent preoccupation with the artist or artist-figure, someone actively engaged in interpreting the human condition: Tuami, the tribal artist in *The Inheritors*; Christopher "Pincher" Martin, the penultimate actor in *Pincher Martin*; Sammy Mountjoy, the guilt-torn painter in *Free Fall*; Dean Jocelin and Roger Mason, creative force behind, and architect of, *The Spire*; Oliver, the confused would-be musician in *The Pyramid*; and Matty Windrove, the naive prophet of *Darkness Visible*.

Viewed in this light, Simon's habitual isolation from the other boys, his obvious inability to communicate to them the "truths" that he grasps intuitively, and finally his death at their hands, reflect the all-too-frequent fate of the artist in society. Of course, all that can be said of the artist's role may be applied to that of the religious or mystic; but again and again in his later works Golding demonstrates that the nature of his unorthodoxy is its basis in that highly eclectic form of mysticism called art. Like many artists before him, he sees the artist as priest, as interpreter of life's mysteries and possible savior of mankind. Unlike many of his predecessors, though, Golding faces squarely the historical fact that the artist—like other saviors—has met with little success. And in this first novel, Simon should be recognized as the first of Golding's "portraits of the artist," embodying both his pride in the high calling and his frustration at the artist's inability to defend himself against the weaknesses of others, or to transcend his own human frailties. Even more important to a reading of his works as a whole is the realization that, for Golding, the artist is representative of humanity at large, and that Golding finds in creativity the source of man's strength and weakness, his good and evil.

In any case, the aftermath of Simon's death is the last point at which *Lord of the Flies* can be said to picture the existence of a calm and ordering vision. Total disintegration of the civilized forces follows swiftly, beginning with the theft of Piggy's glasses—the source of fire and symbol of intellectual power—by Jack and his hunters, and proceeding through Piggy's murder by the brutal Roger to the final hunt for Ralph, who is to be decapitated and sacrificed like a pig to the Beast.

The description of Piggy's death provides an informing contrast to that of Simon's, showing quite clearly, though subtly, Golding's antirationalist bias:

> The rock struck Piggy a glancing blow from chin to knee;
> the conch exploded into a thousand white fragments and ceased
> to exist. Piggy, saying nothing, with no time for even a grunt,

traveled through the air sideways from the rock, turning over as he went. The rock bounded twice and was lost in the forest. Piggy fell forty feet and landed on his back across that square red rock in the sea. His head opened and stuff came out and turned red. Piggy's arms and legs twitched a bit, like a pig's after it has been killed. Then the sea breathed again in a long, slow sigh, the water boiled white and pink over the rock; and when it went, sucking back again, the body of Piggy was gone.

One notes here the same studious reportage of physical fact as in the passage quoted earlier. But this time Golding concentrates on matter-of-fact particulars, eschewing the angle of vision that might place Piggy's death in universal perspective: whereas Simon is described in language befitting a dead saint, Piggy is pictured as a dead animal. Of course, Piggy's actions immediately before his murder are brave in conventional terms; but his rationalist's faith in order and human perfectibility, ironically undercut throughout the book, seems nowhere more misguided than in this scene. The mystic's intuitive recognition that good and evil coexist within man is the spark of his divinity; but the rationalist's denial of such intangible forces chains him forever to the material world of earth and organism.

After Piggy's death, Ralph finds himself being hunted by the other boys. But at the book's climactic moment, just as the "savages" are about to descend on Ralph, a "rescuer" appears in the person of a British naval officer. And at once, in a passage laden with irony, the shrieking painted savages become "a semicircle of little boys, their bodies streaked with colored clay, sharp sticks in their hands . . . standing on the beach making no noise at all." The officer, confronted with this scene of filth and disorder, rebukes the boys lamely (as Lionel Trilling might have noted): "'I should have thought that a pack of British boys—you're all British, aren't you?—would have been able to put up a better show than that—'" And Ralph, the book's Everyman, representative of the world of "longing and baffled common-sense," is left to weep "for the end of innocence, the darkness of man's heart, and the fall through the air of the true, wise friend called Piggy."

Several early critics and reviewers of *Lord of the Flies* assailed the book's ending as too neat, if not actually as a question-begging compromise with lovers of happy endings. However, a reflective reading shows that the "rescue" is no rescue at all: throughout the novel Golding is at pains to point out that the major human predicament is internal; the officer solves Ralph's immediate problem, but "the darkness of man's heart" persists. Practically, of course, as Golding says, in a book "originally conceived . . . as the change from innocence—which is the ignorance of self—to a tragic knowledge . . .

If I'd gone on to the death of Ralph, Ralph would never have had time to understand what had happened to him." And on a more sophisticated thematic level he observes, "The officer, having interrupted a manhunt, prepares to take the children off the island in a cruiser which will presently be hunting its enemy in the same implacable way. And who will rescue the adult and his cruiser?"

Returning to the Simon-Piggy contrast discussed earlier, one might also note that it is Piggy, the misguided rationalist, for whom Ralph sorrows, not Simon, the "saint." Besides subtly underscoring Golding's concern for the fate of the artist-mystic, this fact seems to indicate that Ralph's tragic experience has not finally brought him to the sort of self-knowledge that can save him as a man. The implications for humanity at large are clear and unencouraging. Thus, although the officer seems to suggest a deus ex machina, one will be hard pressed to find a happy ending here.

On a broader front, the plot of *Lord of the Flies* has been attacked as both eccentric and specious, either too far removed from the real world or too neatly microcosmic to be true. The first of these charges, that of eccentricity, may be put aside for the time being. After all, removing one's setting and characters from the larger sphere of civilization has long been an acceptable, if not honorable, practice in almost every literary genre and tradition, as witness the success of Melville and Conrad, whose isolated fictional worlds remain real in both their concrete details and their human significance. The source of the objection seems to be predisposed literary tastes, rather than more rigorous aesthetic standards—preference for the novel as typical history, rather than symbolic vision. However, the related charge—that Golding oversimplifies complex truth through manipulation of his microcosmic world—is on firmer ground. And in speaking to this point, one must necessarily return to John Peter's identification of Golding as a fabulist, as well as to Golding's own wish to be seen as a "myth-maker."

The main concern, then, of both opponents and supporters of *Lord of the Flies* is whether or not it functions adequately on its primary, or "fictional," level; or more simply, is the story told convincingly? Peter, in "The Fables of William Golding," assails the novel for its "incomplete translation of its thesis into its story so that much remains external and extrinsic, the teller's assertion rather than the tale's enactment before our eyes." And indeed, I have detailed several instances of such didactic obtrusions, including some aspects of character and action that seem more concerned with theme than credibility. However, I would qualify Peter's observation rather strongly, noting that such instances seem more vulnerable to the charge of being extraneous than of betraying Golding's "incomplete translation" of his thesis, which is more adequately communicated by the rest of the novel.

And what of the rest of the novel? Is it merely a skeleton of thesis incompletely fleshed by concrete detail? Kinkead-Weekes and Gregor are highly emphatic in answering this question: "Physical realities come first for Golding and should stay first for his readers." They devote a long first chapter in their study to a demonstration of the "complex physical truth" of *Lord of the Flies*, concentrating heavily on the naturalistic clarity and inclusiveness of Golding's description, and arguing that his symbolic representations are often so reflective of life's complexities as to be actually ambiguous, perhaps even too ambiguous to be seen symbolically at all. This latter point is a bit extreme: Golding's main symbolic intentions are clear enough in the novel, even without the many explicit comments he has made since its publication. However, Kinkead-Weekes and Gregor may be excused their overstatement, since so much attention has been paid to the novel's symbolism that its objective vehicles have been too often deemphasized, if not forgotten.

And here, Golding's style becomes a major concern. As Kinkead-Weekes and Gregor demonstrate, Golding's descriptive prose carries the burden of his meaning and—coupled with the inexorable narrative of the boys' descent into chaos—provides the reader with a naturalistically concrete and complex surface world against which to view the symbolic drama. One need only note passages already quoted—the killing of the sow, the deaths of Simon and Piggy—to be convinced that the realities of *Lord of the Flies* live in the flesh, as well as in the abstract, comprising a universe not oversimplified, but paradoxically diverse, in which beauty and ugliness, good and evil, precariously coexist. The main features of Golding's best description are scientific accuracy and objectivity, combined with a felicitous use of simple adjectives and verbs that can transform his tersely pictured scenes into powerful evocations of transcendent beauty or obsessive ugliness. One thinks here of the extremes of such effects before the sow-killing, when "she staggered into an open space where bright flowers grew and butterflies danced round each other and the air was hot and still," and after, when "the pile of guts was a black blob of flies that buzzed like a saw." Without doubt, Golding's world exists compellingly on its primary level: its strained moments seem more like surface blemishes than structural defects, blemishes that catch the eye because of their dissimilarity to the skillfully woven fabric of the whole.

As for Golding's stature as a maker of myth, one must grant him a considerable measure of success. Certainly, if myth "comes out from the roots of things" and evokes age-old and recurrent human patterns, *Lord of the Flies* is much closer to myth than to simple fable. One may trace its literary roots alone back through the more immediate past (*The Coral Island*), to the ancient past (*The Bacchae*), and on a broader plane one may easily see in the story echoes and parallels from both the political and social dynamics of contemporary civilization (the rise of Fascism, anti-intellectualism) and the religious and philosophical foundations of Western culture (the Old Testament, the Fall, the New Testament, the Crucifixion, as well as nineteenth-century rationalism). Indeed, the very profusion of suggestive patterns in the novel should demonstrate that here is no simple allegorical reworking of the materials of *The Coral Island*, and that irrespective of Golding's initial plans, Frank Kermode properly observes: "In writing of this kind all depends upon the author's mythopoeic power to transcend the 'programme.'" And in this first novel, William Golding displays "mythopoeic power" of an impressively high order. The flaws, the didactic interjections and manipulations remain. But, all in all, one may compare Golding to a puppet master who has wrought his marionettes meticulously and beautifully and led them skillfully through a captivating and frightening drama, while only occasionally distracting the audience by the movement of his strings.

PHILIP REDPATH

# Doorways Through Walls:
# Lord of the Flies *and* The Inheritors

The sad truth is that we remain necessarily strangers to ourselves, we don't understand our own substance, we must mistake ourselves; the axiom, 'Each man is farthest from himself', will hold for all of us to all eternity. Of ourselves we are not 'knowers'.

Of all Golding's novels, *Lord of the Flies* and *The Inheritors* have proved the most reducible to definitions about the nature of man. But the quantity of criticism covering these novels can prove a great hindrance to actually reading them. The reductiveness of most interpretations gives the impression that these texts are easily understood or even that just to read the interpretations is sufficient to discover what they mean. Golding is partly to blame for this. His cavalier 'what is trite is true' attitude leads one to expect that these works pose the reader no problems and contain a message that is basic and simple. In a lecture on *Lord of the Flies* he stated that

> Man is a fallen being. He is gripped by original sin. His nature is sinful and his state is perilous. I accept the theology and admit the triteness; but what is trite is true; and a truism can become more than a truism when it is a belief passionately held.

It is not surprising that Kinkead-Weekes and Gregor should say of *Lord of the*

From *William Golding: A Structural Reading of His Fiction.* © 1986 by Philip Redpath.

*Flies* that 'A reader can feel that he possesses this novel in an unusually comprehensive way, and that he could give a lucid, even conceptual account of it.' Ironically, *Lord of the Flies* has provoked more discussion about what it means than all the other novels put together.

If these two texts were making a simple statement about the darkness of man's heart, they would be saying nothing that has not become a religious and perhaps even psychological commonplace. Shakespeare defined this commonplace when he had Prospero in *The Tempest* admit of Caliban 'this thing of darkness I/Acknowledge mine.' In this chapter I will outline the structures of *Lord of the Flies* and *The Inheritors* and will explore the implications of this structure in relation to the nature of man as revealed in both texts. We shall see that Golding's conclusions are nowhere near so well defined or definitive as previous commentators have assumed, and that in the end we are left with suggestions rather than answers. Man's heart is dark perhaps because it cannot be explained away into over-simple moral imperatives. Indeed, it is because Golding has had to leave so much undefined that *Lord of the Flies* and *The Inheritors* open themselves to such a wide range of critical interpretations.

Once the group of young schoolboys, evacuated from a not-too-distant atomic war, have been dropped on to the desert island, the action of *Lord of the Flies* is left to unfold between three areas: the assembly platform, the jungle, and the mountain. The assembly platform is on the beach and is a site of light and space: 'The shore was fledged with palm trees. These . . . reclined against the light and their green feathers were a hundred feet up in the air.' Assemblies are normally held in daylight. The jungle is an area of darkness— 'the darkness of the forest proper'—and suffocation: 'the forest . . . was thick and woven like a bird's nest.' The mountain is 'a stack of balanced rock projecting through the looped fantasy of the forest creepers.' Whereas the assembly platform is an area of discussion in which reason strives to exist, the jungle is an area of physical conflict, of hunting, darkness, and pigs. The mountain overlooks the whole island. It is an area in which reason and unreason confront each other in the forms of the signal fire and the dead airman, and it is a law of the text that whatever force dominates the mountain dominates the novel.

It has not been observed before by previous critics that the narrative is structured around a pattern of assemblies and trips to the mountain. There are six of each of these. The assemblies occur on pages 20–6, 36–42, 86–103, 109–12, 139–42, 188–92, and the trips on pages 27–34, 42–51, 73–82, 105–7, 132–36, 161–62. The first two assemblies are conducted democratically. Names are taken, Ralph is elected leader, tasks are assigned, and the voice of rational debate is provided for: "'I'll give the conch to the next person to speak. . . . And he won't be interrupted.'" The two trips to the mountain confirm that they are on an island and see the signal fire lit there in order to assist in effecting their rescue. Despite the ominous undertones—Jack's 'mortification' at not being leader, his violent threat to kill the pig, talk about a beast, and the fire going out of control—the meetings are based around a rationalism which the boys put into practice by lighting the signal fire. The pattern of assembly-mountain exists when reason is the motivating factor in the boys' behaviour.

From this zenith a descent rapidly takes place. The signal fire is abandoned, the hunters kill their first pig, and real violence is described as the kill is re-enacted:

> 'We hit the pig—'
> '—I fell on top—'
> 'I cut the pig's throat.'

The dead airman which the boys mistake for the beast sits on the mountain and means that the fire cannot burn there. Instead of taking the fire of reason to the mountain, the boys go in search of the beast. The assemblies break down, people do not obey the role of the conch, and the boys vote irrationally in favour of the existence of ghosts. The last four trips and assemblies take place against a growing unreason as fear of the beast dictates events on the island.

If we note down the sequence of assemblies (A) and trips to the mountain (M) according to the pages on which they occur, we find that an order emerges:

| A | M | A | M | M | A | M |
|---|---|---|---|---|---|---|
| (20–6) | (27–34) | (36–42) | (42–51) | (73–82) | (86–103) | (105–7) |

| A | M | A | M | A |
|---|---|---|---|---|
| (109–12) | (132–36) | (139–42) | (161–62) | (188–92) |

Of the six trips and assemblies, the first two assemblies precede the trips. But from the third trip the pattern is reversed and trips precede assemblies. This is significant because with the loss of the ship and the killing of the pig reason loses control on the mountain (the fire goes out), and atavistic fear finally finds its embodiment in the rotting corpse of the dead airman who parachuted to the island after an aerial battle. From then on, the darkness and fear on the mountain has precedence over the rationalism of the assemblies as the beast sits in dominance over the island. This pattern covers a considerable expanse of time. When asked by W. H. Auden if the older boys would not have taken the younger boys in hand, Golding replied:

> They might have done so for a while, but they wouldn't have been able to cope with that vast stretch of time. When time goes on for as long as that, terrible things do happen.

This unreason colours the assemblies which disintegrate into Jack's "'Bollocks to the rules!'" This pattern of assemblies (A) and mountain (M) can be written as a sort of short-hand sentence describing the structure of the novel: A–M A–M/M–A M–A M–A M–A. The overall structure of the novel is therefore based around the antithesis reason/unreason.

*Lord of the Flies* is linear in structure. *The Inheritors* is circular. The epigraph, from H. G. Wells's gospel of rationalism, *The Outline of History*, is vital for it establishes a position from which we read:

> We know very little about the appearance of the Neanderthal man, but this . . . seems to suggest an extreme hairiness, an ugliness, or a repulsive strangeness in his appearance over and above his low forehead, his beetle brows, his ape neck, and his inferior stature. . . .

We enter the novel with this epigraph in our minds. We are then led, for eleven and a half chapters, through the mind of Neanderthal man and view the world from the perspective of a creature incapable of abstraction and inductive logic—incapable, that is, of those attributes that most define us as human beings. In 'The Grisly Folk', a short story about the conflict between Neanderthal man and Homo Sapiens, Wells stated that 'We cannot conceive in our different minds the strange ideas that chased one another through those queerly shaped brains.' But Golding has presented the complex instinctual lives of the Neanderthalers with such enormous immediacy in order to undermine the Wellsian opinion of the Neanderthals. However, from the point of view of the epigraph, what occurs in the Neanderthal mind is clearly something other than rational thought. Janet Burroway has stressed that 'by the end of the novel, deductive reasoning has come to represent the forbidden Tree of Knowledge of Good and Evil.' Lok, the Neanderthal through whose eyes we see the world, shows the first stirrings of deductive thought when he discovers 'like':

> Lok discovered 'Like.' He had used likeness all his life without being aware of it. . . . Now, in a convulsion of the understanding Lok found himself using likeness as a tool as surely as ever he

had used a stone to hack at sticks or meat. Likeness could grab the white-faced hunters with a hand, could put them into the world where they were thinkable and not a random and unrelated irruption.

But in fact Golding has made the Neanderthalers more primitive and the new people more advanced than the accounts given of them in the *Outline*. He has accentuated the gap between the reasonableness of the new people and the Neanderthaler's non-rational view of the world.

Towards the end of Chapter 11 our perspective shifts from Lok's mind to an objective third-person stance in which we see him from the outside for the first time. In Chapter 12 a further shift carries our perspective into the point of view of one of the new people. These are the people Wells sides with in the name of reason against the Neanderthals:

> Man at that time was not a degraded animal, for he had never been higher; he was therefore an exalted animal, and low as we esteem him now, he yet represented the highest stage of the development of the animal kindom of his time.

Unlike the Neanderthals who, except for the baby, are destroyed, the new people lead directly along the evolutionary scale to Wells and ourselves and thereby mark a return to the reason of the *Outline*. The structure of *The Inheritors* is

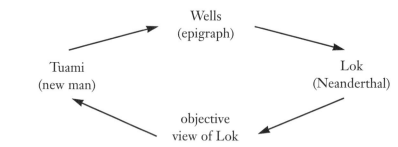

Each sequence can be numbered and given its page reference:

    1.    Wells—epigraph
    2.    Lok—Neanderthal
    3.    objective view of Lok
    4.    Tuami—New man

Sequence 4 always leads back to sequence 1. Both sequences are antithetical

to sequence 2, and sequence 3, a transition between sequences 1 and 4 and sequence 2, acts as a dividing bar between them. An antithesis between the reason of the epigraph and the new people and the unreason of the Neanderthals constitutes the basic structure of the novel.

J. P. Stern says of the structure of *Lord of the Flies*: 'Our imagination being inferior to Golding's, the achieved form of his novel answers our expectations in unexpected ways: his form answers our questions.' It is appropriate for a critic to emphasize the importance of the structure of *Lord of the Flies* and also of *The Inheritors*, but Golding does not answer questions, he raises them. The structural antithesis reason/unreason is closely linked to the antithesis between good and evil. But it is totally inadequate and misdirected to label one side of the antithesis in the novels 'good' and the other side 'evil'. Golding does not intend such an over-simple interpretation of these works. All of Golding's fiction is about the inadequacy of a simple moral attitude to either side of the antithesis.

Rolan Barthes has defined the structure of the antithesis as 'a wall without a doorway'. This 'wall' is the dividing line separating the two sides, and it is the object of *Lord of the Flies* and *The Inheritors* to create a 'doorway' in the wall so that the two sides are no longer held divisively apart, but are merged into an inclusive whole.

Yet schematically to divide each novel into groups representing one or other side of the antithesis is tempting. *Lord of the Flies* is clearly split into those boys who wish to maintain civilized values and do what is right and those who wish to hunt and become savages. The text seems to endorse this division: 'There was the brilliant world of hunting, tactics, fierce exhilaration, skill; and there was the world of longing and baffled commonsense.' In *The Inheritors* the division is even more apparent between the Neanderthalers and the new people. But this simple division and the labelling of one side as good and the other evil is to ignore the complexity created through the novel's structure.

The most obvious drawback to this division is the problem of which side we are to label good and which side evil. In *Lord of the Flies* Ralph and Piggy are those boys who wish to do what is right. Piggy is clearly on the side of morality when he explains what he is going to do in order to get back his stolen glasses: '"I don't ask for my glasses back, not as a favour. I don't ask you to be a sport, . . . not because you're strong, but because what's right's right."' Ralph longs for a return to civilization. He is drawn to becoming a savage, but the idea of rescue and going home is more attractive: '"I'd like to put on war-paint and be a savage. But we must keep the fire burning. . . . Without the fire we can't be rescued."' Rescue, fire, and Piggy's glasses are all linked to civilization, the adult world, and home. The hunters ignore the idea of rescue in favour of irrationality and savagery. When Piggy, without much tact, asks them "'Which is better—to be a pack of painted niggers like you are, or to be sensible like Ralph is?'", they shout him down. To Ralph, the hunters' society is 'demented', their ritualistic belief in and appeasement of the beast seems to him to be the 'breaking-up of sanity.' Clearly, then, reason becomes connected to goodness and those boys who stick by law and order, civilization and rescue, and unreasonable behaviour is linked to evil, the Lord of the Flies, and those boys who become savages.

But in *The Inheritors* the exact opposite is the case. Goodness is a quality possessed by the gentle and innocent Neanderthalers. Samuel Hynes remarks that

> The moral of the novel is not a very complicated one. . . . It offers an anthropological analogue of the Fall, which distinguishes between prelapsarian and postlapsarian man in terms of knowledge of evil and capacity for thought.

Because they do not think rationally and cannot conceptualize, the Neanderthalers belong to the unreason side of the antithesis. They will not kill, their primitive community has moral standards grounded on belief in Oa, a female earth goddess, and, as shown in Hynes's comment, if we consider them in theological terms they are unfallen people. The new people are killers and hunters who have lost their innocence and are beginning to manipulate the world to their own ends. They are postlapsarian man, not so much evil as fallen from innocence, and although, like Ralph and Piggy, their actions are based on their intelligence, they are hunters like Jack and Roger. In a study of the roots of human nature, Mary Midgley points out that

> Man, before his tool-using days, was poorly armed. Without claws, beak, or horns, he must have found murder a tedious and exhausting business, and built-in inhibitions against it were therefore not necessary for survival. By the time he invented weapons, it was too late to alter his nature. He became a dangerous beast.

There is thus a reversal of the moral values aligned to each side of the antithetical structure of the novels. In *Lord of the Flies* reason is linked to civilization and goodness while evil is linked to unreason. But in *The Inheritors* unreason is linked to goodness or innocence and evil linked to reason and the beginnings of civilization. Clearly, if we wish to be consistent, the novels defy any simple moral definitions.

The creation of the beast reinforces this apparent contradiction. It is the littluns, those least influenced by civilized values, who start the idea of a beast on the island. Jack immediately takes this up and unreasonably, since he does not believe in the beast, talks about hunting it: "'There isn't a snake-thing. . . . We're going to hunt pigs and get meat for everybody. And we'll look for the snake too—.'" But it is the twins, Samneric, two of the four reasonable boys left at the end, who give the beast substance and form:

> 'There were eyes—'
> 'Teeth—'
> 'Claws—'

The hunters and all they stand for gain the upper hand because the beast provides a point against which Jack can rally the tribe. He needs the beast as an enemy which his hunters can protect the others from and thereby justify his disregard for the rules. In *The Inheritors* civilization gains the upper hand for exactly the same reasons. It is the intelligent people who create the beast:

> The guard who had run after Fa was dancing in front of the new people. He crawled like a snake, he went to the wreck of the caves; he stood; he came back to the fire snapping like a wolf so that the people shrank from him. He pointed; he created a running, crouching thing, his arms flapped like the wings of a bird.

Like Jack, Marlan needs the beast as a means of keeping his position as leader. As long as he can convince the others that they are safe while he leads he is secure: "'They keep to the mountains or the darkness under the trees. We will keep to the water and the plains. We shall be safe from the tree-dark-ness.'" Both Marlan and Jack need the beast, both need to believe in it, and both belong to different sides of the novels' structural antithesis. Nietzsche, in *The Genealogy of Morals*, described the pervasiveness of the beast within human nature: 'Deep within all these noble races there lurks the beast of prey, bent on spoil and conquest. This hidden urge has to be satisfied from time to time, the beast let loose in the wilderness.'

It is obvious, therefore, that any interpretation of these novels that divides them into two groupings and assigns exclusive moral categories to either would be a misreading. It would not probe deeply enough into what these texts are doing structurally. To say, as one critic does of *Lord of the Flies*, that Golding is 'convinced that without the restraint of social order the human being will sink below the level of the beast', is to neglect that in *The Inheritors* it is the more civilized men with a social order and religious hierarchy who create the beast and murder the innocents. Ralph Freedman exhibits a similarly shallow reading of the novels:

> It would seem . . . that 'light' does not triumph in Golding's universe. But in each novel . . . 'light' is restored in a counterpoint. In *Lord of the Flies* the rescuing naval officer restores identity and order. . . . In *The Inheritors*, our attention shifts from the 'people,' corrupted at last, to the humans, who though corrupt, are rationally aware and capable of taking over control and reorganization of the world.

In other words, civilization in one novel is desired because it acts against the corruption of the savages, and in the other it is desired although it is itself corrupt. The trouble arises from trying exclusively to define either side of the antithesis. This is why terms such as 'reason' and 'unreason' are preferable as a way of speaking about the antithesis rather than the morally and emotionally loaded terms 'good' and 'evil'. If these terms did apply to one or other side of these novels exclusively, they would be no more complex that the clear good/evil dichotomy of a work like Tolkien's *Lord of the Rings*. In this work evil is represented by the powers of Sauron and good by those of Gandalf; there are few, if any characters who cannot be easily defined as good or evil in the trilogy. *Lord of the Flies* and *The Inheritors* are a lot more complex than this.

Throughout *Lord of the Flies* Ralph stands for civilization alongside Piggy. In moral terms this is the side of goodness as opposed to the hunters who act from the darkness of their hearts. But Ralph and Piggy, and therefore the relationship between the two sides of the antithesis, are very ambiguous. Both boys extol the reasonable virtues of the adult world: "'They wouldn't quarrel—'" "'Or talk about a beast—.'" But this adult-worship is misplaced because adults would quarrel; after all, the reason the boys are on the island is due to an adult 'quarrel'. The difference is that the adults would rationalize the beast into an enemy, either nationalistic or ideological, and battle against it. Mary Midgley has beautifully described this process when she argues that

> If . . . there is no lawless beast outside man, it seems very strange to conclude that there is one inside him. It would be more natural to say that the beast within us gives us partial order; the task or perceptual thought will only be to complete it. But the

opposite, a *priori*, reasoning has prevailed. If the Beast Within was capable of every iniquity, people reasoned, then beasts without probably were too. This notion made man anxious to exaggerate his difference from all other species and to ground all activities he valued in capacities unshared by the animals, whether the evidence warranted it or no. In a way this evasion does the species credit, because it reflects our horror at the things we do. Man fears his own guilt and insists on fixing it on something evidently alien and external. Beasts Within solve the problem of evil.

This is ironically what happens to Ralph at the end when the hunters see him as an enemy of the society they have formed around Jack. He becomes the victim of his own glorification of adult behaviour when the savages act like civilized men and hunt down an enemy.

The linking of the forces of reason to the beast is a logical progression throughout the novel. Early on Ralph pretends to machine-gun Piggy: 'Ralph . . . returned as a fighter plane . . . and machine-gunned Piggy.' This prophetically relates Piggy to the beast. Ralph's action reflects the adult world's pursuit of enemies which also parallels the hunters' pursuit of Ralph. Pigs, Piggy, beast and Ralph are gradually merged during the novel. On page 60 Jack asks Ralph if he is '"Coming?"' up the mountain in search of pigs. This prefigures his '"Coming"' when he challenges Ralph to come up the mountain in search of the beast. Pigs and beast are linked, and the tribes' hunting of pigs and then of Ralph relates Ralph to the beast. Indeed, the civilized world has created the beast by providing a corpse which the boys can realize as the beast. Piggy is linked to the beast through Ralph's machine-gunning imitation of the adult world. Reason and the beast, not unreason and the beast, are inseparable. This relationship is made clear from the start by Golding. Piggy's first action on the island is to excrete; when Simon is trying to define the beast he asks '"What's the dirtiest thing there is?"' Jack replies 'shit.' Piggy (reason) and the beast (unreason) are joined. Ralph's belief that without a signal fire the boys will die on the island is wrong. A return to a civilization 'in ruins' and ravaged by atomic war will prove fatal. It was from this rational civilization that the boys were escaping in the first place.

What we have with Ralph is not the development of a heroic insight but a study in failure. He fails when he tries to act reasonably against the hunters because he thinks that adults would act reasonably. But civilization denies the darkness of its heart. It covers it with a veneer of reason and then goes out into the world and fights wars; it acts in the same way as Jack and the hunters, except that it is far, far more destructive. Ralph tries to hide the beast in himself by a worship of the adult world. And yet, if at the end Jack and his painted tribe armed with sharpened sticks reflect the well-armed and uniformed officer and his men, Ralph's advocacy of rational behaviour has been nothing but a misplaced advocacy of an illusion or miscomprehension. He has worshipped the lie behind which man attempts to conceal his true nature. Ralph himself displays the rending of this lie when he finds himself longing to hurt Robert—'The desire to squeeze and hurt was over-mastering'—and when at the end of the novel he has become a very efficient savage. Reasonable naval officer and unreasonable savage are reflections of each other. Ralph's failure is that he does not understand this until the end, and Piggy remains obliviously ignorant of it. We can see that James Gindin has missed the point when he asks, 'If the adult world rescues the boys . . . are the depravity and the brutality of human nature so complete?' Ralph and the officer are not in opposition to the savages; there is no difference between them.

We have shared Ralph's perspective for most of the novel and sympathize with him. The change in point of view to the officer is not just to reveal the officer's lack of insight; it is designed to shock us out of our rationalistic complacency by revealing that *Lord of the Flies* is condemning the point of view it has made us read from. Ralph extols the adult world: his father is ironically a naval officer. But the adult world and the savages are no different from each other except in so far as one lies to itself, denies its unreason, and claims to be civilized. Ralph represents the perspective that would conceal the true nature of man and would rationalize acts of inhumanity. At least Jack is honest: '"We're strong—we hunt! If there's a beast, we'll hunt it down! We'll close in and beat and beat and beat—!"' Ralph is nearly killed because of his faith in the appearance of reason which is useless when contrasted to man's true nature. His rescue is not a rescue at all if it marks a return to a reflection of the society that has tried to kill him on the island. It must represent some kind of a defeat for him in view of what he at last recognizes about the nature of all men.

*The Inheritors* also undermines a too-simple labelling of the Neanderthalers as good and the new people as evil. Whereas *Lord of the Flies*, through Ralph, traced a failure of reason, *The Inheritors*, through Lok, traces a failure of unreason. This failure is shown from the start in the difficulty the disappearance of the log bridge causes the Neanderthals. Hynes believes this episode is important to the novel as

> a model of the Neanderthal mind; the most significant feature of that mind is this, that it cannot conceive of relationships, and we might take this as a tentative definition of the State of Innocence:

man cannot sin until he can both remember and anticipate.

But surely this scene does not so much reveal the Neanderthaler's innocence as their limitation. When Lok speaks 'there was little connection between the quick pictures and the words that came out.' In the Neanderthal mind there is no bridge between words and what they mean, concepts and practice, and this leads to their destruction as inevitably as the log bridge when removed leads to the death of Mal. The Neanderthal philosophy, 'Today is like yesterday and tomorrow,' is less a sign of their innocent incapacity to 'remember and antici-pate' than a formula of stasis and defeat. Time is a dimension through which existence must move; to attempt to live out of time is not to exist at all. This is made apparent from the juxtaposition of the obvious seasonal changes occur-ring in the novel and the Neanderthalers' struggle to cope with their changing world. Johnston claims that 'The bitterness of the winter and other references to climactic changes indicate the dawning of an ice-age that together with other natural catastrophes, threatens the "people's" existence.' But the increased volume of water going over the fall would indicate a thaw, a recession of the ice-cap. Oa, the Neanderthal diety, can be seen as a reversal of Alpha and Omega (Oa/Ao), the beginning and the end. Time for the Neanderthals is seen as coming to an end, and a beginning, symbolized in the climatic spring, is encom-passed in the new people. That time is leaving the Neanderthals behind is plain from the amount of watching they do which emphasizes their helplessness. Between pages 132 and 210 they can only powerlessly watch because there is nothing they can do to act upon their environment or change circumstances. It is their philosophy put into deadly practice.

The Neanderthals' innocence is seen mostly in their reverence for life. They will not kill for meat and dislike eating the carcase of an animal killed by predators. Yet they do not flinch at eating grups. If all life comes from Oa, surely the grubs do as well? When they do find a slaughtered doe they quickly and fiercely tear into it:

> The doe was wrecked and scattered. Fa split open her belly, slit the complicated stomach and split the sour cropped grass and broken shoots on the earth. Lok beat in the skull to get at the brain and levered open the mouth to wrench away the tongue. They filled the stomach with tit-bits and twisted up the guts so that the stomach became a floppy bag.

All this time Lok is lamenting that '"This is very bad. Oa brought the doe out of her belly."' He tries to excuse himself: '"The meat is for Mal who is sick,"' which sounds disarmingly like Piggy trying to wriggle out of responsibility for the death of Simon: "'He was batty. He asked for it.'" Again we see the fusion of the rational and the irrational in the novels and the inadequacy of trying to pin down either of these categories with a moral label.

Golding masterfully allows us to build up sympathy for the Neanderthalers by making us occupy Lok's point of view. But the shift in perspective in Chapter 11 has the effect of undermining our sympathy for the non-rational creature. For the first time we see Lok from the outside:

> It was a strange creature, smallish, and bowed. The legs and thighs were bent and there was a whole thatch of curls on the outside of the legs and the arms. . . . Its feet and hands were broad, and flat. . . . The square hands hung down to the knees. . . . The mouth was wide and soft and above the curls of the upper lip the great nostrils were flared like wings.

Critics have tended to see the Neanderthalers in a too-human light: 'What is perhaps more important to realise about the people of *The Inheritors*', says John Bowen, 'is that they are destroyed chiefly because those who destroy them do not recognise that they are men at all.' But the extinction of this race results from the fact that they are not men at all. Gabriel Josipovici has lucidly described our reading process: 'we rest easily inside Lok's sensibility till the last pages show him to us as we would normally see him: an unalterably alien creature, loping away into the forest.' When we see the Neanderthalers as the new people see them, we can understand their fear:

> This figure was red, with enormous spreading arms and legs and the face glared up . . . for the eyes were white pebbles. The hair stood out round the head as though the figure were in the act of some frantic cruelty.

Although Fa believes that the new people are "'frightened of the air where there is nothing,'" she is horribly mistaken; they are frightened of the non-human Neanderthalers.

The circular construction of *The Inheritors* returns us to the epigraph and the Wellsian perspective. Josipovici is right to state that 'The novel sets out to show not just that Wells is wrong, but also why he should be wrong in just this way.' But we must go further than this. The view of Lok from the outside reveals that we must read from the Wellsian stance because we are human beings and not Neanderthal men, and also why we, like Wells, must always be wrong if we read from this stance and regard ourselves as motivated from purely rational motives. Whilst we see through Lok's eyes, we are shown the inadequacy of the reasonable Wellsian perspective. But Lok and his kind are destroyed because of their lack of reason, and we can only see through his eyes whilst we read the novel. Outside the novel we must regard him as an alien to ourselves. Perceiving from Lok's point of view we see what we are, but only through the eyes of what we are not. The novel reveals to us something about the complexity of man's nature and also shows that he is stuck with that nature because reason and unreason do not simply equate with good and evil.

A close reading—and these novels demand close reading—highlights the impossibility of applying exclusive moral values to either side of these novels' antithetical structures. The reason for this is that both novels over-turn their own structures, break down the antithesis, and replace a too-simple dismissal of themselves as about the evil of man with an ambiguous mixing of darkness and light.

Simon contributes to this breakdown in *Lord of the Flies*, but even so, a great deal of obscurity surrounds his rôle in the novel. His confrontation with the pig's head seems to encompass the message of the text. But a look at this scene shows that in fact he learns nothing from the Lord of the Flies. He dismisses the talking head with the rational formula '"Pig's head on a stick"' which has been described as 'a courageous denial of the head's view of itself'. Throughout the novel Simon has understood the nature of the beast: 'However Simon thought of the beast there rose before his inward sight the picture of a human at once heroic and sick.' He does not need to learn anything from the beast and, indeed, he does not: '"You knew, didn't you? I'm part of you? "'I'm the reason why it's no go? Why things are what they are?"' Simon is not told anything here; a series of questions is posed to which he already knows the answer. Appropriately, the name 'Simon' in Hebrew means 'the one who listens' and we can claim that the head's voice and Simon's are one and the same. But Simon is only raising questions, and these questions, together with the implications of their possible answers, lead to his death. If the beast is in man, reason and unreason belong together, not divided by the bar of the antithesis. Simon's vision overturns the structure of the novel, he creates a doorway through the wall of the antithesis, and for this act he dies. Man tends to regard himself in exclusive moral terms; the reasonable man can rationalize unreasonable and inhuman behaviour against other men by regarding them as an enemy. The death of Simon is thus a further condemna-tion of Ralph who supports rational and civilized values on the island. To reveal man's nature as darkly obscure is to court destruction from one or other side of the antithesis. Simon's powerlessness when possessed of this knowledge shows that all men are at the mercy of their nature, which is basically the same whether applied to Piggy, the officer, or the savages.

In *The Inheritors* it is the artist, Tuami, who makes a doorway in the dividing bar and thus destroys the antithesis. He roughly draws the Neanderthalers in attempts at exorcism and in his drawing creates the beast, conjures up in the new peoples' minds the image they project on the apemen. At the same time he recognizes the futility of killing Marlan. But, as has often been observed, he does experience an artistic vision which resolves the antithesis. Whilst preparing a lump of ivory which he intends to make into a knife, Tuami watches Vivani playing with the Neanderthal baby:

> The rump and head fitted each other and made a shape you could feel with your hands. They were waiting in the rough ivory of the knife-haft. . . . They were an answer. . . . His hands felt for the ivory . . . and he could feel in his fingers how Vivani and her devil fitted it.

Weapon of destruction becomes work of art in which reason and unreason are merged into a comprehensive vision of man (new people) and beast (Neanderthal) together. The knife is a reflection of the novel as a whole. But, like Simon, Tuami is powerless to alter anything even when armed with a knife: 'What was the use of sharpening it against a man? Who would sharpen a point against the darkness of the world?' Tuami with his knife recalls Alex with his razor in Anthony Burgess's *A Clockwork Orange* whose violent nature must be recognized and accepted, because any attempt to change it involved a greater act of violence. Towards the end Alex is 'cured' and restored to his natural self:

> I could viddy myself very clear running and running on like very light and mysterious nogas, carving the whole litso of the creeching world with my cut-throat britva. . . . I was cured all right.

(Despite the muddle over the 'real' ending of *A Clockwork Orange*: Burgess's or Kubrick's) this conclusion is less ambiguous than that of *The Inheritors*. Alex has the choice and chooses to be violent, whereas Tuami must face the fact that whatever he wants to be he is at the mercy of his nature, which is neither good nor bad but a compound of both.

It is not, however, only these two characters whose visions resolve the antithesis of the novels. Simon and Tuami are ineffectual against the circumstances in which they find themselves. Golding has created worlds in both books which undermine the structure of the texts by fusing both sides of the antithesis together. It is because both sides are fused in human nature that

Simon and Tuami are powerless. How can man rationally explain that he is irrational? Hence Golding has ensured that the resolution of the antithetical structure of both texts is taken out of the hands of his characters and embodied in the worlds of the novels.

The island in *Lord of the Flies* is divided into areas in which the antithesis is worked out and resolved. Nature is seen to deny antithetical polarities and to invite visions of unity and wholeness within itself. After his murder on the beach, Simon's body is transformed as the incoming tide dresses his hair with 'brightness' and his 'cheek silvered.' He is carried away, subjected to the mysterious forces of the tides, the earth, and the moon. But the point to which he is carried is the horizontal line of the horizon, a line which symbolizes the breaking of the vertical dividing bar of the antithesis. Here dark night sky flecked with stars is mirrored in the sea sparkling with 'moonbeam-bodied creatures.' Simon is borne to the line where both meet, which is a natural image of his comprehensive vision of the nature of man as heroic and sick. This is emphasized by the fact that the airman too is carried out towards the horizon. The beast, as a part of man, accompanies Simon. Man's being within nature is highlighted by our last glimpse of him:

> Somewhere over the darkened curve of the world the sun and moon were pulling; and the film of water on the earth planet was held, bulging slightly on one side while the solid core turned. The great wave of the tide moved further along the island and the water lifted. . . . [B]eneath the steadfast constellations, Simon's dead body moved out towards the open sea.

The full import of the antithesis between assembly platform and fire and mountain and the beast can now be seen. The mountain is an image of verticality over which the beast presides. This reinforces the antithesis of man as home of the beast and the beast man projects from himself, between reason/unreason. Simon is only fully and individually seen six times—reflecting the structure of the novel: twice on the assembly platform, twice on the mountain, and twice in the forest. This makes clear his mediatory rôle between the antithetical areas and images which accumulate in the novel. He belongs to no particular area, except his sanctuary in the forest through which the boys must pass to get from the platform to the mountain, because his role is to break the antithesis.

Similarly, the Neanderthalers make their way from the horizontality of the sea shore to the vertical fall and overhang:

Beyond the clearing the ground began to rise steeply, earthen, but dotted with smaller trees; and here the bones of the land showed, lumps of smooth grey rock. Beyond this slope was the gap through the mountains, and from the lip of this gap the river fell in a great waterfall twice the height of the tallest trees.

It is appropriate that the antithesis between the Neanderthals and the new people is played out here, and that all the Neanderthalers except Liku and the baby should die on the vertical cliffs.

The new people create the antithesis by displacing the beast from themselves on to the Neanderthals and then regarding them as 'devils' to be destroyed by means of their superior rationality. In this they recall the adult world in *Lord of the Flies*. But our last glimpse of the new people is of them on the horizontal lake heading toward the flat plains, and it is here that Tuami experiences his vision of wholeness:

> Holding the ivory firmly in his hands, feeling the onset of sleep, Tuami looked at the line of darkness. It was far away and there was plenty of water in between. He peered forward past the sail to see what lay at the other end of the lake, but it was so long, and there was such a flashing from the water that he could not see if the line of darkness had an ending.

Although looking along the lake he 'could not see if the line of darkness had an ending', this is only because 'there was such a flashing from the water.' This image of the shore and the water is the most important image in the novel because it summarizes the vision of Tuami. The forest and water form a horizontal bar of darkness and light. But the shore is reflected in the water and the flashing light from the water dazzles Tuami's vision of the shore thereby dissolving the two separate areas of land and water. Hence the novel ends with our seeing through Tuami's eyes an encompassing vision of the natural world with man afloat in the centre of it. He becomes a part of nature which reflects the darkness and light of his own inner nature.

With the resolution of the structural antithesis it is clear that to try to explain the novels with phrases like 'the darkness of man's heart', 'man's fall into guilt', or 'man's loss of innocence', is far too reductive. *Lord of the Flies* and *The Inheritors* are more comprehensive than this. They are also more obscure. They do not tell us that man is evil—that is a commonplace anyway. They make us work towards the conclusion that man is somehow good and evil, that his nature endlessly contradicts itself. Instead of basing our judgements of man upon an either/or hypothesis, we must ground it upon a hypothesis that begins with the premise 'both'. Whatever the beast is in man, it also has its opposite. Given the nature of man, Piggy, a rational reductionist if ever there was one, asks questions which cannot be answered with a simple yes or no: "'Which is better—to be a pack of painted niggers . . . or to be sensible . . . ? . . . to have rules and agree, or to hunt and kill?'" Our reasonable side will claim that to agree, have rules, and be sensible is best, but man still goes out and hunts, kills and destroys whilst claiming to be a rational creature acting in the name of reason. Golding does not intend to define 'good' or 'evil' in the novels, he tries to make us revise our simple categorizations and resee ourselves in a new, more comprehensive way. The novels are maps of man's inner nature, and to experience the resolution of the antithesis is to trace human nature in all its indefinability.

Nietzsche remarked that

> Nobody, up to now, has doubted that the 'good' man represents a higher value than the 'evil,' in terms of promoting and benefiting mankind generally . . . . But suppose the exact opposite were true. What if the 'good' man represents not merely a retrogression but even a danger . . . enabling the present to live at the expense of the future? . . . What if morality should turn out to be the danger of dangers?

These dangers are what Golding draws our attention to. To believe oneself totally good is to justify committing any inhumanity. There is no absolute evil described in *Lord of the Flies* or *The Inheritors*, there are only human beings. In *Something Wicked This Way Comes*, the American writer Ray Bradbury tries to define an absolute evil but has to confine this (literally) to freaks rather than human beings. When he talks about men he comes to the same conclusions as Golding:

> We are the creatures that know and know too much. That leaves us with such a burden again we have a choice, to laugh or cry. No animal does either. We do both, depending on the season and the need.

Golding makes us reassess what we mean by morality when we are so capable of immorality—how a creature that is good and evil can define either good or evil. The effect of this, structurally, as Stinson describes it, is to bring

> opposing rationally assigned categoies . . . into violent interaction only to mix darkly and ambiguously together so as to cast an

ominously foreboding smog over the world as we know it—or
the world as we thought we knew it.

To exist on only one side of the antithesis is not to be human at all. It is a
condition of *Lord of the Flies* and *The Inheritors* being written in the first place
that man occupies the dividing bar where both sides merge and become one
and the other. It is also a condition that allows novels like *Lord of the Flies* and
*The Inheritors* to be read.

JAMES GINDIN

# The Fictional Explosion:
# Lord of the Flies *and* The Inheritors

Given the complexity of Golding's thought, his need to express some fundamental statement about the nature of man in tangible terms, and his tendency to use sharply defined polarities to generate his ideas, his placement of his first two novels as intellectual responses to particular targets is not surprising. His religious impulse requires a heresy or an evil to excoriate; the pressure of his carefully shaped and internal fiction gains its force in reaction against some widely shared or familiar concept. Both the first two novels focus on their targets explicitly: *Lord of the Flies* on R. M. Ballantyne's 1857 novel *The Coral Island, The Inheritors* on H. G. Wells's *Outline of History*.

Ballantyne's *The Coral Island* represents, for Golding, an extremity of Victorian confidence and optimism in the civilised values of English schoolboy society. In Ballantyne's novel, the boys shipwrecked on the island, organise their skills and exercise their imaginations to duplicate the comforts and the values of the society they have temporarily lost. Working with discipline, they build shelters and a boat, make various utensils for their convenience, and find a healthy and interesting variety of animal and vegetable food. With the same kind of devotion to higher powers that characterises the more adult survival in the earlier *Robinson Crusoe*, the boys in *The Coral Island* radiate a confidence in their sense of community and organisation which would seem rather smug were they not also genuinely pious and aware of

From *William Golding*. © 1988 by James Gindin.

their luck. Evil in the novel is externalised, represented by cannibals on the island whom the English boys defeat because they work together and excell in both wit and virtue. Their rescue almost does not matter, for they have essentially recreated the world they can from. Ballantyne draws on a concept of the child that reaches back through the nineteenth century, at least as far as Rousseau and Locke, the child as inherently either good or neutral, manifesting his goodness if left alone and uncorrupted by the adult world or reflecting and recreating the healthy and civilised environment of this initial consciousness. This confidence in civilised Enlightenment, developed from a faith in human possibility in the eighteenth century to a particularly English social achievement in the nineteenth, is precisely what Golding, in *Lord of the Flies*, is determined to reverse. The locus of Golding's attention is the society of boys; the implication is an attack on the naïveté of Victorian confidence in English boys and in public schools, as well as on the whole Enlightenment doctrine about the progress and perfectibility of the human species. Golding's tone, however, is not that of triumphant response to a naïve and mistaken ideology. Rather, his shaping of events and experience on the island, his sense of the inherently predatory and evil characteristics his boys reveal, is dominated by the 'grief, sheer grief' he called the theme of the novel. The 'grief' compounds the presentation of 'sin', for, as Golding has said retrospectively as recently as December 1985, the novel was 'written at a time of great world grief' and that, in addition to the 'original sin' latent in the novel, 'what nobody's noticed is that it also has original virtue'.

Golding's use of *The Coral Island* is direct and unambiguous. He refers to it explicitly several times: once, near the beginning of the novel, when the boys, in momentary agreement, decide they can have a 'good time on this island', like 'Treasure Island', and 'Coral Island'; later, on the last page of the novel, ironically, when they are rescued by the naval officer, who imperceptively comments, 'Jolly good show. Like the Coral Island'. Golding also derives the initial English types of some of his schoolboy characters from Ballantyne's novel. The narrator of *The Coral Island* is named Ralph, a sound and stable boy of 15 (his last name is Rover); the strongest, oldest, tallest boy is named Jack; the third member of Ballantyne's principal triumvirate is Peterkin Gay, a quick, sprite-like, imaginative boy of 14. Golding's Ralph comes closest to following the Ballantyne model, for Ralph, although not the narrator in Golding, is the centrally representative English schoolboy, simultaneously the one who both leads and accommodates to others in terms of the fondly cherished, moderate English tradition. Fair-haired, mild, neither the strongest nor the most discerning of the boys, Golding's Ralph is initially elected to govern the island and to organise building shelters and possible rescue. As the organisation increasingly breaks down, as the boys gradually succumb to dirt, ineptitude, laziness, cruelty and the predatory viciousness of the 'hunters', Ralph reveals something of the same sense of inherent evil within himself (he willingly shares the spoils of the 'hunters' and, however reluctantly and unconsciously, joins in the ritualistic killing of Simon). Finally, hunted by the others, turned from leader into victim, his 'rescue' at the end is far from any reassertion of his moderation. At the end he 'weeps', his confidence shattered, recognising the failure and the irrelevance of the kind of human moderation and civilisation he had thought he embodied. Golding changes the Ballantyne version of the character of Jack, the powerful one outside the communal structure, more immediately and more markedly than that of Ralph. In the first place, Golding's Jack has his own community, his choir of 'hunters', each boy wearing 'a square cap with a silver badge in it': 'Their bodies, from throat to ankle, were hidden by black cloaks which bore a long silver cross on the left breast and each neck was finished off with a hambone frill'. The physical description deliberately suggests the Nazis, the sense of inherent evil institutionalised and made visible in the chanting choir of the predatory. Ballantyne's Jack represented strength absorbed into the civilised community and displayed no sense of evil; Golding's Jack is the aggressive force of evil, acquiring more and more adherents as survival on the island becomes progressively more difficult. Jack imposes a sense of discipline on the others that Ralph can never manage.

The character of Piggy, Ralph's most loyal supporter, is entirely Golding's addition. Physically deficient (he is fat, asthmatic and has a weak bladder), Piggy is the voice of rationalism. He believes in the possibility of rescue by the adult society, in the values of civilisation, and in the possibility of directing human constructive effort. Normally less articulate than Ralph, attempting to endow the symbol of the conch shell, the parliamentary symbol, with silent power, Piggy, in his final scene, eventually poses, to the assembled boys on the pinnacle rock at the end of the island, a series of rhetorical questions that represent his values. He advocates that the boys 'be sensible like Ralph is', 'have rules and agree', and follow 'law and rescue', rather than follow Jack and 'hunt and kill'. In response, Roger, Jack's most vicious lieutenant, high overhead, uses a boulder as a lever to hurl the rock that hits Piggy, casts him forty feet down to hit another rock that splatters his brains before he is washed out to sea. In his death 'Piggy's arms and legs twitched a bit, like a pig's after it has been killed', and Roger had leaned his weight on the lever in the same way he had earlier leaned his weight on his spear to kill the sow. Piggy is the human object, the victim, for the predators. Yet the rationalism and confidence in social organisation does not summarise the function of Piggy's character entirely. He is also fearful, not of the 'beast' the 'littluns' fear, for, unlike the 'littluns', who experience only chaos once

they forget the superficial and carefully taught names, addresses and telephone numbers of identity, Piggy believes in scientific observation, in tracing
patterns of cause and effect. Rather, Piggy is frightened of the 'beast' within
the human being, of people themselves. When, at the end of the novel, Ralph
weeps for 'the end of innocence, the darkness of man's heart, and the fall
through the air of the true, wise friend called Piggy', the sense of Piggy's
wisdom is not an endorsement of Piggy's rationalism or his science. Rather,
Piggy's wisdom, what to fear, in his accurate location of the human evil he
attracts and can do nothing to prevent.

Piggy is not the only scapegoat for the human choir's evil, for both the
rationalist and the visionary, both Piggy and Simon, are destroyed. Simon is
considerably transformed from the model of Ballantyne's sprite-like
Peterkin. In the 1959 interview with Frank Kermode, broadcast as 'The
Meaning of it All', Golding directly indicated how he changed Peterkin into
Simon (citing the New Testament transformation of 'Simon called Peter')
and endowed the sensitive, isolated character, unlike the other boys, with
insight into the unchanging nature of human beings and communities.
Simon is mystic, unable to express what he always knows is man's essential
illness. He is Golding's example of 'original virtue' in the novel. Yet he
isolates himself, building his shelter hidden away within the jungle, gathering
the leaves and fronds he finds as a natural protection against humanity.
Simon, the only one of the boys to approach closely enough to understand
what they fear, actually sees the 'beast' and recognises that the 'beast' is a
dead man from the war outside and above the island, his corpse tangled in
his failed parachute. His recognition, in a forcefully described scene, goes
more deeply than the specific circumstances demand, for it is the 'ancient,
inescapable recognition' that, with the 'white teeth and dim eyes, the blood'
and that 'black blob of flies that buzzed like a saw' on the 'pile of guts', the
'beast' is humanity. Simon imagines the 'beast', 'The Lord of the Flies', as a
schoolmaster. Running to proclaim his discovery to the others, Simon
stumbles into the pig run down the mountainside while the others, led by
the choir, are enacting a ritual of 'kill the pig'. In the rush of predatory
emotion, identities are confused and the 'hunters', even Ralph and Piggy
drawn to the fringes of the dark and crowded scene 'under the threat of the
sky', kill Simon. Simon assumes something of the role of Christ, a Christian martyrdom, sacrifice of self for the truth that is generally unrecog-
nised. Yet Golding's symbolism is suggestive rather than precise. Like the
conch, the shell that cannot support the excessive reliance on it as a parliamentary symbol and becomes worn and bleached white like a skull, the
Christian symbolism is pervasive and dramatic but does not cohere in the
patterns of Christian parable or duplication of the story of Christ. Simon is

his own sort of visionary religious martyr, sometimes seen as more Cassandra-like than Christian, sometimes perhaps as epilectic with his fainting fits, sometimes simply as the odd boy who does not fit the pattern of the school. Similarly complex, 'The Lord of the Flies' is a translation of Beelzebub, the Greek transliteration of the ancient Hebrew word for the Prince of the Devils, an incarnation of evil in both Judaism and Christianity. Yet the figure is also characterised as the 'Lord of Dung', of human refuse. The meanings do not contradict, and both reinforce the pervasive meaning of a symbolic dramatisation of inherent human evil. Yet the cluster of symbolic meanings, both humanly and religiously suggestive, coherent only in the force and tangibility of their metaphorical application to the human condition, make it difficult to push the novel into the total narrative and legendary coherence of parable.

A reading of *Lord of the Flies* as parable is also questionable because of the way in which Golding handles time, space and location. The particular setting, graphically described physically yet unconnected to any knowable geographical location, both invites parabolic or symbolic reading in its absence from specific location and limits or questions that reading in the absence of a consistent narrative of symbolic pattern. The island is described with immediate physical force, Golding providing a strongly visual and emotional sense of the beach, the lagoon, the junglelike tracks to the mountain, and the splinters of precipitous rock at the end of the island opposite from the lagoon. The description of the island does not substantially change, and all the elements are used symbolically, yet a pattern of meaning never coheres from the details. The only coherence is in the implications of illusion or mistaken perception, as when Ralph initially described the island 'like icing . . . on a pink cake'. The geography is always physical and immediate as it simultaneously renders emotional states and ideas, but geography as a coherent entity does not serve to locate parabolic narrative, as would, for example, the desert or the sea in a Biblical parable. Similarly, although the novel describes events moving through time, attention to the fire lighted for rescue gradually subsiding, the claims of the instincts of the 'hunters' rising, and the fragile identities of the 'littluns' evaporating, Golding provides no clock sense, no particular indication of how many or how quickly days or weeks pass. Images of light and dark, day and night, suggest time both physically and symbolically, but the possibility of parabolic coherence through narrative is limited by the vagueness concerning any of our usual temporal increments of days or weeks. We find it difficult to apply any specific sense of change as gradual revelation through narrative. Anticipating *Pincher Martin* in a way, Golding has wrenched usual concepts of time and space away from familiar or conventional patterns.

The force of *Lord of the Flies* emerges less from any form, like parable, than from the strength, immediacy and suggestiveness of the prose Golding writes. He is always a strikingly visual writer, evoking physical sensation. The ritualistic killing of Simon, for example, is powerfully graphic, as the 'crowd . . . leapt on to the beast, screamed, struck, bit, tore. There were no words, and no movements but the tearing of teeth and claws.' As Simon dies from the beating, Golding shifts his attention from the fiery 'hunters' to the victim: 'The line of his cheek silvered and the turn of his shoulder became sculptured marble . . . The body lifted a fraction of an inch from the sand and a bubble of air escaped from the mouth with a wet plop.' A further shift transforms the scene to the cosmic:

> Somewhere over the darkened curve of the world the sun and moon were pulling; and the film of water on the earth planet was held, bulging slightly on one side while the solid core turned. The great wave of the tide moved further along the island and the water lifted. . . . Simon's dead body moved out toward the open sea.

As this passage illustrates, Golding's prose is a remarkable blend of the abstract and the concrete, or, more accurately perhaps, a gesture toward the abstract and symbolic through a strongly visual use of the concrete, the water 'bulging slightly on one side while the solid core turned'. Such passages build structurally in *Lord of the Flies*, connecting the abstract with the concrete in developing, for example, the symbol of the 'beast' and moving it more and more into the centre of the human creature, or in paralleling the dissipation of the echoes of civilisation with the movement toward the human interior. The constancy of the concrete prose holds the variously symbolic novel together.

The linear movement of the novel, the progress of the narration, is symbolically directed toward the human interior, stripping away what Golding sees as the falsity of confidence in civilisation, the representative illusions of Ballantyne, as the novel moves toward its fictional conclusion. References from the very beginning indicate the point of view that sees the story as the process of the gradual erosion of meaning in the paraphernalia of civilisation. On the first page of the novel, before he is even named, Ralph is described in a way that signals a sharp juxtaposition between character and setting: 'The fair boy stopped and jerked his stockings with an automatic gesture that made the jungle seem for a moment like the Home Counties.' Questions about possible rescue are asked from the beginning, sometimes with an underlying confidence, sometimes with the fear that the atomic war has expunged all potential rescuers. Throughout most of the novel, Golding plays the intimations of rescue both ways. At times, the boys' inertia and incompetence seem to prevent rescue, as when they allow the signal fire to go out, see a passing ship that does not stop, and permit their cries for rescue to be drowned out by the ritualistic chant of the choir. At other times, especially when probing the nature of the human creature, the concept of rescue seems trivial and irrelevant. When Roger is first throwing stones near another boy and only 'the taboo of the old life' prevents him from aiming to hit the boy directly, a restraint that will soon disappear, Golding writes that 'Roger's arm was conditioned by a civilisation that knew nothing of him and was in ruins'. The boys become increasingly dirty as the chants of the choir become louder and more atavistic. The feeble rationalist, Piggy, becomes more and more the butt, a link between the echoes of the only superfically civilised schoolboy's world where he 'was the centre of social derision so that everyone felt cheerful and normal' and the island world with none of the veneer of civilisation in which his spectacles are smashed as a dramatic prelude to his total destruction. The twins, 'Samneric', mutually redundant, the last holdout against the choir apart from Piggy and Ralph, 'protested out of the heart of civilisation' just before they were forced to yield to Jack and his 'hunters'. The perspective is rather like that of Conrad's *Heart of Darkness*, a progressive stripping away of the faint echoes of civilisation as the narrative moves toward its conclusion in the centre of human darkness, although Golding refuses, in this novel, to defend Conrad's final palliative of the necessary 'lie'. Golding's perspective is also suffused with human guilt for all those intelligent and rational social constructions, all those various forms of spectacles, that have been unable to overcome or assuage the central darkness.

The directed perspective, moving through narrative time, and its symbolically conveyed moral implications have invited many readers and critics to see *Lord of the Flies* in terms of parable—or, rather, since parable suggests a Biblical or Christian orthodoxy that does not fit the novel, in terms of fable. Fable is also a more useful term than parable in that the religious sources of Golding's imagination are Greek as well as Christian, echoes of the conflict between the Dionysian and the Apollonian or of Euripidean tragedy that Golding has acknowledged. The term 'fable' was first introduced to account for Golding's fictions in an essay by John Peter in 1957, Peter defining fables as 'those narratives which leave the impression that their purpose was anterior, some initial thesis or contention which they are apparently concerned to embody and express in concrete terms.' Peter distinguished the fictional fable, like Orwell's *1984*, from the novel or non-fabulistic fiction like D. H. Lawrence's *The Rainbow*. For Peter, 'the coherence of the fable appears to us as a moral tool, and its patterns become precepts', and this quality distinguished Golding's work from the dearth of value in the fiction of his contemporaries in the 1950s. Later critics, writing in the 1960s, such as Bernard Oldsey and Stanley Weintraub, and Mark Kinkead-Weekes and Ian Gregor, rightly saw 'fable' as too restrictive a term for what Golding was doing. They saw his fiction as too complex and various to be reducible to conclusive moral thesis or to yield to the connection of each important physical detail with a symbolic correlative. Yet 'fable', as a term that was frequently discussed and that still is useful as a means of initiating discussion about *Lord of the Flies*, cannot entirely be ignored.

Golding himself gave the term initial critical credibility by rather equivocally accepting it in so far as 'the fabulist is the moralist' and he always saw himself as the latter. He recognised that the term was not quite right for either the range or the structure of his fiction. In terms of range and suggestability, he said, he aimed for the larger and looser dimensions of 'myth', recognising how difficult and problematic it is to try to create comprehensive myths for one's own contemporaries. In terms of structure, he thought, somewhat humbly, that he reversed some of the implications of linear fable with 'gimmicks' at the ends of his novels. Critics initially often took him at his word: some elevated his work to 'myth', others complained that the 'gimmick' reversed, reduced or palliated the fiction. In perhaps the fullest account of 'fable' as it applies to *Lord of the Flies*, John S. Whitley quotes Golding as saying that where his fable 'splits at the seams' he would like to think the split is the result of a 'plentitude of imagination'. But Whitley, in his careful analysis of the form and his recognition of all the possible adaptations of 'fable', points to all Golding's intrusions, his gestures toward establishing the form and withdrawing from it, realising that the question of 'plentitude' or paucity of imagination is less the point than is the fact that fabulistic form cannot really account for the range of Golding's coherence and appeal. Golding's proportions do not fit his ostensible structure.

The problem of the 'fable' is particularly acute at the end of *Lord of the Flies* in the 'resuce' that, in moral terms, is not really a rescue. A naval officer arrives on the island to pick up the boys and saves Ralph literally from the chanting choir of 'hunters' that destroyed Piggy. Yet the naval officer is as impercipient a representative of the civilised as is any voice of Ballantyne's, for he says, on the final page of the novel, 'I should have thought that a pack of British boys—you're all British aren't you?—would have been able to put up a better show than that', and he still thinks *The Coral Island* an appropriate parallel. Besides, the naval officer is part of the wider world involved in atomic war. The atomic war generated the novel in the first place, was the device to bring the evacuated schoolboys to the island (in this sense, the boys have only duplicated the adult world), and, in the ship and the dead parachutist who is the 'Lord of the Flies', the 'Lord of Dung', and Beelzebub, the war impinges at points throughout the whole novel. Ralph has come to understand something of this, to recognise the central evil of human experience, although he does survive, and Golding, in the final line of the novel, grants him a mysteriously equivocal stance in 'allowing his eyes to rest on the trim cruiser in the distance' without comment. In terms of meaning, symbol and morality, the implications of Golding's perspective are clear: the central darkness and evil the boys revealed reflects a larger human darkness and evil, not only a violation of confidence in what the English public school represents, but also a world at war violating the false confidence of progressive and civilised values. In terms of structure and plot, in terms that 'fable' as comprehensive form would satisfy, the conclusion of the novel (as well as some earlier intrusions) violates the structural expectation that the form should be able to carry all of the novel's meaning. As Whitley sees, this is less a matter of palliative 'gimmick', has fewer of the associations of undercutting or trickery than that term suggests, than the literarily conventional resolution of the plot through a 'deus ex machina'. The form adds a 'deus ex machina' to the fable; the meaning does not require one.

Suggestive as it is for provisional examination, the term 'fable' cannot account for the extraordinarily strong feeling of coherence in Golding's novel. Rather, the coherence is visible in the distinctive and effective language, the explosive pressure of the unique and constant connection between the abstract and concrete. Coherence is also visible in Golding's perspective, his constant probing of civilised illusion, his constant stripping away of facile assurance as he approaches the evil and details the 'grief' he finds central to human experience. These are stong and appealing matters of linguistic and thematic coherence, creations of a world in fiction. The concentrated pressure of Golding's prose also creates an expectation of or hope for formal coherence as well. If, ultimately, 'truth is single', a reader looks for the singular truth in Golding's form as well. And 'fable' is a good term for the kind of formal coherence closest to what Golding is doing. Yet because of Golding's complexity, 'plentitude' or paucity of imagination as it might be, 'fable' is too centred on plot and does not entirely carry the meaning. Golding's sense of formal achievement is not fully satisfied, as it is in some of the later novels. His form, in so far as it is entirely coherent, is conditioned still by the form against which he reacts, the model of Ballantyne's *The Coral Island*. The negative form, the target, provides the points of coherence that a reading as 'fable' cannot quite sustain.

Golding's next novel, *The Inheritors*, reveals a similar formal pattern, as well as a similar interest in exploring the inner nature of the human being. The intellectual target that generates Golding's imagination in this instance is H. G. Wells's *Outline of History*, a passage from which Golding quotes as an epigraph. Elaboration of Wells's prose by including that of someone else he quotes, Golding cites a passage describing Neanderthal man, the human being's evolutionary progenitor, as repulsively strange, short, inferior to man and ugly, 'gorilla-like monsters, with cunning brains, shambling gait, hairy bodies, strong teeth, and possibly cannibalistic tendencies', which 'may be the germ of the ogre in folklore'. This passage alone is, to some extent, a simplification of Wells's point of view, for the balance of *Outline of History* is not quite so confident of human superiority in every moral and aesthetic respect as the quotation itself might suggest. Wells recognised how little we know about Neanderthal man and emphasised evolutionary change and adaptation rather than intrinsic human superiority. Nevertheless, Golding uses Wells to reverse the implications of the epigraph, to show that, in his version of prehistory, the 'monsters' with 'cunning brains' . . . and possibly 'cannibalistic tendencies' are not the Neanderthals but the evolutionary subsequent *homo sapiens*. In framing most of the novel from the point of view of one of the Neanderthals, Lok, Golding tries carefully to duplicate the primitive perspective. The 'shambling gait', for example, is visible on the first page, when Lok is carrying the child, Liku, on his shoulders: 'His feet stabbed, he swerved and slowed.' At other times, he talks of his feet as 'no longer clever', or Golding adds that Lok's following the actions of others in his group is 'affectionate and unconscious parody'. The Neanderthals also flare nostrils grossly and are inhibited by their hairiness. They do not discriminate perceptions sharply and rationally, thinking in a kind of amalgamated metaphor as in describing 'lumps of smooth grey rock' as 'the bones of the land'. This perspective makes the Neanderthal appealing, although Golding could hardly do everything necessary to characterise them through their own eyes. Frequently, he breaks apart from the Neanderthal perspective to add an authorial voice. When Lok, having been hungry and eaten meat, is satisfied and 'became Lok's belly', Golding adds that 'his face shown with grease and serene happiness'. In the next sentence, Golding goes further to show what that is generally human Lok could not do: 'Tonight was colder than last night, though he made no comparisons'. Occasionally, the authorial intrusions become more abstract, as in the confusion Lok shares with Fa, a female member of the group, when they first see a human being and Golding explains that 'There was nothing in life as a point of reference'.

Despite these probably necessary intrusions that interrupt the Neanderthal's point of view and despite what may be oversimplification of Wells,

Golding does build a coherent, appealing and effective fictional portrait of the earlier species. The Neanderthals, or 'people', as they refer to themselves, are made amiable and attractive. Despite their perceptual limitations, the ingeniously conveyed strictures placed on their rational intelligence, the 'people' are warm and responsive. They have a deep and humble sense of their own limitations, as well as a faith in a female divine power (whom they call 'Oa') and in the goodness of the earth. Although we see a group of only eight 'people' (and one of these is a child, another an infant), they enjoy a family life free from fighting, guilt and emotional squabbling. Each has his or her function, carefully defined and limited, each a respect for the other members of the family. Their values are communal rather than individual, for they have no sense of private ownership or sole emotional claim. They all warm the Old Man with their bodies as he is dying. Their sexuality is also communal, for, although Lok and Fa sometimes seem to be mates, Liku is the daughter of Lok and Nil. Nil is the child-bearing woman and Ha the most intelligent man, although the four share sexual relationships, work and spontaneous concern and appreciation for the others. Their emotions centre on what is fundamental: food, shelter and closeness; birth, life and death. They keep and protect the image of Oa, the goddess that the Old Man tells them 'brought forth the earth from her belly. . . . The earth brought forth woman and the woman brought forth the first man out of her belly.' They share a vision of a previous paradise, unlike the colder and more difficult present, a time 'when there had been many people, the story that they all liked so much of the time when it was summer all year round and the flowers and fruit hung on the same branch.' They also have a strongly developed moral sense, not only toward each other but also toward other beings on the earth. When, at one point, out foraging for food, Lok and Fa bring back a deer, Fa assures him that 'A cat has killed the deer and sucked its blood, so there is no blame.'

The 'people' are, however, severely limited in conceptualising themselves. They sometimes split themselves literally into an inside and an outside, as if the two have no connection. Their conceptions of the exterior world are similarly blurred. On their annual migration with which the novel begins, they notice that a log they use to cross a deep stream is no longer there and they assume it has gone away. When the log they find to try to replace it does not hold, they assume the log swims as they assume the sun hides itself. They carry their fire with them, reverently, as if, like Prometheus, they had taken it from the Gods. Their fire is transported as a smouldering spark surrounded by wet clay that they open, blow to flame and feed. Although the fire seems to suit both their needs and their devotion to exterior power, they generally have little capacity as incipient engineers or

organisers of the exterior world to maintain themselves. In the middle of a
process that requires several consecutive steps, like building a bridge, they
sometimes forget the first step before they have finished the second. Some,
like Fa, are brighter than others, like Lok, in maintaining consecutive
memory and in connecting cause and effect rationally. For all of them,
however, language is a commitment that establishes unchangeable reality.
Once something is spoken, it *is*, even when the words are those of the
dying, hallucinatory Old Man who never recovers from the chill he caught
by falling in the water during their inept attempt to reconstruct a bridge to
replace the missing log. Imagination is not conveyed by speech; rather their
imagination takes the form of 'pictures', images of the world that they
dimly apprehend and try to sort out. When something happens outside
their comprehension, they recognise that they have 'no pictures' and,
therefore, no imagination, memory or words. They try, honestly and literally, to construct their world from those 'pictures' that they do observe and
remember, and then to solidify, make permanent, that world through
language.

Golding is most effective in describing the process, the way the minds
of the 'people' try to sort out the 'pictures' of a changing exterior world. The
'people' are invariably direct, working out their perceptions honestly as far as
they can (although they are capable of a warm humour, regarding Lok as the
buffoon of the group when he nonsensically uses words for which he has no
'pictures'). Golding combines the moral respect and sympathy with the insistence on the intellectual limitation, the problems in connecting cause with
effect or the difficulty in summoning a 'picture' and converting it into usable
experience like speech. At times, Golding shows this process operating
through a long scene, as in the one in which Lok and Fa fight off the hyenas
and buzzards for the prize of the doe the cat has killed. Although Fa dimly
understands, as Lok does not, that the feared cat will not return to a kill
whose blood has been drained, she cannot convert her understanding into
speech, although she can express the moral issue in asserting that there is no
blame. The passage works in its compressed complexity, in the sense that
understanding differently, intellectually or rationally separate although
emotionally and morally congruent, one creature fearful, the other not, the
two can work together to bring food home to the family. Golding creates a
stiking *tour de force*, a condensed prose metaphor that uses the 'people', with
all their adequacies and inadequacies, to illustrate the qualities that he sees as
simultaneously prior and fundamental to what we are able to regard only as
human experience. The accuracy of Golding's version of Wells is irrelevant;
we convert the moral and emotional implication of the metaphor into a statement about primal or basic human nature.

*The Inheritors*, however, does not rest in its metaphor of the mind of the 'people', as its action is not confined to the stasis of their decline and evolutionary replacement by *homo sapiens*. Rather, Golding introduces the new species, the human being, at first just as seen from the point of view of the 'people', then, in the short final chapter, with a switch to the human point of view. Human society is full of noise, fights and anger, of provocation, infidelity and betrayal. The individual, understanding and projecting more of his or her imagination, is capable of setting self against community, of trying to gain power or love at the expense of a fellow being. Lok and Fa, looking at the human beings from a distance, can see that they are predatory, that they have 'teeth that remembered wolf'. Lok and Fa are far from able to understand much that they see, although Fa is able to state the moral comment 'Oa did not bring them out of her belly'. Only gradually is Lok able to realise that the long stick he sees from a distance that the human being holds is a bow and the tiny cross-stick that whizzes past his head into a tree is an arrow meant to harm him. He takes even longer to recognise that the human beings have captured Liku; when he does realise this, he thinks they wanted her only as a playmate for one of their children approximately her own age. He tries, at first, to throw food for her. The human beings, however, turn Liku into food, killing her in a ritual sacrifice when their hunt is a failure and devouring her remains. Worship is not respect or devotion but predatory propitiation. Liku, like Simon in *Lord of the Flies* (also like 'you', human beings generically), is the scapegoat, the sacrificial victim to predatory human evil. The 'people' will eat meat only when it is already dead, drained, and they can absolve themselves of 'blame'; human beings, more technologically skilful and rationally intelligent, will eat what they kill no matter how close the species is to themselves. The more intelligently individual and the more accurately self-conscious, the crueller and more evil the species. The 'people' had difficulty in separating themselves from the exterior world; the human being as a post-lapsarian creature, more intelligently divided, more conscious of what the individual self is, makes martyrs and victims out of his own species.

The moral and intellectual contrast between the 'people' and the human beings is not Golding's final statement in *The Inheritors*, for both species are capable of some amount of significant change through experience. The novel is about evolution, not only from one species to another, but of the capacities within each of the species themselves. Golding displays two senses of movement within the novel: from one species to the next; in a quicker, more impacted and interior way, from lesser to greater consciousness within each species. The final chapter shifts to the point of view of

Tuami, one of the human beings. Although still the evil and individualistic human being, he is able to abandon his plot to kill his chief, recognising that the single action of his knife-blade would, at best, be only a sharp point against the overwhelming darkness of the world he would also exemplify. He can feel guilt and 'grief'; he can also recognise the possibilities of love and light. In short, Tuami's consciousness has expanded from a representation of man's essential evil to the suggestion of a more complex representation of fallible human possibility. Tuami, in the log he has made into a boat, ends the novel by looking at the light flashing on the water and 'he could not see if the line of darkness had an ending.' Toward the end of the novel, Lok also learns as he observes the human beings and tries to create 'pictures' of what they are. He begins to imagine similes, and, as Golding comments directly, 'Lok discovered "Like",' which he had 'used . . . all his life without being aware of it'. Through his elementary understanding of simile, Lok begins to establish a prior condition for sorting out individuality, for understanding how creatures are both like and unlike each other. One of his similes seems crucially symbolic: 'They are like the river and the fall, they are a people of the fall; nothing stands against them'. In the final chapter, Tuami watches as Fa (always a few steps ahead of Lok) is precipitated over the falls to her death, a process the now diminished Lok, seen from a distance, is sure to follow. In the process of evolution, Golding symbolically suggests, the Neanderthals have fallen into humanity and attention shifts to the already explicitly human creature who can experience guilt and self-knowledge, just as he can adapt and master the log (suggestions of the 'Tree of Knowledge'), which defeated the 'people' in the initial episode of the novel. The fall into humanity is both a lost innocence and a 'fortunate' fall, fortunate in its recognition of human consciousness and the possibility, however dim, of redemption. The questions of likeness and difference, of one species against the other, have been transformed into a powerfully searching and traditionally religious statement about the nature of the human being.

As Golding's metaphorical statement deepens, the epigraph from Wells seems more a prod that an alternative, a propellant to the fictional explosion. Initially a response to what Golding regards as erroneous simplification in Well's *Outline of History*, just as *Lord of the Flies* was a response to the confidence in civilisation in Ballantyne's fiction, *The Inheritors* becomes a more dense and searching statement about the human condition than any scientifically documentable polarity between Neanderthal and *homo sapiens* might suggest. Golding's account of evolution is simultaneously physical, rational, moral and religious, all conveyed in compact statements of similarity and difference in language that is both concrete and stikingly resonant, explosive prose. A description as 'fable' accounts for *The Inheritors* even less than it does for *Lord of the Flies*, for the pattern of matching action or the progress of narrative to meaning would imply a more simplified and linear process of evolution than that which Golding represents in the novel. The form of the 'fable', in its insistence on the significance of action, would restrict Golding's treatment of the human condition. Nor can one designate *The Inheritors* as 'myth' really achieved, for 'myth', at least in so far as one understands the Classical and Christian myths that echo so strongly through Golding's consciousness, requires an application to and assent from the general litera-ture culture that is difficult to demonstrate in contemporary terms. Perhaps some future age will see Golding's original works as establishing 'myth' with twentieth-century referents (perhaps 'myth', on this level, can only be seen or applied retrospectively), but his powerful fiction seems too individual and idiosyncratic a version of the traditional to operate as the kind of 'myth' to which the literate culture assents. Rather, escaping from both the boundaries suggested by the form of 'fable' and the lines suggested by simple response to the prods and or propellants, the Ballantyne and the Wells, *Lord of the Flies* and *The Inheritors* evolve into distinctive and unique fictions. Without the propellants to set them in action, they might seem incoherent or mysterious, certainly difficult, and the simplified polarity is probably the best point of entrance into Golding's fictional world. But his own kind of form, his own incorporation of literary and religious tradition into an essential statement of the human condition, is not really achieved until his next novel, his next unique and symbolic literary explosion.

PATRICK REILLY

# Lord of the Flies: *Beelzebub's Boys*

There are a number of reasons why this study of the dark epiphany should end appropriately with *Lord of the Flies*, for it recapitulates in a fable immediately resonant to a twentieth-century sensibility the themes that we have traced from Swift onwards: the dread that civilisation is simply a veneer over bestiality; that the self is no more than the fragile product of a particular conditioning which, when the matrix alters, is unnervingly at the mercy of the new situation; that orgiastic surrender to a dark irrationalism is always a temptation and sometimes a fate; that we are shockingly obliged to give psychological house-room to strangers who claim kinship, to the Yahoo, the Pharisee and the sadist, all of whom disconcertingly seem to have equal residential rights with our more decorous, benevolent selves. In its final scene the book supplies us with one of the most explicit renditions of the dark epiphany in modern literature when the newly-rescued Ralph, to the embarrassed incomprehension of his superficial saviour, breaks down and, in thoroughly un-English style, weeps for the end of innocence and the darkness of man's heart.

Golding, as much as his book, seems the apposite terminus for our investigation. If, in fulfilment of Adrian Leverkühn's promise, the twentieth century has pursued a policy of revocation towards the work of its predecessor, it is Golding who has proved himself the most overt and deliberate of

From *The Literature of Guilt from Gulliver to Golding*. © 1988 by Patrick Reilly.

revokers. Almost all of his early work is a taking back, a rescinding of certain long established views and *idées reçues*. His second novel, *The Inheritors*, sets out to invalidate the optimistic view of human development held by H. G. Wells; its epigraph is provided by *The Outline of History* in which Wells celebrates the coming of *homo sapiens* and his victory over Neanderthal Man. Wells presents the latter as a half-witted, blood-thirsty creature, prototype of the cannibalistic ogre of folk-tale, while his supplanter is shown as thoughtful and resourceful, fit ancestor of our superior selves. Even more pertinent to the plot of Golding's book is Wells's short story *The Grisly Folk*, in which the Neanderthal monsters steal a human child and are then, with Wells's total approval, hunted down and destroyed by the new men in an act at once retributive and progressive. *The Inheritors* stands Wells on his head by depicting the Neanderthals as gentle and innocent, the newcomers as vicious and aggressive—man still imagines today that progress and the extermination of his enemies are the same thing. It is man who ruins the garden by introducing evil into it—the serpent is redundant in Golding's revision of Genesis.

His third novel, *Pincher Martin*, does to *Robinson Crusoe* as a myth of human fortitude and tenacity what *The Inheritors* does to *The Grisly Folk*, and is equally outrageous in the reversal it proposes. From Prometheus onward we have come, through culture and inclination alike, to cherish the hero who, rejecting capitulation or despair, pits his isolated, unconquerable self against the overwhelming tyranny of external circumstance. How can we withhold admiration from these champions of the self who cry no surrender even to inexorable reality? Pincher, clinging to his ocean rock after being torpedoed, seems for much of the book yet another irresistible candidate for heroic apotheosis, a worthy son of Prometheus; only gradually do we become aware that another, very different view of the situation is being pressed upon us. A series of flashbacks reveals a nasty, competitive person, bent on self-gratification even if it means destroying others. The snarling man, defying sea and sky, involved in his fierce and cunning struggle to survive, is simply exhibiting the same thraldom to appetite, the same wicked infatuation with his precious self, that caused so much agony to others before his shipwreck. He is not a hero but a damned soul; we learn that he has, in fact, been dead from the first page and that the speciously heroic stand against the self's extinction is, properly understood, a timid and childish refusal to face the truth. What we have deludedly prized as our noblest quality is revealed as a sordid bondage, making us such a woe to ourselves and such a menace to others.

But it is his first and best-known novel, *Lord of the Flies*, that reveals Golding as the supreme revoker, the most obvious abrogator in modern literature, employing the dark discoveries of our century to disclaim the vapid innocence of its predecessor. The target is R. M. Ballantyne's *The Coral Island* and Golding points up the ironic contrast by lifting even the names of his boys from the earlier work. Ballantyne's book could be used as a document in the history of ideas, reflecting as it does a Victorian euphoria, a conviction that the world is a rational place where problems arise so that sensible, decent men can solve them. God has his place in this world but his adversary is pleasingly absent and, with him, the sin which is his hold on humanity. The Home Counties come to the jungle and win easily. Difficulties are confidently overcome, fire is acquired easily and safely, pigs are hunted and killed with neither guilt nor bloodshed. The only troublesome things (cannibals and pirates) come from outside and are bested by British grit and commonsense. What cannibal is as foolish as to eat human flesh in preference to roast pork? All he needs is the proper culinary advice and Ballantyne knows the boys to give it. They, in turn, know nothing of Beelzebub: they are cleanly, godly, sensible, decent and efficient, and their island adventure is gratifying proof that they are just about ready to assume the blessed work of extending the British Empire throughout the savage world.

*Lord of the Flies* was conceived in a very different moral landscape and Golding himself tells us that the horrors of the Second World War were crucial in producing this alteration. When Sammy Mountjoy in *Free Fall* remarks that 'the supply of nineteenth century optimism and goodness had run out before it reached me' and goes on to describe the world as 'a savage place in which man was trapped without hope', one senses an authorial reinforcement behind the words. *Lord of the Flies* springs from the cultural catastrophe of our times and not, as has been foolishly alleged, from the petty rancour of an arts graduate peeved because the scientists today have all the jobs and all the prestige. To attribute the book to a sullen distaste for the contemporary world, to see Golding as another Jack, who, when he can't have his own way, won't play any more and goes off in a huff, all because the scientist has displaced the literary intellectual as leader of society, is dignified by describing it as a *niaiserie*. But it does, at least, help us to focus our attention on Golding's attitude to science. He had started to read science at university on the twin assumptions that 'science was busy clearing up the universe' and that 'there was no place in this exquisitely logical universe for the terrors of darkness'. But the darkness stubbornly refused to scatter and Golding came to suspect (as Bertrand Russell likewise did) that science by itself could not be our saviour and might well, in the wrong hands, become our enslaver. The war confirmed that 'the darkness was all around, inexplicable, unexorcised, haunted, a gulf across which the ladder (science) lay without reaching to the light'. It is, allowing for the heightened mode of expression, much the same perception as Freud's towards the previous war, and no one, surely, is going to accuse Freud of being a disgruntled arts graduate envious of the scientists' acclaim.

Golding's explanation of how his book came to be written seems infinitely more convincing: 'I set out to discover whether there is that in man which makes him do what he does, that's all . . . the Marxists are the only people left who think humanity is perfectible. But I went through the War and that changed me. The war taught me different and a lot of others like me.' Among the lessons learned was that Ballantyne was retailing illusions: namely, that man is basically noble and decent, that reason must extend its empire over darkness, that science is the prerogative of the civilised man. *Lord of the Flies*, by contrast, 'is an attempt to trace the defects of society back to the defects of human nature. Before the war, most Europeans believed that man could be perfected by perfecting his society. We saw a hell of a lot in the war that can't be accounted for except on the basis or original evil.' Orwell's nightmare is a boot in the face forever, a world dedicated to cruelty for its own sake; Camus invites us to contemplate the little-ease and the spitting-cell, the one an ingenious medieval invention, the other the equally masterly device of the most civilised nation in modern Europe. Golding's is the same dilemma as he seeks to discover 'that in man which makes him do what he does'; to dismiss these men as a literary cave of Adullam, a gang of petulant and disaffected *littérateurs* miffed at a scientific takeover, is as foolish as it is impertinent.

Golding has perhaps encouraged his own devaluation by describing himself as a parodist and parody as depending on the mean advantage of being wise after someone else's event. There is a similarly ungenerous self-depreciation in his allusion to a pint-sized Jeremiah, almost as though he were colluding with those who dismiss him as a peddler of doom, content to describe the ruins around us. But *Lord of the Flies* is more than just an inversion of *The Coral Island*, a retelling in realistic terms of a nineteenth-century fantasy, and it is when Golding is most creative that he is also most interesting. *Joseph Andrews* becomes the comic masterpiece it is when Fielding stops burlesquing Richardson and liberates his own imagination. The real triumph of *Lord of the Flies* is not its parodic demolition of Ballantyne but the innovative skill that is most evident in the creation of Piggy, Simon and Roger; it is this that makes it an original work of art, the authentic expression of its age, and not simply a spoof deriving its second-hand force from the work of another era. How sin enters the garden; it is, after all, the oldest story in western culture and Golding's contemporary rendition is a worthy continuation of the tradition.

Piggy is a much more complex character than the simplistic interpretations so regularly adduced will allow; the very fact that his unhesitant commonsense would have chimed in so well with Ballantyne's ethos might make us pause before acclaiming him as the book's hero. This commonsense is evident from the start as when he organises the meeting and tries to make a list of everyone present. It is, significantly, the first question put by the rescuing officer; he wants to know how many boys there are and is disappointed and a little shocked to hear that English boys in particular have not made even this elementary calculation. Yet Piggy is a doubtful hero who, no sooner met, has to rush away from us in a bout of diarrhoea; in addition, he wears spectacles, suffers from asthma, is fat through eating too many sweets in his auntie's shop, can't swim, and, most important of all, his abysmal English reveals him as unmistakably working-class. What, one wonders, was he doing on the plane with boys so clearly his social superiors? Neither Ralph nor Jack would ever have met Piggy back in England except as their employee, for while they are so obviously, in their respective ways, officer material, Piggy is just as obviously born to be an underling all his days.

Yet it is he who has a monopoly of commonsense and practical intelligence. Jack, instinctively recognising him as an inferior and a target of abuse, orders him to be quiet, yet no one else talks such consistent good sense. Ironically, in the increasingly hysterical atmosphere, that turns out to be as much a handicap as his bad eyesight. Yet nowhere is Orwell's description of England as family with the wrong members in control more visibly demonstrated than in the way the leadership contest becomes a straight two-way fight between Ralph and Jack, with Piggy not even considered, far less chosen. Yet who better to elect, given that clear thinking, with a view to maximising the chances of rescue, is the main priority? Jack knows that he should be leader and tells the others why: he can sing high C. The utter irrelevance of this is not meant to expose Jack's folly but his menace: the *Führer*'s lust for power needs no other justification than his own irrational conviction of merit. Yet the choice of Ralph, as Golding makes plain, is just as irrational. Ralph becomes leader because he looks like one—he gets the job on appearance and not ability. His very stillness is charismatic; he only has to sit and look the part.

Piggy lacks the looks but has the know-how. The trouble is that he knows but cannot do, and is relegated, in accordance with Shaw's dictum, to being at best a teacher. He cannot blow the conch himself—the asthma again—but he sees its possibilities and shows Ralph how to do it. He never advances his own claims to leadership nor even thinks of doing so, but is happy to be Ralph's adviser, the thinker and framer of policy. *Lord of the Flies* does not, like *The Admirable Crichton*, depict the rise of a meritocracy, when, following the social upheaval of shipwreck, the supremely efficient butler takes over as leader from the feckless aristocrats and only relapses into subordination when the party is rescued and taken back to the Home Counties from the jungle. Ralph and Jack are the leaders in the jungle as they would be in England. Barrie's aristocrats, recognising the demands of reality, resign themselves to accepting a social inferior as their natural leader; Golding's boys would laugh at the idea of taking orders from Piggy.

What is interesting is the skilful way in which Golding employs the prejudices of the English class system to support his allegorical intention. The allegory requires that the boys should undervalue, ignore and even despise commonsense. How shrewd, in that case, to embody commonsense in a fat, bespectacled, unathletic, working-class boy who is the natural target of upper-class contempt. The language barrier is the crucial thing. Crichton, after all, did at least speak immaculate English, but what gentleman could ever bring himself to take orders from someone who talks like Piggy? Piggy can aspire, at most, to advise and he is to begin with the best adviser that Ralph could get. We must not, of course, push the allegory to the absurd extreme of saying that the working class have all the commonsense, but we are entitled, even obliged to point out that the task set commonsense in the book becomes infinitely more difficult by making its representative a working-class boy among upper-class companions.

The allegorical insistence throughout the book that men prefer passion to practicality and glamour to commonsense (*plutôt la barbarie que l'ennui*) is reinforced by the realism of social antipathy. Piggy, trained to know his place, does not protest, far less rebel against this. From the moment Jack turns up, commonsense takes a back seat, and the reason is unarguably connected with the English class system. Piggy at once stops taking names for his list: 'He was intimidated by this uniformed superiority and the offhand authority in Merridew's voice. He shrank to the other side of Ralph and busied himself with his glasses.' Piggy knows he is inferior just as Ralph and Jack take their superiority for granted. It is this sense of inferiority that makes him deliver himself into the hands of his class enemies right from the start when he fool-ishly tells Ralph his derisory nickname and even more foolishly asks him to keep it a secret. It is perhaps unfair to say that Ralph betrays him, since betrayal implies a confidence solicited and a promise broken, and Ralph does neither, but at almost the first opportunity Ralph blurts out Piggy's secret to the whole world. Even Ralph, so straight and decent, is not above meanness, and his tears at the close for Piggy are an act of contrition for all the insults and injuries, climaxing in murder, which the boys have inflicted right from the start upon their inferior companion. In Ralph, at least, class contempt is gradually and thoroughly overcome; he weeps for the true, wise friend who came to him originally in such an unprepossessing guise.

That Piggy does to some extent bring his troubles upon himself leaves unchallenged his claim to be *the* sensible person on the island. He himself never makes this claim because he only partially realises it. One of his limitations is a tendency to credit others with his own good sense. He keeps attributing to Raph his own practical insights when it is plain to the reader that Ralph is still fumbling around in the dark. He rebukes the other boys for distracting Ralph from what he was about to say and then puts the words into his bemused leader's mouth. There is nothing devious or disingenuous in this. He shares Ballantyne's confidence that commonsense can master any problem and he believes that most people, given the chance, are as logical as himself. When, after Ralph's first speech—Piggy admires it as a model of succinct good sense—the other boys, led by Jack, run off in disorganised excitement to light the signal-fire, Ralph and Piggy are left alone with the conch; then Ralph, too, scrambles after 'the errrant assembly', leaving disgusted commonsense on its own. All Piggy can do is toil breathlessly after them while venting his exasperation in the worst reproof he can imagine: 'Acting like a crowd of kids!' But that's what they are. The book shows that you only get an old head on young shoulders when the shoulders are those of a podgy, unhealthy boy. The adult the boys so desperately need is among them but disguised so impenetrably that there is no hope of his being recognised, let alone heeded. Piggy's continual annoyance and even less justified continual surprise at the foolish behaviour of his companions should surely have led him to suspect that his own commonsense was not so widely distributed as he had imagined, yet right up to his destruction he goes on believing in the power of reason to tame the beast. His most fervent exhortation to the others is that they should stop being kids and instead try to think and act as adults do, for he believes that therein lies salvation. One of the book's major ironies is that the boys finally take his advice: they act like adults and kill him.

Yet in this ambivalent book in which everything is double—fire is both good and bad, faces lit from above are very different from faces lit from below, nature is both beautiful and menacing, the human being is at once heroic and sick—it is fitting that Piggy's handicaps, most notably the asthma, all those things which qualify him as the target for ridicule, should be, in another sense, compensations. Sickness brings its own insights—Simon is, of course, an even more dramatic exemplification of this psychological truth. Long before anyone else Piggy senses the menace of Jack and the element of self-interest in this intuition makes it no less valid. Allegorically, it represents the fact that reason and commonsense are the prey of fanaticism. Piggy is stricken when Ralph talks despairingly of surrendering to Jack: "'If you give up", said Piggy in an appalled whisper, "what'ud happen to me? . . . He hates me. I dunno why.'" On the naturalistic level this is perfectly credible; a little boy, with every cause to be frightened of a bully, expresses his own personal fears, but allegorically we note the impotence of commonsense to check the progress of demented totalitarianism—when Jack is frustrated his eyes are described as bolting, blazing or mad.

Orwell, in what was almost a kind of parricide, attacked H. G. Wells for complacently dismissing Hitler as a jumped-up nonentity doomed to defeat because he was the enemy of reason. Winston Smith has all the commonsense truths of arithmetic and history on his side but they do him no good against O'Brien's fanaticism. Golding shifts the conflict to a school playground, emptied of all teachers, to enforce the same lesson. Piggy perceptively associates his fear of Jack with the sickness from which he suffers: 'You kid yourself he's all right really, an' then when you see him again; it's like asthma an' you can't breathe.' When Ralph tries to pooh-pooh this as exaggeration, Piggy confides the source of his superior insight: 'I been in bed so much I done some thinking. I know about people. I know about me. And him.' If the grammar is faulty, the psychology is sound: Piggy does know about Jack, long before anyone else does, and his knowledge springs from the kind of boy he is. The same thing that has stopped him from being an athlete has encouraged him to be a thinker, though, as we shall see, a thinker of a limited kind.

There is certainly much to admire in Piggy. His liberal-democratic outlook and sense of fair play lead him to the honourable idea that everyone, however lowly, has a right to speak—even a littlun who wants the conch must be given it. Again Jack is the adversary: 'We don't need the conch any more. We know who ought to say things.' This leads straight to a kind of Asiatic court where only the tyrant's voice is heard because all dissenters have been put to death; Piggy supports a polyphonic society, Jack a society of mutes, since men require only ears to hear the master's command.

Piggy, too, is the first to recognise that life entails making certain choices and establishing certain priorities. Ralph, by contrast, tells the boys what mankind has always wished to hear: that there is no troublesome competition among our desires but that all can be simultaneously gratified, that the world will complaisantly minister to all our wishes, that, psychologically speaking, we are like pampered guests in a Hilton hotel where the whole *raison d'être* of the establishment is to provide whatever we want. 'We want to be rescued; and of course we shall be rescued.' Such brash optimism is presumptuous enough, for even though the assembly is 'lifted towards safety by his words', we know that words alone are futile and that the comfort they provide is delusive. But Ralph compounds his offence by presuming still more: 'We want to have fun. And we want to be rescued.' (Fun is a word worth watching in *Lord of the Flies* for on three important occasions when it is used—here by Ralph, by Beelzebub in his warning to Simon, and finally by the unseeing officer—it sets alarm bells ringing.) The conjunction used by Ralph implies a confidence that we can have both things—fun *and* rescue—together. The boys have had a happy accident: they will have a delightful, unexpected, adult-free holiday, with rescue just around the corner the moment boredom begins.

It is the practical Piggy who jarringly introduces the reality principle into this dream of pleasure: 'How can you expect to be rescued it you don't put first things first and act proper?' The grammatical solecism should not conceal the psychological wisdom. Life is not the Hilton but a succession of harsh choices and necessary sacrifices; at the very best, if you are lucky, you will get what you deserve, but windfalls are a pipe-dream. It is the Judaeo-Christian premise upon which western civilisation once rested. You can eat the apple or stay in Eden; not both. You will reach the Promised Land but only after the discipline of an arduous journey through the wilderness. Do you want fun *or* rescue? Piggy introduces the unpleasant idea of an incompatibility between desires; if rescue is our first priority, then fun must come a poor second. If we are serious about rescue, that means work, and work is what we would prefer someone else to do for us: lighting and maintaining fires, building shelters, and all the other tedious chores that the little folk in fairy tales perform for a bowl of milk. Civilisation, says Freud, is based upon the renunciation of instinctual gratification and Piggy is the only Freudian on the island. *Lord of the Flies* depicts, initially, the disintegration of a society whose members play rather than work.

Self-denial is the infallible litmus-test. When Jack goes hunting, he is clearly doing something that is both demanding and dangerous—instinctual gratification is not necessarily immersion in sybaritic hedonism. The point is that Jack is doing what he wants, not what he ought; he relishes the danger of the chase and the excitement of the kill. Piggy does not criticise Jack for doing what is easy, but for putting his own pleasure above the priority of rescue. Stalking pigs is thrilling, tending a fire is dull, so Jack opts for Yahoo excitement in preference to Houyhnhnm tedium—that's what makes him the foe of civilisation and Piggy alike. The trouble is that Jack is more representative than Piggy and his outlook prevails, even though not all of the defaulters are pursuing pigs with the indefatigable hunter—many have plumped for Tahiti, for fruit, swimming and sunbathing. At assemblies they all vote dutifully for the laudable resolutions because people love to talk, but they do not love to work: 'We decide things. But they don't get done . . . people don't help much.' And so the huts, vital to civilised survival, are either unbuilt or ramshackle. It is hard to be civilised, deleteriously easy to be savage. Work is irksome, and, in terms of this Kantian definition, Jack is a layabout, even if he chased pigs from dawn to dusk.

We must, accordingly, be careful not to be too harsh on Piggy for being such a bore; even Ralph, despite their growing friendship, sees this failing: 'his fat, his ass-mar and his matter-of-fact ideas were dull'. Piggy *is* depressingly literalist, totally lacking in a sense of humour, taking everything so seriously. But the book exists to demonstrate the superiority of dull decency to the heady intoxication of evil—the Yahoos pay a swingeing price for all that life they are supposed to possess. The two worlds are strikingly contrasted when Jack, the bloodied knife in his hand, fresh from his first, elated kill, confronts Ralph, fuming because the chance of rescue has been lost: 'the brilliant world of hunting, tactics, fierce exhilaration, skill' versus the antithetical world of 'longing and baffled common-sense'. We *must* choose between pigs and huts, hunters and builders, fun and rescue. If Piggy is dull, he is also right.

Only to a certain degree, however, because Piggy's intelligence is seriously limited. The sole, damaging occasion when he agrees with Jack is to deny the beast's existence. Jack initially insists, with fine positivist arrogance, that there is no beast—he has hunted all over the island and 'if there were a beast I'd have seen it'. Piggy ominously joins his enemy in scouting the idea of a beast—'of course there isn't nothing to be afraid of in the forest'—though he approaches Simon's intuition in stating that 'there isn't no fear . . . unless we get frightened of people'. But Piggy is handicapped by an unfounded trust in a rational universe administered by rational man: 'Life is scientific, that's what it is. . . . We know what goes on and if there's something wrong, there's someone to put it right.' Everything comes right in the end: it is the root fallacy of the liberal mind that Orwell identified and pilloried in *Nineteen Eighty-Four*. Piggy has joined up with the complacent optimists he formerly rebuked.

It is Simon, a character not to be found, however faintly, in Ballantyne's story, whom Golding uses to highlight Piggy's shortcomings. The distance separating Piggy from Simon (who clearly embodies Golding's highest values) is indicated in Piggy's shocked incomprehension when Simon hesitantly suggests that perhaps there *is* a beast and that 'maybe it's only us'. Piggy indignantly rejects this as 'Nuts!' Simon's mystical speculations are beyond Piggy's limitedly sensible mind; he cannot and, more to the point, will not assist Simon in the latter's inarticulate effort to express man's essential illness. For Piggy, man is *not* ill—he just has a foolish but corrigible habit of following Jack when he should be taking Piggy's sensible advice. Piggy is still handing out this sensible advice when the stone crushes him to death. Simon's stumbling attempt to explain the beast provokes general derision in which Piggy participates, but, as the book shows, it is Simon who is right and the mockers who are wrong.

Ralph reveals a similar incapacity for Simon's insight and reproaches him for voicing such a distressing thought: 'Why couldn't you say there wasn't a beast?' Tell us what we want to hear or say nothing at all. But Piggy characteristically supplies the rationale for dismissing Simon as demented. There is no beast for the same reason that there are no ghosts. ''Cos things wouldn't make sense. Houses an' streets, an'—TV—they wouldn't work'. Piggy will pay for this empty faith with his life, but, even as he speaks, the argument is sorrily unconvincing. Golding ironically emphasises this by having the other boys, led by Jack, chant and dance like savages while Piggy is making his pitiful profession of faith.

Ralph and Piggy both fail to see that, in silencing Simon, they are in effect delivering themselves into Jack's hands. The book traces three routes for mankind: Piggy's commonsense, Jack's irrationalism, and Simon's mysticism. But commonsense is intimidated by irrationalism—Piggy is terrified in Jack's presence. The paradox is that the mystic way, which strikes Piggy as outrageous mumbo-jumbo, is the only sensible, practical solution. That the mystic is, astonishingly, the practical man is made evident when the boys huddle in crazed despair after the appalling discovery of the beast on the mountain. Ralph has just gloomily announced that there is nothing to be done when Simon reaches for the conch. Ralph's irritation is plain: 'Simon? What is it this time?' Bad enough to be leader in such a predicament without having to listen to a crackpot, but what Simon says takes the all-time gold medal for sheer looniness: 'I think we ought to climb the mountain.' Piggy receives this with open-mouthed incomprehension and no one even bothers to answer the idiot when he asks, 'What else is there to do?' Piggy's solution, applauded by the boys as a stroke of intellectual audacity, is to concede the mountain to the beast and shift the signal-fire to a safer place. Yet Simon's is the truly intrepid invitation in every sense of the word, intellectually, morally and psychologically, for it *is* the only thing to do: we must outstare Medusa, face and outface whatever we fear or be afraid forever. Either the beast rules us or we rule it—surrendering the mountain to the beast is admitting that the contest is over. One might as well go the whole way and join Jack in devil-worship, in full propitiation of the demon.

Simon knows how to deal with the beast because he knows who the beast is: 'However Simon thought of the beast, there rose before his inward sight the picture of a human at once heroic and sick.' Piggy is incapable of such an intuition. In his secret place among the leaves Simon's recognition of the beast enables him to solve the problem that leaves the others in baffled anguish. It is while Simon is unlocking the secret that Ralph is asking why things have gone so terribly wrong and making one more vain appeal to commonsense. Surely if a doctor told the boys to take medicine or die, they

would do the sensible thing? Why, then, can't they see the equal importance of the signal-fire? Why do you have to beg people to save themselves? The mystery tortures him without respite: 'Just an ordinary fire.
You'd think we could do that, wouldn't you? Just a smoke signal so we can
be rescued. Are we savages or what?' It echoes Swift pondering in angry
perplexity the insensate behaviour of the self-destructive Irish. Ralph
appeals piteously to Piggy: 'What's wrong? . . . what makes things break up
like they do?', but Piggy's answer shows how sadly limited his own understanding is, for all he knows is to blame Jack. This is true only in the allegorical sense, but Piggy, of course, not knowing that he's a character in an
allegory, blames Jack as an individual and this is totally inadequate. Jack is
to blame only in the sense that he lives in all of us, that we are all guilty
because mankind is sick.

Simon is the one exception to this general condemnation. The epilectic
is the one spiritually sound person on the island, and, further paradox, it is
his sickness that helps to make him a saint. Simon is not interested in leadership or any other form of competitive self-assertion—the nature of reality,
not the promotion of the self, is his preoccupation. He is one of the meek, of
the poor in spirit, who are promised the kingdom of heaven, not the congratulations and rewards of earthly assemblies. He is a surprising and anachronistic addition to the one-time commonplace tradition which affirmed the
peculiar sanctity of the sick, the weak and the dying. His very debility is to
be seen as a mark of the divine at work in him. While Ralph and Piggy
wrestle in vain with the *mysterium iniquitatis*, Simon is shut up in audience
with the Lord of the Flies. Piggy is only partially right: there is nothing to
fear in the forest because the beast is within man; the only forest of fear is the
heart of darkness. 'Fancy thinking the Beast was something you could hunt
and kill! . . . I'm part of you? Close, close, close! I'm the reason why it's no
go? Why things are what they are?' From the first men in *The Inheritors* to
the atomic killers of our own day persists the same root delusion: evil is
external and other; we, innocent and threatened, will pursue and destroy it.
Beelzebub warns the boy who has broken the secret not to interfere with the
'fun' about to take place or else 'we shall do you', and it is significant that the
'we' includes Piggy and Ralph as well as Jack and Roger; Simon is the sole
immaculate conception in Golding's fable. When he ignores the threat and
tries to bring the good news to the other boys, Beelzebub's promise is
hideously fulfilled.

'What else is there to do?' Despite Beelzebub's warning and the indignation of his companions, Simon climbs the mountain to face the beast and
finds instead the rotting parachutist, 'harmless and horrible'. He at once sets
out to bring to the others as quickly as possible the news of salvation, and,

stumbling into the predicted 'fun', is murdered by his frenzied friends, Piggy and Ralph included. The representatives of commonsense and decency are just as eager as anyone else to take a place in the ritual of 'this demented but partly secure society'. Simon is killed while 'crying out something about a dead man on a hill', and, however different from Christ the parachutist is, the words cannot fail to evoke an image of the corpse on Calvary, with Simon's own death just as clearly intended as a recapitulation of that ancient sacrifice. Nothing changes in the way men treat their redeemers.

Despite the fact that *Gulliver's Travels* was written by the Dean of St Patrick's, and despite *The Fall*, with its significant title and its pervasive Christian themes and images, it is, of all the texts we have considered, *Lord of the Flies* that is closest in spirit to Christianity. There is no hint of redemption in *The Fall* and it is pointless to speculate as to what Camus might have gone on to write had he not been so tragically killed. His last book is unrelievedly pessimistic and we have no right to assume that in producing so dark a text Camus was either propelling us towards the church door or preparing to enter it himself. It may be a propaedeutic for Christianity but it may also be nothing of the kind. *Lord of the Flies* is different and the difference is Simon, for either he is imbecile or he has a 'supernatural' insight into reality denied to the other boys. The novel forbids the first alternative. Simon clearly *has* some mystical, prophetic power, as when he tells Ralph that he *knows*, in some incommunicable way, that Ralph will get home again—Ralph, be it noted, not himself. Simon is awkward in that he confounds all simplistic interpretations of the novel, for example, that it is an Augustinian or 'tory' book, arguing for law and order against anarchic misrule and licentious freedom. All of the boys, so it is argued, removed from the pinfold of civilisation, inevitably regress to savagery. But Simon doesn't regress to savagery; it is in the jungle that he becomes prophet and redeemer, and it would be foolish in the extreme to argue that he inherits these roles as a result of a sound education in the Home Counties. Simon is not one up for civilisation in its quarrel with nature—if anything, the beautiful resumption of his body by the ocean might lend support, here, if nowhere else, to nature's advocates.

But it is misleading to use him as a counter in the culture versus nature debate, for he transcends both to become, in the religious sense, a new creation. Why did Golding create him and why is the hideous death followed by so beautiful a *requiescat*, in almost brutal contrast to the curtly realistic disposal of the dead Piggy? Only the determinedly deaf will miss the religious reverberations echoing through the passage describing the transfiguration of the dead Simon—the gentle escort of his body towards the infinite ocean is as close to a resurrection as any novel dare come, is far more 'religious' than Sydney Carton's self-sacrifice, despite the explicitly Christian context in which Dickens invests the latter. Simon's transformation—the silvering of the cheek and the sculptured marble of the shoulders—is, to begin with, beautiful in the way that the transformation described in Ariel's song in *The Tempest* is beautiful. But more than simply a sea-change is depicted in Simon; this beauty is clearly the servant of some greater purpose—it points to an alternative world opposed to the nightmare world of blood and taboo, a world, in Hopkin's words, charged with the glory of God. The passage provides a sacramental guarantee that creation is not just some haphazard collision of atoms but the product of an organising power, a power which promises not simply rest but resurrection to those who sacrifice themselves for its sake. The rhythm and imagery make it impossible to believe that Simon's death is merely another bloody atrocity, pointless and inane, clinching proof in this dark book that life is a tale told by an idiot. The sense of peace informing the passage is not simply that which Macbeth envies in Duncan. Simon *is* out of the madness, *is* at rest—after the fever of the island he sleeps well—but not just in the negative sense of Macbeth's longing; the peace that concludes Simon's sacrifice is much more akin to the promise of the Sermon on the Mount: blessed are the pure in heart for they shall see God. Simon is now at one with whatever strong, beautiful power it is that sustains creation, the power that will continue to maintain 'the stead-fast constellations' when all the hagridden acolytes of Jack have followed Macbeth to vacuous death. It is an arresting *peripeteia*: the dark epiphany is pierced by a shaft of light from that other epiphany promising salvation and for once Dame Julian's assurance that all shall be well is echoed in the century of revocation.

But only momentarily. We are taken from the glory of resurrection back to fallen humanity, to the 'befouled bodies' of Simon's friends, Ralph and Piggy. It is now that Piggy's moral limitations are most fully exposed: the failure to climb the mountain is a metaphor for the failure to face truth. He will not even talk about Simon: 'We got to forget this. We can't do no good thinking about it, see?' Truth must be placatory or it is unwelcome. He searches desperately for any defence against the accusation, for the essential thing is to maintain one's innocence. The darkness, the dancing, the storm all combined to thrust the boys into an act they never intended. One recalls Swift's icy disdain for the shifts of alibi-seeking men, incriminating Satan for their own misdeeds. Ralph, more honest than Piggy, denies that he was afraid and seeks in vain to name the emotion that drove him to attack Simon—the reader has no difficulty in identifying it as bloodlust. 'Didn't you see what we—what they did?' The change of pronoun deceives no one, himself included, for even as he speaks 'there was loathing, and at the same time a kind of feverish excitement in his voice'. Piggy denies complicity: he wasn't in the circle and his poor eyesight prevented him from seeing what happened. By now he is hopelessly entangled in evasions, contradictions and lies: perhaps Simon isn't dead, perhaps he was only pretending, the boys' fear absolves them from all responsibility, it was an accident, Simon deserved what he got for crawling out of the dark. Any one of these excuses on its own would be flimsy—jumbled together in one self-exculpating torrent they are pitiful, indicating merely his frantic attempt to blot out the memory of what happened.

Ralph is frightened 'of us', but Piggy still insists that he is victim and not culprit, and he finally persuades Ralph to tell the lie that preserves innocence: 'I was on the outside too.' We did and saw nothing; Jack and the others committed the crime—it is always the others who are guilty. Yet the Lord of the Flies included Ralph and Piggy among those who would 'do' Simon, and this is one occasion when the father of lies speaks true. And the boys know it: when Piggy touches Ralph's bare shoulder, Ralph shudders at the human contact. Simon in death is proved correct; there is no salvation for those who will not climb the mountain. Jack is just as evasive; they didn't kill Simon, for it was really the beast in disguise and the beast in unkillable. But Piggy's self-deception is much more hurtful, for, while Jack's irrationalism thrives on lies, Piggy's practical intelligence must respect truth or it is good for nothing.

Piggy starts off short-sighted, becomes one-eyed and, finally, his glasses stolen, is completely blind; it is, in terms of the allegory, a depressing view of the value of commonsense. His reverence for the conch is at once exemplary and absurd, touching and ludicrous. As with his commonsense, he tends to attribute his own values to everyone else. Thus, despite Jack's unconcealed contempt for the conch from the start, Piggy foolishly believes that the purpose of Jack's raid was to seize the conch and not the glasses. To the end Piggy clings to the delusion of legitimacy. The blind boy demands, with heroic obtuseness, to be led by his friends to the fortress of the savage chief where he will confront the tyrant with 'the one thing he hasn't got', i.e. the precious conch. He will use decency to shame power; right will confront might and right will prevail. Piggy's passionate willingness to carry his talisman against all the odds is at once a tribute to his liberal commitment and the guarantee of his eventual destruction. No wonder the savages giggle derisively when Ralph tells their chief that he isn't 'playing the game', that in stealing Piggy's spectacles Jack has broken some schoolboy code. Has Ralph forgotten that he's speaking to Simon's murderer? The twins' protest at being taken prisoner is equally absurd: 'Oh, I say!' It would be farcical if it were not tragic, for what have these gentlemanly reproaches got to do with the demented doings of the island?

Appealing to Jack's sense of decency is like asking for fair play in Dachau. Piggy's commonsense is still trying to prevail in bedlam: 'Which is better— to be a pack of painted niggers like you are, or to be sensible like Ralph is? . . .' The logic is irrefutable but the questions are addressed to the wrong company, as misplaced as they are reasonable. Piggy insists on treating the savages like a crowd of scatter-brained kids, implying that if only they behaved like adults all would be well. When Roger, looking down on the bag of fat that is his view of Piggy, releases, 'with a sense of delirious abandon-ment', the great rock that kills the advocate of adult commonsense, he is not acting like a kid but like the corrupt adults who have plunged the world into atomic war in the first place. Commonsense and the conch perish together and there is nothing healing or transfiguring about this death.

Yet, even after all this, the frenzied slaughter of Simon and the calcu-lated killing of Piggy, Ralph still tries to persuade himself that the savages will leave him alone. His first thought, remembering his dead friends, is to assume that 'these painted savages would go further and further', but it is a thought too hideous to entertain and he instinctively rejects it: 'No. They're not as bad as that. It was an accident.' It is easy to believe what we want to believe. His wish to think well of his fellows, despite all the contrary evidence, springs from fear for himself, for if they *are* as bad as their actions, he is as good as dead. The incentive to repeat Piggy's mistake of denying truth for the sake of comfort is massive—there can be a vast emotional investment in delusion when the truth is too terrible to accept. Only when he hears the chilling news that Roger has a stick sharpened at both ends does he brace himself for the appalling truth that his erstwhile friends intend to treat him as they did the pig: skewer, roast and eat him while leaving his head as an offering to the Lord of the Flies. Both Golding and Orwell know that the worst thing in the world can and will happen unless man unearths some undisclosed resource, some as yet untapped or neglected potency, to deflect the disaster.

This deliverance is shown by the text to be far more difficult than some of its more simplistic interpreters will allow. It is facile to present the book as a straight opposition between civilisation and savagery, city and jungle, with Golding upholding the former and all its salutary disciplines against the chaotic free-for-all of the latter. Certainly, this opposition is present but the solution is not nearly so easy as the mere election of one over the other. The first page presents the two states, jungle and Home Counties, which are apparently so remote from each other. The boys are ecstatic at their mirac-ulous relocation. To be on an adult-free, coral island means 'the delight of a realized ambition', conveyed in the 'bright, excited eyes' and 'glowing' faces, the elated boyish exclamations, the sense of glamour and adventure at escaping civilisation. We hear that 'the cause of their pleasure was not obvious', for Ralph, Jack and Simon are at this point hot, dirty and exhausted, but that only makes it more plain that internally they feel exhilaratingly emancipated. It is a good island and it is theirs, empty of adult restriction. 'Until the grown-ups come to fetch us we'll have fun.' The island is not to be a permanent home but a storybook holiday.

Almost immediately reality breaches the idyll. The marvellous sun burns, the convenient fruit causes diarrhoea, irrational fears come with darkness. The bigger boys deride the littluns' terrors—'But I tell you there isn't a beast!'—but privately they share them. Soon taboos have infiltrated paradise: 'snakes were not mentioned now, were not mentionable'; 'the glamour of the first day' wears increasingly thin. The jungle is now threat rather than playground; even Jack, besotted with hunting, senses that in the forest he shockingly exchanges the role of hunter for hunted, 'as if something's behind you all the time in the jungle'. Ralph is scandalised, but Jack's personal courage is never in question and no one knows better than he the jungle atmosphere. The holiday camp becomes a hellhole as the idyll plummets towards nightmare. 'The best thing we can do is get ourselves rescued.' Life in a real jungle educates the boys to appreciate civilisation: the rescue once so casually postponed is now ardently desired, the missing adult supervision is no longer cause for celebration but grief.

'With a convulsion of the mind', Ralph discovers dirt and decay. Everything breaks down: the shelters collapse, the simplest repairs are too taxing, the basic rules of hygiene are ignored, the habit of disciplined work is lost as lazy, feckless man succumbs to nature. The boys understandably blame this collapse on the absence of adults, but the text denies the reader so simple an explanation. Ralph, Piggy and Simon, left alone as the others slide into savagery, can be forgiven for craving 'the majesty of adult life', for believing that with adults in control none of the insanities would have occurred. Adults, they assure themselves, would not quarrel or set fire to the island; what the boys fail to see is that children are but men of a smaller growth, that the child is father to the man, for they would not be on the island at all but for the fact that adults have quarrelled in an atomic war which may set the whole world ablaze. It is the discovery analogous to that announced by Freud relating to the First World War. The state, which insists on internal peace, is externally the greatest criminal of all; the adults who would make the children behave, handle their own enemies with a sophisticated ferocity that makes Jack look like a mere dabbler in destruction. When the boys pray for a sign from the adult world—'if only they could get a message to us'—their prayer turns into an ambush. 'A sign came down from the world of grown-ups'; the dead parachutist descends upon the island and is catalystic in toppling the already disintegrating society into gibbering demon-worship.

Everything has come full circle. Ralph pines now for the once unheeded benefits of civilisation like a bath or toothbrush, while Simon the prophet can bring Ralph no more joyous tidings than to assure him that 'you'll get back to where you came from'. The island is now a prison, Eden become Gehenna. Ralph's dreams reflect his altered view of reality and the reversal of priorities which the island experience has produced in him. He turns away from wild Dartmoor and its wild ponies—'the attraction of wildness had gone'; far better 'a tamed town where savagery could not set foot'. *Lord of the Flies* was clearly not written to encourage a flight to the jungle, and the nature it exhibits is certainly very different from that mediated by Wordsworth or Rousseau. Yet it would be unwise to conclude that it must be a plea for civilisation, at least in its existing form, for, just as clearly, it exposes the delusion that 'civilisation' is civilised and that Jack can only be found in the jungle.

Jack is not a proponent of savage disorder but of stern totalitarian discipline. Far from disliking rules, he loves them too much and for the wrong reasons: '"We'll have rules!" he cried excitedly. "Lots of rules! Then when anyone breaks 'em—"' Those critics who find the book upholding Augustine against Pelagius should reflect that Jack is a confirmed Augustinian with a zest for retribution. From the outset his authoritarianism is glaringly evident. That is why it is such a disastrous concession when Ralph, to appease his defeated rival, tells him that 'the choir belongs to you, of course'. Jack, as leader of the hunters, becomes invincible as the lord of the food supply. The need to hunt and kill leads to the formation of an army and the democratic process is undermined by this alternative power-structure. Ralph's bitterness when he lashes the hunters for throwing away a chance of rescue should include himself as target, for he is not blameless. Nor does he emerge with credit from his showdown with Jack, for he finds the lure of meat as irresistible as anyone else. His resolve to refuse the costly meat crumbles and he is soon gnawing as voraciously as the others. It is a crucial victory for Jack, as his triumphant cry announces; 'I got you meat!'

This is not, as is sometimes mistakenly said, a slide from society into savagery, but the replacement of one kind of society by another. Jack's exultant claim is the announcement of a new totalitarian contract in which freedom is the price of meat. The Grand Inquisitor (who was certainly not advocating a return to nature) declared that men will fall down and worship anyone who guarantees to feed them and his chief complaint against Christ is that he will not use food to secure obedience. Jack would have won the Grand Inquisitor's approval. The provision of meat becomes a key element in the establishment of his new society. The democrats can stay and get diarrhoea with Ralph or defect to Jack and a full table, at the trifling cost of their freedom. The meat-giver wins hands down; a hungry democracy cannot compete with a well-fed tyranny. The meat which in Ballantyne is the means of redeeming cannibals becomes in Golding the infallible resource for transforming citizens into slaves—slaves rather than savages. Even Ralph and Piggy, all their fine principles notwithstanding, are driven by hunger towards Jack's camp where he sits among piles of meat 'like an idol'. The dictator, as lord of the feast, contemptuously permits the shamefaced pair to eat. When, later, the quarrel rekindles and Ralph attacks them for running after food, Jack needs only to point to the accusatory bone still in Ralph's hand. It is analogous to that devastating moment in *Nineteen Eighty-Four* when O'Brien, exploding Winston's claim to moral superiority, plays back the incriminating tape on which the 'good' man has promised to commit the very atrocities which he denounces Big Brother for committing. In each case, the hero, in compromising himself, has forfeited the right to condemn his opponent.

Those who cite the book as proof of how people, removed from the ramparts and reinforcements of civilisation, so easily regress into savagery, have failed to see that, for Golding, our much vaunted civilisation is little more than a sham in the first place. 'We're English; and the English are best at everything.' Such hubris is asking to be chastised and the book duly obliges. Our alleged civilisation is, at best, a mere habit, a lethargy, a conditioned reflex. Jack, longing to kill the piglet yet unable to do so, is simply unlearning a tedious half-taught lesson; three chapters later he has overcome the rote indoctrination as he sniffs the ground while he tracks his prey, obsessed with a lust to kill, more avid for blood than for meat. The island, like a truth-serum, makes us tell the truth about ourselves, the truth that hitherto lay hidden within—it is, in the etymological sense, an education, and its prime lesson is to confirm Renan's belief that we are living on the perfume of an empty vase. Roger is simply the most frightening instance of the emptiness of civilisation; to say that he retreats from it misleadingly implies that he was ever there at all. But the island does not change people so much as liberate them to be their real selves. Jack would be just as arrogant in England, though his aspiration to command would necessarily take a different route. Roger would have the same sadistic drives at home but the island allows them to be indulged with impunity, as he finds himself in the serendipitous position of a psychopath promoted to chief of police. It is, however, not only in the jungle that psychopaths become chiefs of police.

To begin with, Roger, throwing stones to miss, is still conditioned by a distant civilisation now in ruins. The old taboo is still just barely effective. Lurking darkly behind a tree, 'breathing quickly, his eyelids fluttering', longingly contemplating the vulnerable littlun, so temptingly defenceless, Roger is a masterly depiction of barely controlled perversion. Even Ralph, in the roughhouse of the mock ritual, is not immune from the 'sudden, thick excitement' of inflicting pain on a helpless creature. But what is a shocking, fleeting visitation for Ralph is Roger's permanent condition. It is appropriate that, during the killing of the sow with its explicit sexual overtones, he should be the one to find a lodgement for his point and to force it remorselessly 'right up her ass!' Who else but the pervert should lead those pursuing the sow, 'wedded to her in lust', and, at her death, collapsing 'heavy and fulfilled upon her'? Orgasmic release for Roger is always a matter of hurting someone else.

He is a much more frightening figure than Jack, for whereas the latter's cruelty springs from fear—the unfortunate Wilfred is going to be beaten because the chief is angry and afraid—Roger's sadism is the pure, unadulterated thing, with pleasure as its motive. When he hears the delectable news of Wilfred's beating, it breaks upon him like an illumination and he sits savoring the luscious possibilities of irresponsible authority; it is a sadist's elysium—absolute power and a stock of defenceless victims. The rescuing officer arrives just in time to prevent a supplantation, for, as the connoisseur in pain, Roger is already beginning to shoulder the chief aside to practise his hellish craft. Significantly, the sharpened stick meant to take Ralph's life is carried by Roger and not Jack. But we do the island an injustice if we blame it for producing Roger, for he exhibits, rather, the two ostensibly contradictory truths which the book advances: how far the boys have moved away from civilisation and what a tiny journey it is. By the book's close little Percy Wemys Madison has completely forgotten the talismanic address chanted throughout to console him in his ordeal; it is a sign at once of how perilously fragile the civilised life is and of how thoroughly abandoned it can become.

Whatever flimsy excuse can be offered for missing the implicit indictment of civilisation recurring throughout the text is irreprievably cancelled by the unmistakable irony of the climax. Yet some readers uncomprehendingly dismiss this as a gimmick, Golding sacrificing the text's seriousness to a piece of sensationalism. The truth is that the final startling change of perspective is integral to the book's meaning. Ralph, fleeing in terror, falls, rolls over and staggers to his feet, 'tensed for more terrors and looked up at a huge peaked cap'. The long desiderated adult has finally arrived and the bloodthirsty savages seeking Ralph's life dwindle to a semicircle of little boys indulging in fun and games; Jack, from being a manic dictator, is reduced to a dirty little urchin carrying some broken spectacles at his waist. This has been astonishingly misinterpreted as an unprincipled evasion of the problems posed by the fable: the horror of the boys' experience on the island is finally only a childish, if viciously nasty, game; adult sanity has returned and the little devils will have to behave themselves again. Human nature cannot be so irremediably bad if the arrival of one adult can immediately put everything to rights—the problem is, apparently, a mere matter of classroom control.

But such obtuseness in face of the text's irony is inexcusable. Ralph is saved but that does not exempt us from scrutinising his saviour or assessing the fate that awaits the rescued boy. The officer seems a doubtful redeemer; his cruiser and sub-machine gun are the sophisticated equivalent of the primitive ordnance used by Jack and his followers. Killers are killers, whatever their implements, sharpened stick or atomic missile, and it is no more a proof of progress to kill technologically than it is for a cannibal to use a knife and fork—the unkempt savages are the counterparts of the trim sailors, not their opposites. We must be gullible indeed to be taken in by evil simply because it comes to us well groomed and freshly laundered. The officer stands embarrassed as Ralph weeps—English boys should surely behave better than this—but this merely betrays his imperception, which is replicated in that of certain critics. Ralph, weeping for the end of innocence and the darkness of man's heart, is weeping for all men, the officer and his crew included. Because the officer cannot see this does not entitle the reader to be equally blind. The idea that when the cruiser arrives the beast slinks back abashed into the jungle to wait for the next set of castaways is so preposterous that it scarcely deserves refuting.

There is no happy ending nor anything optimistic about the final scene. Whatever we may wish, it is not legitimate to infer from the text that society, the *polis*, is man's salvation. The book is not an implicit tribute to the humanising power of social institutions nor does it offer us the city as a refuge from the jungle. Perhaps the city is essential, but it very much depends what kind of city it is—Cain's city will not help us. If man regresses in nature, that does not mean that social man is necessarily good; Swift detests the Yahoo but abhors the 'civilised' Yahoos of London and Dublin even more. Of course, man needs a structured community in which to develop his humanity; of course, the city should be the safe and decent haven. But 'should' is not 'is'; in *King Lear* the castle is where man should be safe, the wild heath where he should be endangered, but Lear and Gloucester do not find it so. Golding likewise knows that all too tragically in our century the city itself has become, paradoxically, a jungle, the wild place in which man finds himself born. In any case, Golding's concern is with the defects of man and not those of society, because man is more important than society. Simon is again the decisive figure, for, while not anti-social, he cannot ultimately be defined in social terms—when he goes apart from his fellows to meditate alone, Golding is affirming the superiority of man to men. This is an auspicious point upon which to end this study. Salvation is not in the city but exists, if anywhere, within man himself, the individual human being transcending social roles, however important those may be. From Swift to Camus we have contemplated the darkness of man's heart. *Lord of the Flies*, continuing this tradition, supplies yet another striking instance of the dark epiphany, but shows, too, the possibility of a brightness within. It would be presumptuous to demand more. Dame Julian may seem altogether too serene for a troubled century like ours; but, if we cannot be certain of salvation, perhaps it is enough to sustain us if we know that the darkness need not prevail.

S.J. BOYD

# *The Nature of the Beast:* Lord of the Flies

And Jesus called a little child unto him, and set him in the midst of them,
And said, Verily I say unto you, Except ye be converted,
and become as little children, ye shall not enter the kingdom of heaven.

St Matthew 18. 2–3

As flies to wanton boys, are we to th' Gods;
They kill us for their sport.

*King Lear*

*Lord of the Flies* has become almost compulsory reading for those enduring the painful process of growing up. One has the impression that *everyone* has studied and been impressed by this novel in the latter part of schooldays. It is not difficult to give reasons for this popularity: its protagonists are schoolboys, drawn with a remarkable awareness of the realities of the playground world, its unhappy theme 'the end of innocence'. The loss of innocence for which Ralph weeps at the novel's close is not, however, a matter of transformation from childish goodness to adolescent depravity, is not a growing into wickedness. It is rather the coming of an awareness of darkness, of the evil in man's heart that was present in the children all along. To acknowledge the

From *The Novels of William Golding*. © 1988 by S.J. Boyd.

presence of this darkness in one's own heart is a necessary but devastating condition of growing up, of becoming fully and yet flawedly human.

Golding's concern is to present us with a vision of human nature and also of the nature of the world which we inhabit through the experiences of a group of children cast away on a desert island. The two quotations above represent polar opposites of optimism and pessimism with regard to the nature of children (which we might take to be representative of essential or pristine human nature) and the nature of the universe in which we live. In the words of Jesus in St Matthew childhood is presented as a state of innocent goodness, a state which may be regarded as the kingdom of heaven on earth. As adults, fallen from this happy state, we may well hanker after a return to it and the possibility of such a conversion is held out to us in this passage by Jesus. There is room for optimism about human nature then, and there is considerable cause for optimism about the nature of our universe, for the speaker has traditionally been regarded as the creator and loving ruler of the universe, come down to earth to suffer and die so that we might be redeemed or rescued from our wickedness and restored to the original purity and happiness we see in children and remember, or think we remember, as our experience of childhood.

The tragic universe of *King Lear* is at its darkest in Gloucester's terrible words: we live in a cruel world which can only be governed by malevolent demons whose delight is to torture us; if we wish to see an image of these dark gods or devils we need look no further than children or our own childhood, need only examine 'the ghastly and ferocious play of children', where we see how little devils torture and kill insects for fun, playing god with flies. From within and without we are beset by evil, 'All dark and comfortless'. *King Lear* is not everywhere so hopeless in outlook but it does seem to force us to accept that nature provides no evidence of beneficent paternal care for us and that in our human nature there is a terrifying propensity towards wanton cruelty which is evident even in children.

It scarcely needs to be said that the picture of childhood, of human nature, and of the nature of things, which emerges from *Lord of the Flies* is closer to that expressed by Gloucester than that in the passage from St Matthew, though in Golding's novel and in Shakespeare's play, as we shall see, some redeeming features are suggested which have much to do with the life of Jesus. The bleakness of the novel's vision has been eloquently encapsulated by Golding himself in a sentence which recalls the despair of Lear in its bludgeoning repetitions: 'The theme of *Lord of the Flies* is grief, sheer grief, grief, grief, grief'. The grief which Golding expresses and powerfully elicits in the novel is grief at man's very nature and the nature of his world, grief that the boys, and we too, are 'suffering from the terrible disease of being human'. Shakespeare's tragedy and Golding's novel both present us with a fearless and savage close-up of human nature, a stripping-down of man to what essentially he is. The effect is appalling and humiliating: we are, in Golding's words, a species that 'produces evil as a bee produces honey'. As naturally as the humble insect produces sweetness, we produce the wickedness and violence which sour our lives. In *King Lear* the burgeoning evil of Lear's daughters and Cornwall finds extravagant expression in the blinding of Gloucester: in *Lord of the Flies* Jack and his gang with comparable callousness steal Piggy's glasses: "'That's them," said Piggy. "They blinded me. See? That's Jack Merridew."' Piggy has been blinded and his complaint indicates that this action of blinding was an expression of the essential nature of Jack Merridew and friends. The blinded Piggy has been granted insight. The darkness of Gloucester's experience leads to his despairing suicide attempt at the Dover cliff. He is, however, saved from death and despair by the loving care of his son: his heart, we are told, 'Twixt two extremes of passion, joy and grief,/Burst smilingly.' Piggy too is led to the rocks at the island's tip—'"Is it safe? Ain't there a cliff? I can hear the sea."'—but for him there is to be no comforting or consolation. The deathsman Roger wantonly knocks him over the cliff and his head bursts messily: 'His head opened and stuff came out and turned red'. Piggy's experiences seem to recall those of Gloucester, but his end is more terrible. The crass prose that records his end matches the callousness of Cornwall in transforming Gloucester's eye to 'vile jelly', which is exactly what Roger has done to Piggy's brain.

The evil of Cornwall and Roger transforms humanity into vileness. The compulsive viciousness of Roger might well provoke us to adapt Lear's exclamation concerning Cornwall's accomplice Regan: 'let them anatomise *Roger*; See what breeds about *his* heart.' Roger's evil is inexplicable, in part because he is a shadowy character about whose background we know almost nothing, but Golding is determined, as was Shakespeare in *King Lear*, that we should confront the Roger or Regan within us, "'the reason why it's no go."' He has himself spoken of this characteristic determination to anatomise 'the darkness of man's heart':

What man *is*, whatever man is under the eye of heaven, that I burn to know and that—I do not say this lightly—I would endure knowing. The themes closest to my purpose, to my imagination have stemmed from that preoccupation, have been of such a sort that they might move me a little nearer that knowledge. They have been themes of man at an extremity, man tested like a building material, taken into the laboratory and used to destruction; man isolated, man obsessed, man drowning in a literal sea or in the sea of his own ignorance.

In *King Lear* the trial by ordeal of human nature takes place on the inhospitable landscapes of a storm-blasted Dark Age Britain; the laboratory in which Golding's schoolboys are used to destruction is the apparently more idyllic world of a tropical island. As we shall see, there are many islands, both real and metaphorical, in Golding's fiction: in *The Inheritors* the new people (i.e. we humans) are first discovered on an island and it is characteristic of them that they are isolated from each other in a way that the Neanderthal people are not; in *Pincher Martin* the central figure finds himself utterly alone and forgotten on a mere rock in the ocean; to Jocelin in *The Spire* the great ship of the cathedral seems to offer insulation against the evils of the dangerous sea of the world; Wilfred Barclay in *The Paper Men*, despite his credit-card-given ability to travel anywhere at anytime, is isolated from his fellow man and from his own past by his alcoholism and his spiritual crisis occurs on one of the Lipari islands. Isolation is everywhere.

In confining the boys to a small island in *Lord of the Flies* Golding is using a long-established literary method of examining human nature and human polity in microcosm, as in Shakespeare's *The Tempest* or Thomas More's *Utopia*, in Defoe's *Robinson Crusoe* or Swift's *Gulliver's Travels*. These books provide a literary background to the boys' adventures on their island. In such works we find a tendency to present human nature at an extreme: in More's utopian fantasy and in Aldous Huxley's *Island* we see human nature and society at their best. In his introduction to the former Paul Turner remarks:

> The old-fashioned method of getting to Utopia is to be wrecked on an island, preferably in the South Seas, and Huxley's last essay in the genre [*Island*] is to this extent traditional. So is William Golding's *Lord of the Flies* . . . , which may, I think, be considered a rather individual form of Dystopia.

The South-Sea island setting suggests everyone's fantasy of lotus-eating escape or refuge from troubles and cares. But for Golding this is the sheerest fantasy: there is no escape from the agony of being human, no possibility of erecting utopian political systems where all will go well. Man's inescapable depravity makes sure 'it's no go' on Golding's island just as it does on the various islands visited by Gulliver in Swift's excoriating examination of the realities of the human condition.

*Robinson Crusoe* belongs in part to the world of sheer escapist boys' adventure stories which also contribute to the literary background of *Lord of the Flies*. The castaway boys themselves are reminded of *Treasure Island, Swallows and Amazons* and Ballantyne's *The Coral Island*: prompted by the mention of these works, Ralph assures them: "'It's a good island. Until the grown-ups come to fetch us we'll have fun.'" The boys imagine that they can have fun not only in swimming and hunting but in imposing decent, civilised English values upon their island, as Ralph, Jack and Peterkin Gay had done on Ballantyne's island and as Robinson Crusoe had done by converting his island to an English gentleman's country estate. But their efforts in this direction are a dismal failure. Things fall apart, or 'break up' in Ralph's phrase, into atavism, savagery and bloodshed. The boys regress to what might be called a state of nature, but the experience of this is not of an earthly paradise but a hell on earth.

Golding is determined to disabuse us not only of naive optimism about the nature of children but also of the sort of faith in the goodness of all things natural described by Aldous Huxley in his essay 'Wordsworth in the Tropics':

> In the neighbourhood of latitude fifty north, and for the last hundred years or thereabouts, it has been an axiom that Nature is divine and morally uplifting . . . To commune with the fields and waters, the woodlands and the hills, is to commune, according to our modern and northern ideas, with the visible manifestations of the 'Wisdom and Spirit of the Universe'.

Such an optimistically Romantic view of the beneficence of the natural world is not confirmed by the visit of Golding's northern boys to the tropics. Golding has remarked of Huxley: 'I owe his writings much myself, I've had much enjoyment and some profit from them—in particular, release from a certain starry-eyed optimism'. Huxley proposes in 'Wordsworth in the Tropics' that a visit to the tropics would cure any Wordsworthian of his faith in nature. The tropical island of Golding's novel, which seems to the boys paradisial in its unspoilt wildness, proves to be an inferno, a sort of pressure-cooker heated by a vertical sun which aims blows at the boys' heads in its violent intensity, which fires 'down invisible arrows' like an angry or malevolent god. It is just as Huxley describes: 'Nature, under a vertical sun, and nourished by the equatorial rains, is not at all like that chaste, mild diety who presides over . . . the prettiness, the cosy sublimities of the Lake District.' Prettiness and cosiness are important elements in Ralph's memories of natural wildness back in England, but Ralph's experience of nature is hopelessly limited and naively comfortable: 'But the remembered cottage on the moors (where "wildness" was ponies, or the snowy moor seen through a window past a copper-kettle . . . ) is utterly out of reach and unreal; a flimsy

dream.' The reality of nature in the tropics is profoundly sinister and threatening. From their experience of this natural environment the boys derive a
sort of religion, but their theology is a demonology, their lord or god is a
devil. In this they merely conform to the ways of indigenous jungle-dwellers
as described by Huxley: 'The sparse inhabitants of the equatorial forest are
all believers in devils.'

The boys' physical surroundings are terrifying and encourage in them
a belief in a malevolent god; the boys' own physical condition also is not
improved by their stay on the island. Their return to a state of nature, insofar
as it implies a lack of toilet facilities and wholesome food, has a very
unpleasant effect on them. The 'littluns' in particular quickly become 'filthy
dirty' and are affected by 'a sort of chronic diarrhoea'. One of Ralph's problems as a chief is that the boys fail to abide by the rule that only one clutch
of tide-washed rocks should be used as a lavatory: 'Now people seem to use
anywhere. Even near the shelters and the platform'. Man seems to be a
natural producer of filth as well as evil, and the one is a symbol of the other.
Of this aspect of the boys' plight Leighton Hodson writes: 'the odour of
decay pervades life from the diarrhoea of the littluns . . . to Jack hunting the
pigs by following their steaming droppings; the association of the Beast, evil,
excrement, and blood is both overpowering and purposeful.' This physical
degeneration is matched by an upsurge of cruelty, bloodlust and violent
rapacity as the Beast, which they take to be a spirit or monster outside of
themselves, rises up within them and takes over their lives. Overwhelmed by
the horrors that have entered their lives, littluns will isolate themselves to
wail, gibber and howl at the misery of their condition. Were Lemuel Gulliver
to land on the island, he would instantly recognise that he had returned to a
land inhabited by Yahoos.

In Book Four of *Gulliver's Travels* the hero lands on an island dominated by the Houyhnhnms, a nation of intelligent horses whose name signi-
fies '*the perfection of nature*' and whose generally very admirable way of life is
lived in accordance with nature or, more precisely, with reason, which they
take to be the supreme gift of nature. The peacefulness, cleanliness and
reasonableness of their lives make their society an ideal towards which we
humans might well wish to aspire. The humanoids of the island, however,
have no such aspirations for they are, as Gulliver is mortified to discover, a
disgusting race of passionate, violent, irrational, greedy and lustful creatures:
these are the Yahoos. Their appearance and presence are rendered particularly offensive by 'their strange disposition to nastiness and dirt'. They
wallow in their filth, symbolising their propensity towards evil and the dark,
perverse psychological forces which make them incapable of behaving
reasonably or organising and maintaining a rational society. Swift thus gives

us a painfully simple sketch of the human condition: we aspire to reason-ableness and would like to construct and live in rational societies, but the nature of the beast within us, the innate propensity toward violence, cruelty and selfish and self-destructive wickedness, makes such optimistic schemes incapable of realisation. Swift rubs our noses mercilessly in our own filth. John S. Whitly has suggested that 'the Hebrew word "Beelzebub", though it means literally "Lord of flies", might be rendered in English as "lord of dung", that substance around which flies gather'.

The Yahoo-nature inevitably brings about misery. It is not surprising that even the insensitive, brute Yahoo is driven at times 'to retire into a corner, to lie down and howl, and groan' like the half-demented littluns on Golding's island. The transformation form schoolboys to Yahoos forces upon us the bitter truth of *Gulliver's Travels*, that we are creatures whose nature renders us incapable of maintaining rational, equable and peaceful societies such as that of the Houyhnhnms. Ralph and Piggy attempt to create such a society on the island. Piggy in particular has great faith in Houyhnhnm-like values, believing in government by persuasion, deciding issues by debate, above all in reason itself. For Piggy the world is reasonable: at one point he seems amusingly reminiscent of René Descartes: 'I been in bed so much I done some thinking'. But Piggy's rationalism is as inadequate as his grammar. His reason cannot control the boys, his belief that science can explain every-thing makes him unable to comprehend the reality of the Beast, his democ-racy crumbles before the onslaught of the atavistic Jack, intuitively adept at using the Beast for his own ends. Piggy may be the brains of the outfit but the Beast in Roger, by smashing his skull, makes those brains useless. Piggy's body is quickly swallowed by the sea, which in the chapter 'Beast from Water' was suggested as a possible dwelling-place of the Beast. When Ralph first inspects the spot where Piggy dies, the sea's motion is described by the narrator as 'like the breathing of some stupendous creature', 'the sleeping leviathan'. The sea is an insuperable obstacle to the boys' escape and one is tempted to detect a reference to Thomas Hobbes' *Leviathan*, wherein the life of man in a state of nature is characterised as being just as Yahoo-like as the boys discover it to be. It is, in Hobbes' famous phrase, 'solitary, poor, nasty, brutish, and short'. *Lord of the Flies* insists that this is a truth, a grim reality, from which there is no escaping.

The boys' return to nature, then, is not an idyll but a nightmare. It is tempting to see their misadventures as a regression from the Houyhnhnm-like values of our civilisation into the caveman world of the Yahoos. This is Piggy's view of the matter: if only they would behave like grown-ups all would be well; if only a ship carrying grown-ups would spot them they would be saved. This is a comforting view of the book since it seems to put us

grown-ups on the side of the angels and endorse the view that our civilisation is rational, peaceful and even salvific. To take such a view is, however, to
fall into what Golding suggests is one of the most dangerous of errors: to
attempt to deny that the Beast is in us and to limit its existence or presence
to some other time, place, or group of people. Such a reading of the book is
untenable. Piggy's faith in grown-ups is shown to be sadly misplaced. Here,
displaying typical common sense and faith in the known laws of science, he
tries to reassure Ralph: "'The trouble is: Are there ghosts, Piggy? Or beasts?"
"Course there aren't." "Why not?" "'Cos things wouldn't make sense.
Houses an' streets, an'—TV—they wouldn't work."' But the horrible truth
is that man's organised civilisation and sophisticated systems of communication have failed to work, have been destroyed or have broken down in the
nightmare of nuclear war.

Civilised values *are* endorsed by the novel—it is heartbreaking to see
how friendship and fair-play are replaced by hostility and tyranny—but our
actual civilisations are condemned as barbaric and monstrously destructive.
Ralph and Jack, chiefs of rival gangs or tribes on the island, are 'two continents of experience and feeling, unable to communicate'. They are thus an
image of the tragic state of world politics in the mid-twentieth century and
of the seemingly eternal need of civilisations to find rivals with whom to
quarrel, the perennial argy-bargy of history which Joyce in *Finnegans Wake*
sums up as 'wills gen wonts'. When the Lord of the Flies himself, the focus
of evil in the book, condescends to speak, it is with the voice of a schoolmaster, whose duty it is to instil the values of our civilisation into developing
children. That these values are, to say the least, defective is made very clear
by an outburst from Piggy just before his fatal fall: "'Which is better—to be
a pack of painted niggers like you are, or to be sensible like Ralph is?"' Piggy
*in extremis* lets slip that being 'sensible' may well involve adhering to tribal
values and loyalties, regarding whomever is judged to be alien with contempt
or loathing and treating them accordingly. But then Piggy knows what it is
to be an alien, because he is made an outsider in part by his being physically
unattractive but also as a function of that prominent feature of English civilisation, the class system.

Golding's later novels, especially *The Pyramid* and *Rites of Passage*, make
abundantly clear his deep bitterness at and hatred of the evils of class. But
even in this first novel, even on a desert island, this Golding obsession is in
evidence. The novelist Ian McEwan has written of his adolescent reading of
*Lord of the Flies*: 'As far as I was concerned, Golding's island was a thinly
disguised boarding school.' At one point the narrator seems to claim that
class is of no importance in the alienation and persecution of Piggy: 'There
had grown up tacitly among the biguns the opinion that Piggy was an

outsider, not only by accent, which did not matter, but by fat, and ass-mar, and specs, and a certain disinclination for manual labour'. But the narrator implicitly admits that accent, a mark of class, *is* an alienating factor ['not only'] and actually mocks, in passing, Piggy's way of speaking. The view that class does not matter in Piggy's misfortunes is scarcely borne out by events. From the very outset Piggy is isolated, stranded on an island within the island, by being lower-class. On the book's first page Ralph's 'automatic gesture' of pulling up his socks makes 'the jungle seem for a moment like the Home Counties' and unfortunately Piggy just does not fit into the middle-class ambience implied thereby. Ralph is a good-natured boy, but in this initial scene he seems very reluctant to accept the friendship of the one companion he has so far found on the desert island: '"What's your name?" "Ralph." The fat boy waited to be asked his name in turn but this proffer of acquaintance was not made'. One has the uncomfortable feeling throughout this scene that Ralph has been conditioned to be unfriendly towards boys who talk like Piggy. Ralph is not slow to inform Piggy that his father is officer-class, but in response to the crucial question '"What's your father?"' Piggy can produce only the poignant reply: '"My dad's dead," he said quickly, "and my mum—."' The unseemly haste with which Piggy announces that his father is dead suggests a reluctance to reveal his place in life and the blank after the mention of his mum speaks unhappy volumes. Piggy has failed to produce satisfactory credentials. It is at least partly for this reason that Piggy is doomed to become 'the centre of social derision so that everyone felt cheerful and normal'. Life seems cheery and normal provided there are the likes of Piggy around to be looked down on and derided.

Piggy's main persecutor is Jack, who from the first evinces contempt and hatred for Piggy, whom he seems to regard as an upstart. Jack's education appears to have instilled in him the belief that it is his right to give commands, to rule: '"I ought to be chief," said Jack with simple arrogance, "because I'm chapter chorister and head boy."' His privileged choir-school background has no doubt taught him much about the necessity of hierarchies, including the notion that head boy from such a school ought to be top man anywhere. Whitley comments: 'This assumption of leadership, bred by being part of a civilised élite, is maintained when he becomes a member of a primitive élite. The perfect prefect becomes the perfect savage.' It would be difficult to imagine anything more suggestive of innocence than a group of cathedral choristers, but we first see the choir as 'something dark' in the haze, as 'the darkness': the choir is from the outset associated with evil. A cathedral choir connotes also a certain English middle-class cosiness, a social world 'assured of certain certainties'. Here is Jack at his most 'sensible', declaring some important certainties: '". . . We've got to have rules and obey them. After all, we're not savages. We're English; and the English are best at everything."' Golding has written that such cosy English chauvinism was something he particularly wished to attack in *Lord of the Flies*:

> One of our faults is to believe that evil is somewhere else and inherent in another nation. My book was to say: you think that now the war is over and an evil thing destroyed, you are safe because you are naturally kind and decent.

The English error is to objectify and externalise the Devil, as the boys do, and this self-congratulatory attitude is dangerous because it allows the Devil to go to work, evils to be perpetrated, under cover of the belief that English people are good, decent and fair-minded. The classic jingoistic expression of such an attitude might be: 'Come off it! This is *England*! Something like that couldn't happen in England!' Whoever adopts such an attitude blinds himself to the evils which do exist in English life, prominent among which is the class system. Golding tries to expose the truth about this evil by translating it from England to a desert island: Jack's hatred of and violence towards Piggy is the raw naked truth about English social organisation. Classist attitudes not only ensure that under the motto of fair play a very unfair deal is given to most members of a society, they also bring about the reification of people. Thus a person may be treated not on the merits of his complex make-up as an individual but merely in accordance with his being recognised as a component of a mass class-group. The final blow dealt to Piggy transforms the extraordinary and miraculous complexity and beauty of his brain, the seat of consciousness and what makes him the particular and unique person he is, into mere 'stuff'.

The treatment meted out to Piggy makes the view that the boys' story is one of simple regression and degeneration a very difficult one to hold. But such a view is completely undermined by the adventitious arrival of the naval officer at the close. Every reader of the novel must have felt profoundly relieved when Ralph stumbles upon this white-clad saviour. All will be well now that the authority and values of civilisation have returned in the figure of this man, who might indeed almost be Ralph's father come to rescue them all. Critics have long recognised, however, that this warrior who stops the boys' war is anything but snowy-white morally. Virginia Tiger sums the matter up thus:

> There is no essential difference between the island world and the adult one and it is the burden of the fable's structure . . . to make it clear that the children's experiment on the island has its constant counterpart in the world outside.

The officer is a warrior, a killer, and he is right to regard the boys' war as mere 'Fun and games', because compared to the massive death-dealing of the nuclear war in which he is involved it is very small-scale indeed. But the officer is nonetheless dismayed that a group of British boys should have degenerated into savages, should have failed 'to put up a better show than that'. Show, the keeping-up of a good appearance, is what this ultra-English officer is all about. The white uniform, the gold buttons, the 'trim cruiser' of the closing sentence are all signs of the officer's belief in orderliness, cleanliness, and of his and his nation's belief in their moral rectitude. The officer's first, and apparently kindly, thought about Ralph is that he 'needed a bath, a hair-cut, a nose-wipe and a good deal of ointment'. An advocate, no doubt, of the stiff upper lip, he is embarrassed by Ralph's heartbroken tears. The officer is no saviour at all. He is doubly guilty: of being a warrior on behalf of one of the world's two tribes and of sanitising the killing, the vast butchery, involved in such conflicts, of cleaning and dressing it up so that it seems sane and sensible. He is able to masquerade as a peacemaker, a bringer of light to the savages. He dislikes the blood and filth of the boys, he is embarrassed by Ralph's open display of emotion, but the blood and filth are the true symbols of war or warriors and Ralph's grief is an absolutely human and appropriate reaction to the revelations of the island.

The officer comes ashore like Lemuel Gulliver to discover a pack of Yahoos. Like Gulliver, hs finds them distasteful. But Gulliver gradually comes to see that supposedly civilised humans are worse than Yahoos because they have all the filth and vices of the Yahoos, though they hide these under clothes and a clothing of pride in their own supposed moral rectitude, and have abused what reason they have by employing it in the invention of new ways in which to express their viciousness. It is a uniform-wearing Yahoo that has come to rescue the boys: there is even more reason than Ralph thinks to weep for 'the darkness of man's heart'. The phrase describes succinctly enough the central concern of Swift's writing but asks us specifically to think of Conrad. The overall picture of man's nature which emerges from *Lord of the Flies* is indeed similar to the one we find in *Heart of Darkness*. A return to the state of nature, an escape into primitivism such as that attempted by Conrad's Kurtz, leads only to the unleashing of brutality, greed for power, and sadism in the most naked and brutal forms, to the horror of orgiastic and murderous midnight dances and human heads stuck on poles. But the forces of civilisation, clad in shiny white to proclaim their moral excellence, are mere whited sepulchres, every bit as guilty as Kurtz and lacking even the honesty of open savagery. Both books offer this grim view of the human condition: there is no rescue, no way out, and the ending of *Lord of the Flies* is anything but happy. To regard it as such would be to ignore the prophetic voice of Simon.

In *The Coral Island* Ballantyne's three young adventurers had the names
Ralph, Jack and Peterkin Gay. In Golding's novel we find a Ralph and a Jack
but two boys seem to share the derivation of their names from the third
member of Ballantyne's jolly-sounding trio: Piggy's name is an approximate
and unpleasant contraction of Peterkin Gay, but the name Simon, we know
from the Bible, was the original name of St Peter, so Simon has a claim too.
Simon and Piggy are, indeed, alike in sharing a role in *Lord of the Flies*, the
role of outsider, scapegoat and victim of murder. Though the two are alike
in this way, however, they are otherwise very different from one another and
represent, indeed, two mighty opposites, two warring ways of looking at the
world, which occur again and again in Golding's fiction. Faith in science and
rationality, with a marked disbelief in anything supernatural, is characteristic
of Piggy. Simon, by contrast, is intuitive, introspective, other-wordly; his
central insight is gained in a vision or trance; Simon represents and has
access to a dimension of experience it is proper to call religious. Piggy cannot
understand Simon and thinks him mad.

This conflict between the contrasting world-views of science or ratio-
cination and religious or visionary experience, between worldly commonsense and otherworldly mysticism, is dramatised time and again by Golding:
in the figures of Nick Shales and Rowena Pringle in *Free Fall*, in Roger
Mason and Jocelin in *The Spire* and in Edmund Talbot and Robert James
Colley in *Rites of Passage*. This conflict is clearly of great importance to
Golding and it would be true to say that, though he is at pains to be fair to
and make a strong case for the scientific or worldly side, his sympathies ultimately lie with the Simons, Jocelins and Colleys. In an essay on education he
writes: 'it cannot be said often enough or loudly enough that "Science" is not
the most important thing'. This too has a Swiftian air to it. In Book Three
of *Gulliver's Travels* Swift demonstrates powerfully that the analytical intellect, alone and unaided by any higher insight, cannot even begin to offer
solutions to the problems of being human. Golding has expressed admiration
for Copernicus, whom he characterises as a man devoted to the quest for
scientific truth but who nonetheless bears the signs of an inclination towards
mysticism. In *Lord of the Flies* Golding's bias in this matter is perhaps most
clearly seen in the differing degrees of respect accorded to Piggy and Simon
by the narrative in their deaths. Leighton Hodson describes this succinctly:

> Golding manages to deepen his meaning of what the boys' atti-
> tudes represent by providing them, in their common ends, with
> descriptions that correspond to the limited practical intelligence
> in the case of Piggy—dry in tone—and the intuitive depth of
> understanding in the case of Simon—eloquent and transfiguring.

The limitations of Piggy's practical intelligence are, indeed, particularly highlighted by comparison with Simon. Piggy's clever and sensible schemes fail to bring about the rescue the boys desperately need; his rational approach is unable to sway the mass of boys in debate or preserve order among them; above all, he rejects Simon's suggestion that the Beast is a reality within the boys themselves. Piggy rightly condemns the notion that there is an external Beast that lives in the forest or the sea, but under great pressure comes to believe that Jack is the Beast or Devil, failing to see that this too is an externalisation, an avoidance of his own guilt. Piggy's scientific views dictate that there is no Devil in the world, but if he must allow that there is evil he is determined to 'believe that evil is somewhere else' and in someone else. He is himself, however, involved in the murder of Simon, for all his predictable attempts to exculpate himself and explain the killing away as an accident.

Simon is murdered by the boys when he emerges from the forest into the frenzy of their dance, supposedly a charm against the Beast. Their defence against an imagined external Beast allows the beast within them to gain absolute control and transform them into murderers. Simon had come to tell them that the creature on the mountain they thought to be the Beast was merely the horribly damaged body of a pilot, evidence of the effects of the beast within us in the world of warring adults. Simon had come to bring them confirmation of the truth that he had proposed earlier and for which he had been shouted down and derided, the dark truth that the Beast is within them, each and every one of them. The reception he is given proves his point once and for all. The truth which Simon offers is a grim one, but Simon himself is not at all a grim or dark figure. He is affectionate, gentle and kind, helping the littluns to find good fruit, for example, but also a loner, a 'queer' boy who isolates himself in a forest glade reminiscent of a church and goes into reveries. It is small wonder that the other boys regard this youthful mystic as mad or 'batty', a fool. We must take Simon a great deal more seriously. The traditional role of the prophet is to awaken men to the truth of their own sinfulness: this Simon does, and he also succeeds in fulfilling the popular view of the prophet's task by foretelling the future. He tells Ralph that he will get home safely and his voice comes back to Ralph just before he is in fact rescued. The boys are living in the dangerous error of believing that the Beast is an evil creature at the mountaintop, so Simon the prophet goes to the mountain to discover the truth. On his way he finds a forest glade desecrated by a sow's head on a stick, a gift for the Beast. Simon falls into a fit, or hallucination, or vision, in which the Lord of the Flies, the Devil, speaks to him through the foul mouthpiece of the head and tells him that he is '"part of you"'. He warns Simon to go back and fall into line or the boys will 'do' him. Simon defies the threat, climbs the mountain, finds the parachutist and descends to the beach to be slaughtered.

Amidst the bloody chaos of the storm and the demonic dance we are told that 'Simon was crying out something about a dead man on a hill' as he is being assaulted. He refers of course to the parachutist, but we must hear also a suggestion of the death of Christ on Calvary and realise that, in killing the true prophet who had come down to reveal to them their real nature, their sinfulness, and thus set them on the road towards saving themselves, the boys are re-enacting the crucifixion of Jesus Christ. Simon's life and death are an imitation of Christ. In ascending the mountain and returning to the boys, despite the warnings of the Lord of the Flies about what will happen to him, he takes up and shares the Cross like his namesake from Cyrene: "'Simon. He helps'", as Ralph earlier remarks. His self-sacrifice does not, however, achieve an instant conversion of the boys to goodness. Nor did Christ's with regard to mankind as a whole. Piggy blames him for bringing his death on himself: "'Coming in the dark—he had no business crawling like that out of the dark. He was batty. He asked for it'". He walked right into his own death, so he must have been mad, a fool, a Simple Simon.

To suggest that a person or character is a fool would normally undermine any confidence we might have that the person or character concerned had wisdom to offer us. Here this is not the case. Simon imitates the folly of that supreme fool Christ, who allowed himself to be crucified and whose teaching must seem foolish to the worldly-wise. Christ the holy fool is admirably described by Erasmus in the *Praise of Folly*:

> Christ too, though he is the wisdom of the Father, was made something of a fool himself in order to help the folly of mankind, when he assumed the nature of man and was seen in man's form . . . Nor did he wish them to be rendered in any other way save by the folly of the cross and through his simple, ignorant apostles, to whom he unfailingly preached folly.

To those in darkness, to those under the sway of the Lord of This World who is the Lord of the Flies, the wisdom of Christ must indeed appear utter folly. Simon is the first of Golding's holy fools, characters who in many respects are holy or Christ-like and yet, almost by that very token, are ill-fitted for survival in the world of fallen man: two clear examples, whom we shall examine later, are Nathaniel in *Pincher Martin* and Matty in *Darkness Visible*. The holy or prophetic fool dares to challenge the cosy but delusive beliefs of the majority and so must be laughed at, dismissed, driven out or slaughtered by that majority.

The message or wisdom which Simon offers—that the Beast is in us, that we must acknowledge the 'thing of darkness' as our own—is disturbing and negative. He does not appear to bring the good news of redemption or salvation. But his life and death offer some hope in the book's pervasive gloom inasmuch that among all the boys, so to say, at least one good man has been found, one person who is capable of imitating Christ's redemptive example. At the mountain top he is able to free the dead pilot, according to Golding a symbol of the nightmare of human history, and allow him to fly off, just as Christ, from an orthodox point of view, changed the nature of history by freeing man from the bondage of sin, offering the *possibility* of escape from the endless backsliding and tribulations of human and personal history. There is, furthermore, the 'eloquent and transfiguring' description of the sea's disposal of Simon's body. Simon is carried 'towards the open sea' by the tide, attended by 'strange, moonbeam-bodied creatures with fiery eyes' who weave a halo of brightness around his head. These beautiful and seemingly magical little entities we have seen before in broad daylight:

> There were creatures that lived in this last fling of the sea, tiny
> transparencies that came questing in with the water over the hot,
> dry sand . . . Perhaps food had appeared where the last incursion
> there had been none; bird droppings, insects perhaps, any of the
> strewn detritus of landward life. Like a myriad of tiny teeth in a
> saw, the transparencies came scavenging on the beach.

But there is no beauty or magic or mystery. The creatures are simply the lowest point in the ugly world of living nature, vile scavengers as coldly destructive as sawteeth. It is Simon's self-sacrifice that transforms them to beauty, goes some way towards redeeming the world of nature and reestablishing its beauty and harmony.

What light there is in the book does, indeed, seem to be concentrated around Simon. There are, however, certain other aspects of the novel which may be seen as mitigating the generally excoriating treatment of human nature. 'I am by nature an optimist' Golding has remarked 'but a defective logic—or a logic which I sometimes hope desperately is defective—makes a pessimist of me'. Though this is rather a dark utterance, it does make explicit that tension between optimism and pessimism, between hope and despair, which is characteristic of Golding's fiction. Indeed, from *The Spire* onwards it seems appropriate to characterise his fiction as broadly tragi-comic. Though comedy is a grotesquely inappropriate term to apply to *Lord of the Flies*, the outlook of the novel is not entirely pessimistic.

There is first the essential decency of Ralph, 'the fair boy' whose eyes proclaim 'no devil' and who tries to keep the other boys' eyes on the values of civilisation, tries 'to keep a clean flag of flame flying'. Though the book suggests that we should be sceptical about such an ocular proclamation and about 'Rally round the flag, boys!' sentiments, there is no doubt that Ralph does strive earnestly and sincerely to be fair and decent. There is also the goodness, the sheer vitality, of the twins Samneric, Ralph's most loyal supporters. Not only are they kind, loyal and generous, but their apparent blending into one another makes them seem representative of average everyday man, the 'man on the Clapham omnibus'. Moreover, we sympathise strongly with this group and abominate Jack and Roger. It seems that we can at least say of ourselves that we would *like to be* decent, fair and good. Our sympathy or even identification with Ralph is also very effective in intensifying the 'thriller' aspect of the novel: in the final chapter we have the very unpleasant feeling that *we* are being hunted by Jack and Roger. How we fear and loath their extravagant and insatiable evil! There is some comfort to be taken in this, but we must remember that Ralph and Samneric, those models of decency, were involved in the murder of Simon and, like another decent man caught up in evil, they try to wash the innocent martyr's blood from their hands by their denial that they were present at the killing. Further, Samneric are coerced into joining Jack's tribe and in Ralph's final interview with them they have become, for all the kindness towards Ralph which they cannot quite fight down, guardians of a régime where all rules have disappeared except the rule of sadism. Samneric, like other ordinary men before them, have been transformed into concentration camp guards, porters at the Gate of Hell. Ralph's conversation with them at the Castle Rock is perhaps the most heartrending section of the entire book and there is every reason why that should be so.

Just as we sympathise with the nature of Ralph, Samneric and, indeed, even Piggy, so too we are attracted to the democratic system they create. The gentle, exhortatory paternalism of Ralph and Piggy seems both fair and sensible as a way of organising government. It is manifestly preferable to Jack's absolutist tyranny. Again our hearts seem to be in roughly the right place. And yet Jack's system has greater attraction for the boys, who desert Ralph's tribe in droves. In fairness to Jack it must be said that in certain important respects his reign of terror is a more effective form of government than Ralph's. He gives the boys meat and he is able to keep them in order, to put a stop to quarrels, fragmentation and even sheer laziness in a way which Ralph was not: '"See? They do what I want"', he pointedly remarks to Ralph, who has just become a one-man tribe. Once again the Leviathan raises its head: Hobbes' pessimistic view is that human fractiousness requires to be quelled and governed by an absolute monarch. *Lord of the Flies* could never be said to advocate Jack's monarchy however, since though in some ways it clearly 'works' it also panders to and is an expression of the worst aspects of human nature; greed, cruelty and lust. Like a vicious Roman emperor he provides food and entertainment for his mob, entertainment taking the form of beating littluns, murderous ritual dances, and the obscene and rapacious violence of the hunt: 'The sow collapsed under them and they were heavy and fulfilled upon her'. Jack intuitively knows all about the lowest and vilest elements in our nature and how to exploit them:

> Simon became inarticulate in his effort to express mankind's essential illness. Inspiration came to him.
> "What's the dirtiest thing there is?"
> As an answer Jack dropped into the uncomprehending silence that followed it the crude expressive syllable. Release was like an orgasm . . . The hunters were screaming with delight.

Obscenity can be delightful: that is a symptom of our essential illness.

Jack may be successful in satisfying in the short-term certain basic and base human cravings, but his system offers no hope of rescue. Behaviour such as Jack indulges in and encourages seems to preclude redemption or salvation, even if salvation is no more than the imitation of Christ in *this* world which we see in Simon, whom Jack and his minions kill. The symbol of this terrible régime is the stick sharpened at both ends, the support of the totem Lord of the Flies, a weapon which seems to suggest that its killing-power may rebound against the user. It is a symbol which reminds us of the self-defeating nature of the weaponry deployed for nuclear war by those who build fortresses and bunkers against imagined external threats and evils in the world outside the island. The spear is sharpened by Roger and, for all that has been said about Jack's ability to command obedience, it is not difficult to imagine this sinister figure returning Jack's violent means to power upon him and completing his bloody and Macbeth-like career by sticking *his* head on a pole.

At the close the naval officer arrives to find the island paradise lost and burning, the scene 'with dreadful faces thronged and fiery arms'. Coming from his warship, he is a veritable *deus ex machina* descending from the 'above' of the adult world to set things right and rescue the erring children. Despite the sinister associations of the naval officer, might he not still be seen as the caring and omnipotent God who finally intervenes in man's world to stop the course of the bloody history of fallen man and restore peace forever? Such a view would offer a glimmer of religious light at the end of the tunnel. Such a reading is perhaps allowable, but there is evidence in the novel which counts against it and which ought not to be ignored. There seems to be no haven for the boys to be rescued *to*. We are told much earlier that 'Roger's arm was conditioned by a civilisation that knew nothing of him and was in ruins'. When the boys first spot a passing ship on the horizon the narrative speaks of 'the smoke of home' beckoning to them, a touching phrase since it suggests both the homeliness the boys long for and the smoking ruins that are all that remain of home. Having been terrified by the dead parachutist that seems to be the Beast, Ralph complains that the 'thing squats by the fire as though it didn't want us to be rescued', and the corpse is, indeed, a sign that the civilisation which might rescue them has been destroyed by war. The naval officer has played a part in that war. Perhaps there is no comfort in seeing him as an image of God, because the image is of a flawed and irresponsible god, perhaps like the forgetful or lazy creator of the island's reef: 'The coral was scribbled in the sea as though a giant had bent down to reproduce the shape of the island in a flowing, chalk line but tired before he had finished'. The creator's signature does not inspire confidence in his character and evidences from nature generally, as we have seen, from the 'enmity' of the sun, that traditional symbol of the Godhead, downwards, are not such as to encourage faith in absolute beneficence. The weight of evidence would seem to indicate that any creator must be a cruel selfish wielder of power, that the gods are indeed as Gloucester described them, swatting men like flies with an ease the naval officer might well envy or might even match, a source of no comfort or hope. What desperate hope the book offers is simply the example of Simon, the acknowledgement of our guilt, of the 'thing of darkness' within us, and the overcoming of this guilt and darkness in generous, if unsuccessful, self-sacrifice for the sake of others. Simon, like Cordelia, allows a little room for hope, but the book's abiding impression remains like that of *King Lear*: 'grief, sheer grief, grief, grief, grief'.

L.L. DICKSON

# Lord of the Flies

Of Golding's nine novels, *Lord of the Flies* is most clearly an allegory. It has been criticized as both too explicit and too ambiguous. Walter Allen's skepticism is typical: "The difficulty begins when one smells allegory." More accurately, Golding's *Lord of the Flies* combines the best features of realistic and allegorical fiction; the novel allows for "the simultaneous operation of the factual and the fabular."

The tension between realistic novel and allegorical fable is established in the setting for the action in *Lord of the Flies*: the isolated island provides an appropriate stage for the survival story of the deserted boys, but also suggests a universal, timeless backdrop for symbolic action. Golding creates a microcosm, a procedure common "to the great allegorists and satirists," and then "examines the problem of how to maintain moderate liberal values and to pursue distant ends against pressure from extremists and against the lower instincts." The protagonist's ironic "rescue" by a naval officer, who is himself engrossed in the savage business of international warfare, reveals that the chaotic island-world is but a small version of a war-torn adult world. The novel does not imply that children, without the disciplined control of adults, will turn into savages; on the contrary, it dramatizes the real nature of all humans. The nightmare world, which quickly develops on the island, parallels the destruction of the outside world through atomic warfare. The dead

From *The Modern Allegories of William Golding*. © 1990 by the Board of Regents of the State of Florida.

parachutist, whom the boys mistake for the Beast, is a symbolic reminder of the human history of self-destruction; the parachutist is literally and figuratively a "fallen man."

At first, the island world is compared to Eden: the boys "accepted the pleasure of morning, the bright sun, the whelming sea and sweet air, as a time when play was good and life so full that hope was not necessary and therefore forgotten." But this setting is simultaneously sinister and hostile. The boys are scratched by thorns and entrapped by creepers. "The ground beneath them was a bank covered with coarse grass, torn everywhere by the upheavals of fallen trees, scattered with decaying coconuts and palm saplings. Behind this was the darkness of the forest proper and the open scar." Eventually the island becomes a burning hell: "Smoke was seeping through the branches in white and yellow wisps, the patch of blue sky overhead turned to the color of a storm cloud, and then the smoke bellowed around him" [Ralph, the protagonist]. The island is a microcosm from the adult world; indeed, "you realize after a time that the book is nothing less than a history of mankind itself."

The personified agents in *Lord of the Flies* are developed in all the four ways discussed in the first chapter. First, the analogy through nomenclature is the most obvious method by which the characters take on additional dimensions. Golding's novel represents an ironic treatment of R. M. Ballantyne's *The Coral Island*, a children's classic that presents the romantic adventures of a group of English schoolboys marooned on an Edenlike South Sea island. By mustering their wits and their British courage, the boys defeat the evil forces on the island: pirates and native savages. Not only is Golding's island literally a coral island where the boys "dream pleasantly" and romantically, but there are specific references to Ballantyne: "'It's like in a book.' At once there was a clamor. 'Treasure Island—' 'Swallows and Amazons—' 'Coral Island—.'" At the conclusion of the novel, the dull-witted naval officer who comes to Ralph's rescue makes an explicit comparison: "Jolly good show. Like the Coral Island." Golding uses the same names for his main characters as Ballantyne did. Ralph, Jack, and Peterkin Gay of *The Coral Island* become Golding's Ralph, Jack, and Simon ("Simon called Peter, you see. It was worked out very carefully in every possible way, this novel"). Golding's characters, however, represent ironic versions of the earlier literary work, and their very names, inviting comparison to Ballantyne, add ironic impact to the characterization.

The change of Peterkin's name to Simon better supports that character's function as a "saint" figure in Golding's novel. Obviously Piggy's name contributes to the symbolism: Piggy will become identified with a hunted pig, and eventually will be killed too, as the boys' savage hunt turns to human rather than animal victims. When Piggy falls to his death, his arms and legs twitch "like a pig's after it has been killed." Jack's name is a variant of John, the disciple of Christ, and indeed Jack is an ironic distortion of the religious connotations of his name, in the same manner as is Christopher Martin, the egocentric protagonist of Golding's third novel.

Second, the characters in *Lord of the Flies* become allegorical agents through the correspondence of a state of nature with a state of mind. The more the boys stay on the island, the more they become aware of its sinister and actively hostile elements. The description of the pleasant *Coral Island* fantasy world quickly dissolves into images of darkness, hostility, danger. The boys accept "the pleasures of morning, the bright sun" and the unrestricted play, but by afternoon the overpowering sunlight becomes "a blow that they ducked." Though dusk partly relieves the situation, the boys are then menaced by the dark: "When the sun sank, darkness dropped on the island like an extinguisher and soon the shelters were full of restlessness, under the remote stars."

The boys' attitude of childish abandon and romantic adventure changes to a much more somber one when the possibility of a beast is introduced. At that point the island is transformed into a dark haven for unspeakable terrors. The boys' increasing apprehension about their immediate physical safety parallels the gradual awareness that is taking shape in the minds of Simon, Piggy, and particularly Ralph, concerning the *real* evil of the island. The boys mistakenly project their own bestiality on an imaginary animal roaming the island, but Simon hesitantly speculates, "maybe it's only us." The others do not understand. They look into the blackened jungle for signs of the beast's movement. The darkness is "full of claws, full of the awful unknown and menace." Simon's inner vision, however, tells him that it is the human being who is "at once heroic and sick." When Simon confronts the Lord of the Flies, the pig's head on a stick, it tells him (but really he tells himself), "Fancy thinking the Beast was something you could hunt and kill! . . . You knew, didn't you? I'm part of you?" The hostile island and its dark mysteries are only a symbolic backdrop reinforcing the images of savagery, bestiality, and destruction that describe, and reveal, the boys themselves.

A third method by which the characters assume allegorical significance is through the implicit comparison of an action with an extrafictional event. James Baker was the first to point out similarities between Euripides' *The Bacchae* and Golding's novel. The mistaken slaying of Simon recalls Pentheus's murder at the hands of the crazed bacchantes of Dionysus. Pentheus's pride and his inability to recognize Dionysus's powers lead to his downfall: "This same lesson in humility is meted out to the schoolboys of

*Lord of the Flies*. In their innocent pride they attempt to impose a rational order or pattern upon the vital chaos of their own nature. . . . The penalties (as in the play) are bloodshed, guilt, utter defeat of reason."

Both the novel and the play contain a beast-god cult, a hunt sequence, and the dismemberment of the scapegoat figure. Though Simon is the clearest equivalent for Pentheus, Piggy and finally Ralph are cast in similar roles. Piggy is destroyed, though not dismembered, by Jack's forces. Ralph is chased by frenzied hunters but is "saved" (by a deus ex machina process similar to that of the end of Euripides' play) from the prospect of beheading. Ralph fittingly becomes Golding's version of Agave. The boy, like Pentheus's mother, mistakenly takes part in killing and then must live sorrowfully with the knowledge of his, and all humanity's, capacity for blind destruction.

The actions that help establish parallels to religious events emphasize biblical analogues. Ralph's first blowing of the conch, proclaiming survival after the crash on the island, recalls the angel Gabriel's announcing good news. Inasmuch as the boys' "survival" is quite tentative, however, the implied comparison to Gabriel is ironic. Simon's fasting, helping the little boys, meditating in the wilderness, going up on the mountain—all these actions solidify the Christ parallel. The recurring pattern of falls—the falling parachutist, Piggy's fall to his death, the destruction of the conch in the same fall, Ralph's tumbling panic at the end of the novel—emphasizes the fall of humankind motif.

The extrafictional event pertaining to classical mythology or to Christ's passion enlarge the surface action with additional symbolic meanings.

The fourth and final technique for intensifying allegorical agents concerns the manifestation in an action of a state of mind. In *Lord of the Flies* a series of hunts, for either pigs or humans, symbolically demonstrates the boys' gradual deterioration into savages. Moral order is corrupted and the end result is chaos. William Mueller has established convincingly that "the book is a carefully structured work of art whose organization—in terms of a series of hunts—serves to reveal with progressive clarity man's essential core." Mueller identifies six "hunts," but there are at least nine separate instances where this symbolic act occurs: (1) the first piglet, "caught in a curtain of creepers," escapes when Jack is mentally unable to kill the helpless creature; (2) a second pig eludes the hunters, much to Jack's disgust; (3) Jack is successful the next time, and the hunters conceive the ritual chant of "Kill the Pig. Cut her throat. Spill her bood"; later Maurice briefly pretends to be the pig; (4) during a mock ceremony that gets out of hand, Robert plays the role of the pig, in a scene that sinisterly foreshadows the transition from nonhuman to human prey; (5) after another successful hunt, the boys smear themselves with animal blood, and Maurice plays the pig while Robert ritually pokes him with a spear, to the delight of Jack's hunters; (6) Jack and Roger play hunter and pig respectively, as Piggy and Ralph "find themselves eager to take a place in this demented but partly secure society"; (7) Simon is mistaken for the beast and is torn to pieces; (8) Piggy is killed by Roger, who acts "with a sense of delirious abandonment"; (9) and finally Ralph is the object of the last murderous hunt.

The two fundamental patterns by which allegorical action is resolved are those of "progress" and "battle." The journey motif is first established by the plot circumstances of the opening chapter. A group of boys has been taken by airplane from a war-threatened England to a safer territory, but in the process their plane is attacked and they have been dropped to safety on a deserted island. Their thwarted flight is mentioned in the opening exposition. Though their physical, outer journey has ended, they soon begin a more recondite "journey." Through their quest for the beast, they (or at least Simon and Ralph) discover the real beast, humanity's own predilection for evil.

The structure of *Lord of the Flies* provides for a gradual revelation of insight, as Ralph sees his friends slowly turn into beasts themselves. The significance of the final scene, in which the naval officer reestablishes an adult perspective, is not what James Gindin once contended: "a means of cutting down or softening the implications built up within the structure of the boys' society on the island." The officer's presence does not reaffirm that "adult sanity really exists," nor is it merely a gimmick that "palliates the force and the unity of the original metaphor." On the contrary, it provides the final ironic comment: Ralph is "saved" by a soldier of war, a soldier who cannot see that the boys have symbolically reenacted the plight of all persons who call themselves civilized and yet continue to destroy their fellow humans in the same breath.

The irony of this last scene is consistent with Golding's sarcastic treatment of Ballantyne, and it also emphasizes the universality of Ralph's experience. There is no distinction between child and adult here. The boys' ordeal is a metaphor for the human predicament. Ralph's progress toward self-knowledge culminates in his tears: "Ralph wept for the end of innocence, the darkness of man's heart, and the fall through the air of the true, wise friend called Piggy." Because Piggy represents the failure of reason, the use of "wise" offers a further irony.

The battle motif is developed in both physical confrontations and rhetorical "combat." Initially, the pig hunts are ritualized tests of strength and manhood, but when the hunters eventually seek human prey (Simon, Piggy, and finally Ralph) the conflict is between the savage and the civilized;

blind emotion and prudent rationality; inhumanity and humanity; evil and good. This conflict is further established in the chapter entitled "The Shell and the Glasses," when Jack's hunters attack Ralph's boys and steal Piggy's glasses. Jack carries the broken spectacles—which have become symbolic of intellect, rationality, and civilization—as ritual proof of his manhood and his power over his enemies: "He was a chief now in truth; and he made stabbing motions with his spear." In the "Castle Rock" chapter, Ralph opposes Jack in what is called a "crisis" situation: "They met with a jolt and bounced apart. Jack swung with his fist at Ralph and caught him on the ear. Ralph hit Jack in the stomach and made him grunt. Then they were facing each other again, panting and furious, but unnerved by each other's ferocity. They became aware of the noise that was the background to this fight, the steady shrill cheering of the tribe behind them."

More subtle form of "battle"—debate and dialogue—are dramatized in the verbal exchanges between Jack and Ralph. Golding emphasizes their polarity: "They walked along, two continents of experience and feeling, unable to communicate." Later when Jack paints his face and flaunts his bloodied knife, the conflict is heightened: "The two boys faced each other. There was the brilliant world of hunting, tactics, fierce exhilaration, skill; and there was the world of onging and baffled commonsense." When Ralph does not move, Jack and the others have to build their fire in a less ideal place: "By the time the pile [of firewood] was built, they were on different sides of a high barrier." Different sides of the wood, different continents, different worlds—all these scenes intensify the symbolic as well as physical conflict. Here we encounter "a structural principle that becomes Golding's hallmark: a polarity expressed in terms of a moral tension. Thus, there is the rational (the firewatchers) pitted against the irrational (the hunters)."

In both chapter 2, "Beast from Water," and chapter 8, "Gift for the Darkness," the exchange of views about whether there is a beast or not "becomes a blatant allegory in which each spokesman caricatures the position he defends." Ralph and Piggy think that rules and organization can cure social ills, and that if things "break up," it is because individuals are not remembering that life "is scientific," rational, logical. Jack hates rules, only wishes to hunt, and believes that evil is a mystical, living power that can be appeased by ritual sacrifice. Simon feels that evil is not outside but rather within all human beings, though he is "inarticulate in his effort to express mankind's essential illness." He uses comparisons with excrement and flith to describe his notion of human inner evil.

Simon's confrontation with the pig's head on a stick, the Lord of the Flies, is another instance of allegorical dialogue. At first, Beelzebub seems to triumph: Simon is mesmerized by the grinning face; he is warned that he is "not wanted," for Simon is the only boy who possesses a true vision of the nature of evil; and finally he faints. However, Simon recovers, asks himself, "What else is there to do?", discovers the dead parachutist, and then takes the news about the "beast" to the rest of the boys. The entire scence with the pig's head represents the conflict that is occurring within Simon's own consciousness. The Lord of the Flies is only an externalization of the inner evil in all humans. Later when Ralph comes upon the pig's head, "the skull [stares at] Ralph like one who knows all the answers and won't tell." Though Ralph does not understand the significance of the pig, he does feel a "sick fear." In desperation he hits the head, as if breaking it would destroy the evil on the island. However, the broken pig's head lies in two pieces, "its grin now six feet across." Rather than being destroyed, it ironically has grown. In the final pages of the novel, when Ralph is desperately fleeing from the hunters, he runs in circles and retraces his steps back to the broken pig's head, and this time its "fathom-wide grin" entirely dominates the burning island.

Four patterns of imagery reinforce the symbolism in *Lord of the Flies*. Images pertaining to excrement, darkness, falling, and animalism help define the human capacity for evil and savagery.

The many references to excrement, and also to dirt, underline thematically the vileness of human nature itself. As the boys' attempts at a sanitation program gradually break down, the inherent evil in human nature is symbolically manifested in the increasing images that refer to dung: "the two concepts merge in Golding's imagination—covertly in *Lord of the Flies* and manifestly in *Free Fall*, which is a literary cloaca, full of that revulsion psychologists try to explain in terms of the proximity and ambiguity of the apertures utilized for birth and excreta."

Images associated with excrement (and more generally, dirt) are used in a negative sense, depicting human corruption. The conch makes "a low, farting noise." Johnny, the first "littlun" Ralph and Piggy meet, is in the act of defecating. Pig droppings are closely examined by Jack's hunters to determine how recently the pig has left a particular place; the temperature of feces has become the central subject of interest. Ralph slowly loses his battle against filth: "With a convulsion of the mind, Ralph discovered dirt and decay, understood how much he disliked [his own long, dirty hair]." Even when Piggy tries to clean his glasses, the attempt is in vain. He is appalled at the increasing filth on the island: "'We chose those rocks right along beyond the bathing pool as a lavatory. . . . Now people seem to use anywhere. Even near the shelters and the platform. You littluns, when you're getting fruit; if you're taken short—' The assembly roared. 'I said if you're taken short you keep away from the fruit. That's dirty.'"

Weekes and Gregor recognize the realistic level of description here—
eating nothing but fruit does indeed bring on diarrhea—but they add, "The
diarrhea might seem to invite allegorical translation—the body of man is no
longer fit for Eden." At one significant point, the inarticulate Simon tries to
think of "the dirtiest thing there is" in order to describe the fallen human
condition, and Jack's answer, "one crude expressive syllable," reaffirms the
metaphor of excrement, which prevails throughout the novel. The area near
the decaying, fallen parachutist is "a rotten place." When the pig's head is
mounted on the stick, it soon draws a "black blob of flies"; it is literally a lord
of the flies, as well as figuratively Beelzebub, from the Hebrew *baalzebub*,
"lord of flies." Sometimes this name is translated "lord of dung." By the end
of the novel, Ralph himself has been reduced to a dirty, piglike animal.

Golding uses light-dark contrasts in a traditional way: the numerous
images of darkness underline the moral blackness of the boys' crumbling
society. The normal associations with the sinister, with death, with chaos,
with evil are suggested by this imagery. Decaying coconuts lie "skull-like"
amid green shadows; Jack's choirboys are clothed in black; the beast is naturally associated with the coming of night; the "unfriendly side of the mountain" is shrouded in hushed darkness. Roger is described as a dark figure: "the
shock of black hair, down his nape and low on his forehead, seemed to suit
his gloomy face and make what had seemed at first an unsociable remoteness
into something forbidding."

With a Hawthornesque touch, Golding describes the subtle change
that has come over all the boys' faces, after the group has become largely a
hunting society: "faces cleaned fairly well by the process of eating and
sweating but marked in the less accessible angles with a kind of shadow." Jack
is described as "a stain in the darkness." Generally, the coming of night turns
common surroundings into a nightmare landscape of imaginary horrors:
"The skirts of the forest and the scar were familiar, near the conch and the
shelters and sufficiently friendly in daylight. What they might become in
darkness nobody cared to think."

Images of light and brightness are identified with spirit, regeneration,
life, goodness. The description of Simon's dead body as it is carried out to
sea suggests transcendence: "Softly, surrounded by a fringe of inquisitive
bright creatures, itself a silver shape beneath the steadfast constellations,
Simon's dead body moved out toward the open sea." The contrast between
the bright, gaudy butterflies and the black flies on the pig's head emphasizes
the symbolic conflict between good and evil used throughout the novel. The
bright butterflies are drawn to the sunlight and to open places; they surround
the saintly Simon; they are oblivious to the brutal killing of the sow: "the
butterflies still danced, preoccupied in the centre of the clearing." In this

particular instance, they remind the reader of those indifferent seagulls in Stephen Crane's "The Open Boat"—simply a part of nature, not threatened by the environment, and a mocking contrast to the violent predicaments that human beings either perpetuate or suffer. But the butterflies represent a more positive force, and significantly they desert the open space dominated by the grinning pig's head.

Golding's obsession with the fallen human state permeates the imagery of *Lord of the Flies*. The opening chapter is typical. Ralph appears amid a background of fallen trees. He trips over a branch and comes "down with a crash." He talks with Piggy about coming down in the capsule that was dropped from the plane. He falls down again when attempting to stand on his head. He pretends to knock Simon down. In addition to the descriptions of the fallen parachutist, Simon's fainting spells, Ralph's "nightmares of falling and death," and his final collapse at the feet of the naval officer, the act of falling is closely associated with the idea of lost innocence. Ralph weeps for "the end of innocence . . . and the fall through the air" of Piggy.

Animal imagery reinforces the boys' transformation into savages and subhumans. Predictably, evil is associated with the beast, the pig's head, or a snake, but as the story progresses, the boys themselves are described with an increasing number of animal images.

The boys' disrobing early in the novel at first suggests a return to innocence, but as the hunters become more and more savage, their nakedness merely underscores their animalism. Sam and Eric grin and pant at Ralph "like dogs." Jack moves on all fours, "dog-like," when tracking the pig; during the hunt he hisses like a snake, and is "less a hunter than a furtive thing, ape-like among the tangle of trees." Ralph calls him a "beast." Piggy, whose very name suggests an obvious comparison, sees that the boys are becoming animals; he says that if Ralph does not blow the conch for an assembly, "we'll soon be animals anyway." Without his glasses, Piggy laments that he will "have to be led like a dog." When he dies, his body twitches "like a pig's after it has been killed." Simon, hidden in the shadows of the forest, is transformed into a "thing," a "beast," when the narration shifts to the other boys' view.

Ralph's transformation is slower than the others, but it is clearly discernible. Early in the novel, he viciously accepts the hunters' raw pig meat and gnaws on it "like a wolf." He is caught up in the savage ritual when Roger plays the pig; he is part of the unthinking gang that murders Simon. When Piggy is killed, Ralph runs for his life and obeys "an instinct that he did not know he possessed." In the last chapter, Ralph is little more than a cornered animal. Ironically he sharpens a stick in self-defense and becomes a murderous hunter himself: "Whoever tried [to harm him] would be stuck, squealing like a pig." We are told that he "raised his spear, snarled a little, and waited." Ralph's transformation is both shocking and saddening. Alone in the forest, he brutally attacks the first adversary he meets: "Ralph launched himself like a cat; stabbed, snarling, with the spear, and the savage doubled up." When Ralph is trapped in the underbrush, he wonders what a pig would do, for he is in the same position.

Related to these animal images is the continual reference to the word *savage*. In *Lord of the Flies* the distinction between civilized human being and savage becomes increasingly cloudy and a source of further irony. Early in the novel Jack himself proclaims, "I agree with Ralph. We've got to have rules and obey them. After all, we're not savages." Piggy asks more than once, "What are we? Humans? Or animals? Or savages?" followed by the double irony, "What's grownups going to think?" The painted faces of the hunters provide "the liberation into savagery," an ironic freedom to destroy society; and the animal imagery contributes to this idea.

Several "levels" of meaning operate in *Lord of the Flies*, apart from the surface narrative. First, from a particular psychological viewpoint, the tripartite organization of the human psyche—ego, id, superego—is dramatized symbolically in the characters of Ralph, Jack, and Piggy, respectively. The conflict between Ralph, the level-headed elected leader of the boys's council, and Jack, the self-appointed head of the hunters, corresponds to an ego-id polarity. Ralph realistically confronts the problem of survival and works out a practical plan for rescue. Jack is quick to revert to savagery, dishonesty, violence. Piggy, the fat, bespectacled rationalist, reminds Ralph of his responsibilities, makes judgments about Jack's guilt, and generally represents the ethical voice on the island. Since Piggy does not acknowledge his own share of guilt for Simon's death, Oldsey and Weintraub conclude that this inconsistency "spoils the picture often given of Piggy as superego or conscience." However, the many times Piggy reminds the weakening Ralph of what must be done far outweigh this one reversal.

A second level of symbolism emerges from the archetypal patterns in the novel. The quest motif is represented by Ralph's stumbling attempts at self-knowledge. His is literally an initiation by fire. Ironically the knowledge he acquires does not allow him to become an integrated member of adult society, but rather it causes him to recoil from the nightmare world he discovers. He is a scapegoat figure who must be sacrificed as atonement for the boys' evils. Simon and Piggy are also variants of the scapegoat symbol. Simon is most clearly the saint or Christ figure. The Dionysian myth is also reworked, as the boys' blindness to their own irrational natures leads to their destruction. As James Baker has observed, Euripides' *Bacchae* "is a bitter allegory" of not only the degeneration of society but also of essential human blindness: "the failure of rational man who invariably undertakes the blind ritual-hunt in which he seeks to kill the threatening 'beast' within his own being."

On still another level, *Lord of the Flies* accommodates a political allegory in which Ralph represents democracy and Jack totalitarianism. Golding has often stressed the impact of World War II on his own life and his change from an idealist who believed in human perfectibility, to a more skeptical observer who had discovered a dark truth "about the given nature of man." In his most explicit statement about the effect of the war on his estimation of humanity and its political systems, Golding says:

> It is bad enough to say that so many Jews were exterminated in this way and that, so many peopled liquidated—lovely, elegant word—but there were things done during that period from which I still have to avert my mind lest I should be physically sick. They were not done by the headhunters of New Guinea, or by some primitive tribe in the Amazon. They were done, skillfully, coldy, by educated men, doctors, lawyers, by men with a tradition of civilization behind them, to beings of their own kind. . . . When these destructive capacities emerged into action they were thought aberrant. Social systems, political systems were composed, detached from the real nature of man. They were what one might call political symphonies. They would perfect most men, and at the least, reduce aberrance.
>
> Why, then, have they never worked?

Such statements not only define Golding's own social background but also illuminate his use of the microcosmic island society in *Lord of the Flies*.

Golding's own comments about *Lord of the Flies* continually focus on the potentials and the limitations of the democratic ideal. Though he supports a democratic doctrine, he recognizes its weaknesses: "You can't give people freedom without weakening society as an implement of war, if you like, and so this is very much like sheep among wolves. It's not a question with me as to whether democracy is the right way so much, as to whether democracy can survive and remain what it is." By giving up all its principles, the island society of *Lord of the Flies* demonstrates the inefficacy of political organizations that attempt to check human beings' worst destructive instincts. It is only by first recognizing these dark powers that democracy can hope to control them.

The fourth level of meaning is the moral allegory, which focuses on the conflicts between good and evil, and encourages philosophical or theological interpretations. Golding is defining the nature of evil. Whether it is embodied in a destructive, unconscious force, a mistaken sacrifice that unsuccessfully atones for the boys' collective guilt, or a dictatorial power opposing the democratic order (corresponding to the psychological, archetypal, and politico-sociological levels, respectively), the problems of moral choice, the inevitability of original sin and human fallibility, the blindness of self-deception create a fourth level of meaning in the novel.

The island is not only a stage on which characters must make crucial moral decisions but also a microcosm for the human mind, in which ethical conflicts similarly occur. Because Golding believes that "a fabulist is always a moralist," he assigns a significant pattern of imagery to Ralph, "the fair boy," who unties the "snake-clasp of his belt." Ralph possesses a "mildness about his mouth and eyes that proclaims no devil"; he rallies the boys to the open, sunlit part of the island; his conch sounds a Gabriellike note unifying (if only temporarily) his followers. Jack, on the other hand, is identified with darkness and violence: when his band of choirboys first appears, it is described as "something dark," like a "creature"; the black caps and cloaks hide their faces; Jack's red hair suggests a devilish element; his impulsive decision to be a hunter and kill pigs foreshadows his demonic monomania for destruction; when he first meets Ralph, Jack is sun-blinded after coming out of the dark jungle.

However, because Golding complicates the characterization and shows Ralph to be susceptible to evil forces and at times paradoxically sympathetic to Jack, the reader recognizes ambiguities not easily compatible with a neat but rigid system of symbols. If *Lord of the Flies* "teaches" through its moral allegory, it is the lesson of self-awareness: "The novel is the parable of fallen man. But it does not close the door on that man; it entreats him to know himself and his Adversary, for he cannot do combat against an unrecognized force, especially when it lies within him."

JOHN F. FITZGERALD AND JOHN R. KAYSER

# Golding's Lord of the Flies: *Pride as Original Sin*

"Just as the mathematicians say the rainbow is an appearance of the sun
embellished by its reflection into a cloud, so the present myth is the appearance of a reality which turns the mind back to other thoughts."

—Plutarch
*Isis et Osiris*

In "Fable," William Golding avers that *Lord of the Flies* is a multilayered
work and open to various interpretations. The novel has been plausibly
interpreted as a Christian parable and Greek tragedy, and less plausibly with
reference to neo-Freudian, Jungian, and Marxian concepts. In what has
become the authoritative interpretation of *Lord of the Flies*, James R. Baker
and Bernard Dick, who base their respective arguments on textual evidence
and Golding's professed admiration for Greek tragedy, conclude that the
form and substance of Golding's myth owes much to Euripides's *Bacchae*.
Both Baker and Dick argue that *Lord of the Flies* is an allegory on the disintegration of society due to a tragic flaw in human nature: man fails to recognize, and thereby appease, the irrational part of his soul.

Ralph at the end of the novel, on the precipice, stares uncomprehendingly into the irrational darkness of his soul. He cries for the loss of

From *Studies in the Novel* 24:1 (Spring 1992). © 1992 by the University of North Texas.

innocence. He cries for the loss of his rational friend Piggy, who also denied the irrational. The boys have committed the sin of Pentheus, according to Baker, by trying to impose "in their innocent pride" an order on the "vital chaos of their own nature." Their attempt took the form of a parliamentary government, and it failed. They regress into barbarism. The plight of the boys becomes an allegory for the plight of modern man, who denies and fears the irrational. Mankind's essential illness is irrational fear.

But such a conclusion does not adequately account for Golding's emphasis on "off-campus history", the concept through which he explores the meaning of *Lord of the Flies*. Indeed, Dick candidly admits that he is "vexed" by Golding's emphasis. Off-campus history, which Golding distinguishes from academic history, is characterized by prejudice for and pride in one's own. The partisan and the sport-fan alike are moved by the fortunes of their heroes; their passion for their own agitates them and clouds their judgment, whereas the scholar's objectivity inures him to partisan passions. Fear, the dead parachutist, and the various other manifestations of the beast are symbols of off-campus history and point to the vital core of this fabulist's tale.

No interpretation of *Lord of the Flies*, however, has sought an Egyptian influence. Yet Golding's interest in ancient Egypt and the Osiris myth is well documented. This myth apparently left an indelible impression upon Golding, and its influence reverberates in the symbolism of *Lord of the Flies*. But most importantly, an Osirian interpretation illuminates man's fallen nature, while explaining the importance attached by Golding to off-campus history. The "trite, obvious and familiar" moral lesson of Golding's novel is that we are capable of the most heinous cruelties in the service of our pride.

The "beastie" appears to the reader in a variety of guises: as a "snake-thing," "beast from water," "beast from air," and, finally, as an aspect of human nature. The nature of the beast is also implied by the suggestive symbolism of the title, *Lord of the Flies*. The "lord of the flies," or Beelzebub, has been associated with the Christian devil. Leaving aside the pregnant symbolism of the decaying pig-head, the beastie as a snake-thing invites comparison to the serpent of the Garden of Eden. However, in the Osiris myth the Egyptian daemon Set-Typhon is also represented by "snakes," and with the ascent of Christianity he was transfigured into Baal or Beelzebub.

A biblical interpretation of the symbolism of the snake is not at variance with an Osirian interpretation. Golding imputes that the fallen nature of man is related to his temptation by the subtle serpent in mythical Eden. Mankind's fallen nature is his desire to be "wise" and "as gods." This would reduce the fallen nature of man to pride. May we then attribute man's ills, including war, to his vanity?

Set-Typhon, intriguingly, is also associated with the sea. The "beast from the air" comes, as it were, from "a sudden bright explosion" carried by the changing winds to its resting place on the island. Typhon, who is also regarded as "fire," later became the god of winds. The narrator also informs us that the boys arrived on the island by some "enchantment. Some act of God—a typhoon perhaps." It strikes us as more than coincidental that typhoon is derived from Typhon. Moreover, this passage appears to refer to the arrival of the boys, or Ralph, on the island. Given the construction of this passage, "his" could refer to the arrival of a god.

The beast's manifestations as "from the sea," "from the air," and "in us" are all associated with war. Rescue, long awaited and desperately needed, comes in the form of a trim warship off-shore; that is, rescue comes from the sea. The dead parachutist bears a message from the adult world, to the boys, from a "battle fought at ten miles' height." This sign descends upon the boys just as their society is disintegrating, and just as Ralph cries out for a sign from the supposedly well-ordered adult world, a world which, the narrator informs us, is embroiled in a cataclysmic war. Our diseased nature, the beast "in us," leads the boys to war and barbarism just as it does in the adult world.

The Osiris myth accounts for the emergence of discord and, hence, war. It thereby demonstrates the precariousness of civilization. According to Plutarch, while reigning as king on earth, the god Osiris gave the Egyptians civilization by introducing laws, worship of the gods, marriage, and agriculture. Before Osiris gave them agriculture the Egyptians had been savages and cannibals. Osiris's brother, the daemon Set-Typhon, filled with envy and pride, sought to usurp his throne. Frustrated in his attempt to take his brother's place, Typhoon tricked Osiris and drowned him. Isis, the wife of Osiris, searched for the body, regained it and concealed it in the woods. Typhon, while hunting pig during a full moon, discovered and mutilated it. A war, punctuated with "terrible deeds" and "confusion," ensued until Horus, son of Osiris, appears to have defeated Typhon. But as Plutarch notes, although "weakened and shattered [the] power of Typhon still gasps and struggles."

Plutarch informs us that the wise interpret the myth as an explanation of entirely natural phenomena: the Nile is Osiris, Isis the earth, and Typhon the sea. The yearly inundation of the Nile valley marks the victory of Osiris and Horus over Typhon. But Plutarch also makes it quite clear that a strict allegory is an insufficient guide to understanding. The "wisest," Plutarch continues, "think that nature must contain in itself the creation and origin of evil as well as good." Osiris, then, represents good in the universe and Typhon evil. The creative, fertilizing, and nourishing aspects of nature are represented by Osiris as is the order of the universe. Typhon symbolizes "everything harmful and destructive in nature."

Plutarch also states that this myth, "because it is inbred into the body and into the soul of the universe," reverberates with meaning for the soul of man. Osiris represents reason and mind (*nous kai logos*) in addition to creativity. Moreover, Plutarch concludes that Osiris and Dionysus are the same diety. They either represent the same qualities within the soul or have the same origin and source. The identification of Osiris with both the reasonable and creative elements of the soul poses a problem, because Osiris as both creative principle and dispassionate reason questions our modern disassociation of reason from creativity or reason from intuition.

Typhon represents "the element of soul which is passionate, akin to the Titans, without reason, and brutish." He personifies the overpowering, violent, and proud. On account of these qualities, Typhon lusted after Osiris's preferred position. His desire to garner power was described by Plutarch as a "mad frenzy." The ritual slaughter of animals becomes identified with Typhon through this myth.

The dramatic movement of the Osiris myth flows from the character of the daemon Typhon. Typhon's desire to rule leads him to wage war against his brother. If this myth does speak to the soul of man, and man like nature contains both Osirian and Typhonic traits, then we can conclude that man is by nature proud. Man can, therefore, be said to be a fallen creature because of his desire to be preferred. Pride leads some, in this myth Typhon, to heroic exertions, but also to harm others. Thus, Typhon may be said to be heroic and sick. Pride leads to war.

The Typhonic element of human nature, in *Lord of the Flies*, is represented by Jack. Jack is red-haired, freckled, hence ruddy, and prone to blush when angry and frustrated. Typhon, according to the tradition, is described as red and ruddy. Indeed, red-haired men were burned and abused in ancient Egypt because they represented Typhon. When Jack's face "blushes with mortification," on the election of Ralph, he can be said to be red. And as Golding again describes, after the second vote, "Jack turned, red in face," because he had been outwitted. Jack desires to be preferred, and when his pride is offended he blushes. It should also be noted that when Ralph's moral superiority is in doubt he too blushes. Thus, blushing appears as a manifestation of wounded pride. Golding's depiction of the character Jack, and blushing, accord well with Plutarch's description of Typhon as envious, proud, and red.

Jack's soul is also Typhonic. He evinces an overweening ambition and a burning desire to be chief, demonstrated by his competition with Ralph both when the boys first selected a chief and when Jack calls for a vote of "no confidence" in Ralph. After his second parliamentary defeat, Jack responds by creating his own society and waging war on Ralph's. Jack's successful society is dedicated to hunting, war, protection from the beast, but most importantly to placating Jack's ego. Jack's regime reverts to savagery, and the narrator describes it as "demented." It is the antithesis of the society he opposes, the society made possible by Piggy and his specs.

Ralph seems to be the civilized counterpart to Jack: Osiris to Jack's Typhon. Ralph blows the conch, articulates the idea for a rescue fire, and, according to Jack, "gives the orders." Ralph certainly looks the part of a leader and, unlike Piggy, he comes from the class expected to lead. He insists that the boys must have and follow rules.

Yet after arriving on the island, Ralph does not know how he got there. The opening conversation makes it pellucid that Piggy does. Although Ralph discovers the conch, Piggy knows what it is and how to use it. But perhaps, most important of all, Piggy sees the need for a meeting. Once the boys are gathered, Piggy "moved among the crowd asking names and frowning to remember them." Not Ralph, but Piggy knows the importance of assemblies. Piggy can, for these reasons, be deemed the true founder of the parliamentary society created by the assembly. At the start of the novel, the narrator states, "what intelligence had been shown was traceable to Piggy."

Damning to the interpretation that Ralph is the reasonable character is his attraction to the seduction of hunting, fierce exhilaration, and ambition. In the incident where Ralph almost maims Robert in the ecstasy of a pig killing ritual, he was "carried away by a sudden thick excitement" and overmastered by a "desire to squeeze and hurt." More damning is his participation in yet another pig killing ritual: the murder of Simon. His self-forgetting in the irrational, frenzy of the boy's orgiastic rituals conspires against the *Bacchae* interpretation, discussed above, for the authors of that interpretation concluded that Ralph was Pentheus who tried to repress irrationality causing his downfall. He demonstrates that he too can be carried away by mad frenzy.

If Ralph does not represent the Osirian elements, what does he represent? Following Golding, we agree that Ralph is "the average rather more than average, man of goodwill and commonsense." Ralph represents better than average humanity; his tale is ours.

Golding represents the duality of Osiris's nature with Simon and Piggy. They together embody that mixture of reason and intuition, which is the root of creativity. It should be recalled that the distinction made in Plutarch's *Isis et Osiris* was between the destructive and passionate, on the one hand, and creative and rational, on the other. Again, unlike modern perceptions, the Osiris myth, does not disassociate reason and creativity. Golding insists that art and reason are connected. As he related: "this business that the artist as a sort of starry-eyed inspired creature, dancing along with his feet two or three feet above the surface of the earth, not really knowing what sort of prince he's leaving behind him, is nothing like the truth."

Golding may have felt it necessary to bifurcate Osiris to make this myth accessible to a modern audience. Golding has supported this "reduction" of Simon and Piggy to the same root by stating that Simon is "Simon called Peter," and that this character was derived, in part, from the character Peterkin Gay of Ballantyne's *Coral Island*. Piggy is also an odd contraction of Peterkin's name by combining the first initial and one vowel of each part of his name to form PiGy.

An Osirian interpretation also avoids the difficulty of explaining why Golding deviated from Euripides over the choice of "scapegoats." Golding, according to the authors of the "*Bacchae*" interpretation, assigned the scapegoat role to Simon, but from the logic of their analysis the scapegoat should have been Ralph, "the Pentheus in embryo." Neither Dick nor Baker offer a satisfactory solution to this problem of Golding's choice. Golding also passionately denies that Simon is a scapegoat.

From the moment we first see the boys on the island, Piggy appears as a knower. Piggy has an inkling of the chaos into which the adult world has fallen. He understands that their coming to be on the island is linked to the war raging outside. He attempts to dispel the irrational fear of the littluns by offering a rational account of fear and the beast. Speaking of "doctors . . . for the inside of your mind," Piggy concludes that fear is in the beholder; it does not result from a healthy apprehension of the unknown. The author has Piggy proclaim the credo of scientific humanism, "Life is scientific, that's what it is."

Piggy's knowledge is, however, quite limited. Its roots are modern science and deductions from empirical observations. Only that which can be demonstrated in the light of day is real and rational. Piggy, moreover, lacks practical wisdom; he doesn't understand people. For example, he questions whether the island can sustain a beast. He asks, "What would a beast eat?" The obvious, and ironic, answer is that it would eat pig. He goes on to precipitate the debate that marks the boy's undoing by asking Phil to recount his experience of the beast. Phil's tortured rambling initiates a chain of events that would lead the narrator to relate, "That the world, that understandable and lawful world, was slipping away." Had Piggy been an acute observer of men, or boys, he would have realized how fragile the island society had become and foreseen the impact of Phil's tale.

Piggy's lack of prudence points to another fatal flaw in his understanding. He proves incapable of diagnosing the disease that afflicts the boys:

he cannot see the beast for what it is. Piggy refuses to admit that Simon's death was murder. Calling it an accident, he refuses even to acknowledge his participation. He rationalizes the entire incident by arguing, "He hadn't no business crawling like that out of the dark. He was batty. He asked for it." Piggy denies the moral implication of their collective guilt. He coldly declares, "We never done nothing, we never seen nothing." Piggy's reason ill-equips him to understand the nature and origin of evil. Indeed, Piggy's scientific humanism precludes him from seeing the beast in us.

Scientific humanism, which is faith in the progressive and liberating power of science and man's ability to rationally posit values, has stripped man naked of the religious context which gave his life meaning. Confidence in mankind's ability to conquer nature and prejudice gave modern man the sensation that hitherto undreamed of possibilities were now opened to him. However, recent history and the myriad of variations on the philosophy of Friedrich Nietzsche indicate that scientific humanism precludes us from positing any value; that is, it precludes us from seeing evil for what it is. The scientific humanist, the "model intellectual," is "literally in a state of free fall."

However, there is one character who sees, but the status and nature of his understanding disturbs modern sensibilities. Golding's "saint" Simon knows the truth about the beast. He arrives at the novel's truth about the fallen nature of man. As the lord of the flies asserts:

> "There isn't anyone to help you. Only me. And I'm the Beast."
> Simon's mouth labored, brought forth audible words.
> "Pig's head on a stick."
> "Fancy thinking that the beast was something you could hunt and kill!" said the head.
> For a moment or two the forest and all the other dimly appreci-
> ated places echoed with a parody of laughter. "You knew didn't
> you? I'm part of you? Close, close, close! I'm the reason why it's
> no go? Why things are what they are?"

This truth comes to Simon in the form of a revelation. He had also intuited it earlier. In the disastrous assembly, which signaled the collapse of Ralph's regime, we learned that Simon knew the truth about the beast. But the boys, principally Piggy, shout him down.

Simon attempts to articulate his vision of the beast with, "What is the dirtiest thing there is?" Jack's crude, monosyllabic response literally ruins Simon's effort. The reader is left to wonder what the dirtiest thing is, Jack's response, and how they relate to the beast. From the vantage point of a young boy we may infer that excrement, which can be conveyed in one crude syllable, is the dirtiest thing. "Shit" is in us, entirely natural, and yet invisible like the beast. Like the beast, it too evokes revulsion when it becomes manifest. Simon's inspired image and Jack's reply are altogether apt. Simon may not be able to articulate his message, because, by its very nature, it can not be rationally defended. Simon would have been unable to persuade the other boys even if he could find the words. He is ridiculed, later mistaken for the beast, and eventually beaten to death for his insight and effort.

Simon's death symbolically marks the death of the god Osiris by the power of Typhon. Just as Simon's murder is prefigured by the pig-hunting ritual, by moonlight, so too is Osiris's body discovered by Typhon during a moonlit pig hunt. A similar fate befalls Piggy, the rational face of Osiris, in the mad, ego-driven frenzy that sweeps away the last vestiges of sanity. Again, on the surface, both the similarity of Pig to Piggy and that animal's association with Osiris support an Osirian interpretation. The sea claimed the battered bodies of Piggy and Simon just as the sea had claimed the body of Osiris.

We are not, however, offering up either Simon or Piggy as scapegoats. A scapegoat unwillingly becomes a surrogate for the god; he appeases the god by being sacrificed to him. Given the situation on the island at the time of their deaths, we witness the stuff out of which new cults and their attendant rituals are made. We observe the death of the "gods," not their scapegoats who will come later. The return of "civilization" in the guise of the naval officer neither precludes the destruction of Western civilization, as we know it, nor that Ralph will pass on his new found knowledge in the form of a myth.

Golding appears to contradict the foregoing interpretation by insisting that Simon is a saint. His depiction of Simon as a "saint" carries definite Christian connotations. But a saint is, as Chesterson revealed, "a medicine because he is an antidote. Indeed that is why the saint is often a martyr; he is mistaken for a poison because he is an antidote." Simon represents the antidote for a rationalism that cannot see. Simon's insight into the beast offers the boys the possibility of salvation on the island, not, insofar as we know, in heaven. Simon's knowledge, had it been believed, would have made up for the defects in Piggy's. Piggy's knowledge coupled with the ability to see beyond mere appearance would have made Ralph's regime resilient to the inroads of Jack's barbarism.

As Leo Strauss observed, "The very life of Western civilization is the life between two codes [the biblical and Greek philosophic], a fundamental tension." The separation of rational and revelatory knowledge, from Golding's perspective, is both the essence and the illness of the West. It "has begotten that lame giant we call civilization as Frankenstein created his monster." The ascendancy of scientific humanism, its inability to see to posit eternal verities, leaves modern man free falling in the abyss of nihilism. We confront, through our excavation of Golding's myth, the value problem. Until Simon and Piggy together comprise an Osiris, Western civilization cannot diagnose, let alone cure, its essential illness.

The narrator reveals mankind's essential illness with compelling clarity in the following scene:

> "This was fascinating to Henry. He poked about with a bit of stick, that itself was wave-worn and whitened and a vagrant, and tried to control the motions of the scavengers. He made little runnels that the tide filled and tried to crowd them with creatures. He became absorbed beyond mere happiness as he felt himself exercising control over living things. He talked to them, urging them, ordering them. Driven back by the tide, his footprints became bays in which they were trapped and gave him the illusion of mastery."

Henry, who is a child, the modern apotheosis of innocence, seeks mastery over other living things, and he too is marked by the beast. The root of his will to mastery is vanity. Henry may be distinguished from Jack, or Typhon, but only in power and magnitude. This is the terrible, dark truth that resides at the heart of *Lord of the Flies*.

Pride has various manifestations, among them honor, prestige, fame, and wealth. Off-campus history, or nationalism, is but one manifestation of this deeper tragic flaw. But perhaps even more troubling for modern man, pride in our ideas has "thrust our world into a mental straitjacket from which we can escape only by the most anarchic violence." The virulent, global atrocities of the twentieth century were caused by both ideological pride and nationalism. But these otherwise impressive edifices are merely projections out from the self, which seeks to have its view sanctified. They are mirrors, if you will, that reflect back to us our own petty prejudices. Modern man, who can explain everything in entirely antiseptic, sanitary ways cannot, no matter how often he cleanses himself, rid himself of the decay that comes from within.

LAWRENCE S. FRIEDMAN

# *Grief, Grief, Grief:* Lord of the Flies

*Lord of the Flies* opens in Eden. Ralph, fair-haired protagonist, and Piggy, faithful companion and resident intellectual, look about them and pronounce their island good. And so it is, for William Golding has set his young castaways down upon an uninhabited Pacific island as lush as it is remote. Fruit hangs ripe for the picking; fresh water flows abundantly from a convenient mountain; and the tropical climate soon prompts the boys to throw off their clothes. Ralph joyfully stands on his head, an action he will repeat at moments of high emotion. It is easy to forget that the world is at war, and that the plane that carried Ralph, Piggy, and the many other English boys stranded on the island, was shot down by the enemy.

As war and plane crash recede from memory, the visible world shrinks to the desert island and its populace of six- to twelve-year-old boys. Because of the island's fecundity and mild climate the boys are largely exempt from the struggle for food and shelter; because of their youth they are exempt from sexual longing and deprivation; because of their isolation they are exempt from adult constraints. Free to live as they choose, they can act out every boy's dream of romantic adventure until their eventual rescue. *Lord of the Flies* begins, therefore, as a modern retelling of R. N. Ballantyne's Victorian children's classic, *Coral Island*. Indeed Golding traces his book's genesis to a night when he had finished reading just such an island adventure story

From *William Golding*. © 1993 by Lawrence S. Friedman.

to his eldest child. Exasperated by the familiar cutout characters and smug optimism of the original, he conceived of breathing life into a moribund genre by isolating boys on a desert island and showing how they would really behave. Ballantyne's shipwrecked boys, somewhat older than Golding's, lead an idyllic life on their remote South Seas island. Tropical nature is benign, the boys' characters conventionally innocent. What evil exists on Coral Island enters in the form of such adult intruders as savage cannibals or pirates. Ballantyne's vision is doubly optimistic: man is inherently good; and good will win out in the end. Like most fairy tales, *Coral Island* is an amalgam of faith and hope.

On Golding's coral island, Piggy's allusions to atomic war, dead adults, and uncertainty of rescue barely ripple the surface of Ralph's pleasant daydreams. Soon the boys recover a conch from the lagoon. More than a plaything, the conch will become a means of communication, and ultimately a symbol of law and order. Instructed by the wise but ineffectual Piggy, Ralph blows on the conch, thereby summoning the scattered boys. Possession of the conch ensures Ralph's election as chief. Later the assembled boys agree that whoever wishes to speak must raise his hand and request the conch. Cradling the conch in one's hands not only confers instant personal authority but affirms the common desire for an orderly society.

Read as a social treatise, Golding's first chapter seems to posit notions of fair play and group solidarity familiar to readers of *Coral Island*. But the same chapter introduces us to Jack Merridew marching at the head of his uniformed column of choirboys. Clad in black and silver and led by an obviously authoritarian figure, the choirboys seem boy Nazis. Frustrated by Ralph's election as chief, Jack barely conceals his anger. The chapter ends with Jack, knife in hand, reflexively hesitating long enough on the downward stroke to allow a trapped piglet to escape. The civilized taboo against blood-letting remains shakily in place as the angry boy settles for slamming his knife into a tree trunk. "Next time," he cries.

It is the exploration of Jack's "next time" that will occupy much of the remainder of *Lord of the Flies*. By fixing incipient evil within Jack, Golding reverses the sanguine premise of nineteenth-century adventure stories that locate evil in the alien or mysterious forces of the outside world. According to Golding his generation's "liberal and naive belief in the perfectibility of man" was exploded by World War II. Hitler's gas chambers revealed man's inherent evil. His followers were not Ballantyne's savage cannibals or desperate pirates whose evil magically dissipated upon their conversion to Christianity. Rather they were products of that very Christian civilization that presumably guarantees their impossibility. Nor does it suffice to accept Ballantyne's implication that his boys' Englishness, like their Christianity, marks them as inevitably good. "We've got to have rules and obey them. After all, we're not savages. We're English, and the English are best at everything. So we've got to do the right things." Coming from Golding's Jack, these words effectively shatter Ballantyne's easy optimism. Conditioned no less by the theology of man's fall than by Nazi atrocities, *Lord of the Flies* traces the spreading stain of man's depravity from its first intimations in Jack to its near-total corruption of the boys and their social order. "I decided," explained Golding, "to take the literary convention of boys on an island, only make them real boys instead of paper cutouts with no life in them; and try to show how the shape of the society they evolved would be conditioned by their diseased, their fallen nature."

Too immature to account for the enemy within, the boys project their irrational fears onto the outside world. The first of these projections takes the shape of a snakelike "beastie," the product of a small boy's nightmare. One side of the boy's face "was blotted out by a mulberry-coloured birthmark," the visible sign of the dual nature of fallen man. More by force of personality than by reason, Ralph succeeds in exorcising the monster from the group consciousness. Now the boys struggle to drag logs up the mountain for a signal fire, Ralph and Jack bearing the heaviest log between them. Jack's momentary selflessness combined with the manipulation of the lenses of Piggy's spectacles to start their fire—as well as the very act of fire building itself—signal a resurgence of civilized values. But the fire soon rages out of control; exploding trees and rising creepers reinvoke cries of "Snakes!, Snakes"; and the small boy with the birthmark has mysteriously disappeared. The seed of fear has been planted. Reason has failed to explain the darkness within, and the island paradise begins its fatal transformation into hell.

Soon Ralph and Jack find communication impossible, the former talking of building shelters, the latter of killing pigs. Increasingly obsessed with his role as hunter, Jack neglects his more important role as keeper of the signal fire. Painting a fierce mask on his face he is "liberated from shame and self-consciousness." Shortly thereafter he and his frenzied followers march along swinging the gutted carcass of a pig from a stake to the incantory chant, "Kill the pig. Cut her throat. Spill her blood." Abandonment to blind ritual has displaced the reasoned discourse governed by the conch. Meanwhile the untended fire has gone out, and a ship has sailed past the island. Lost in blood lust, Jack's thoughts are far from rescue, and he at first barely comprehends Ralph's anger. When he does, he strikes out at the helpless Piggy, shattering one of his lenses. Reason henceforth is half-blind; the fragile link between Ralph and Jack snaps; and ritual singing and dancing resume as the boys gorge themselves on the slaughtered pig. That Ralph and Piggy join in the feast indicates the all-too-human failure to resist the blandishments of mass hysteria.

Killing marks the end of innocence. It is a wiser Ralph who "found himself understanding the wearisomeness of this life where every path was an improvisation and a considerable part of one's waking life was spent watching one's feet . . . and remembering that first enthusiastic exploration as though it were part of a brighter childhood, he smiled jeeringly." Here at the beginning of the important fifth chapter, "Beast from Water," the regression and initiation themes converge. On the basis of his newfound knowledge, Ralph assembles the boys to discuss such practical matters as sanitation, shelter, and, most crucially, the keeping of the fire. But the tension among the boys is palpable, and Ralph soon confesses, "Things are breaking up. I don't understand why. We began well, we were happy." And he concludes, "Then people started getting frightened." Piggy's theory that life is scientific is countered by new reports of a beast from the sea. Neither Piggy's logic not Ralph's rules can hold the boys together, and the meeting scatters in confusion.

E. M. Forster pleads in his introduction to the 1962 American edition of *Lord of the Flies* for more respect for Piggy. Of course he is correct. Faced with specters of water beasts and Jack's authoritarian violence, who could fail to opt for Piggy's rationalism? Yet unaided reason cannot tell Ralph why things go wrong; it can only deny the physical reality of the beast. It is left to Simon, the skinny, inarticulate seer to "express mankind's essential illness" by fixing the beast's location: "What I mean is . . . maybe it's only us." Golding's moral—that defect in human society can be traced back to defects in human nature—can be illustrated by the fable of the scorpion and the frog:

> "Let me ride across the pond on your back," pleads the scorpion.
> "No," replies the frog, "for if I let you on my back your sting will prove fatal."
> "Listen to reason," cries the scorpion. "If I sting you, you'll sink to the bottom of the pond, and I'll drown."
> So the frog takes the scorpion on his back and begins swimming. Midway across the pond, he feels the scorpion's fatal sting. "How could you," gasps the frog with his dying breath. "Now you'll drown."
> "I couldn't help it," sighs the scorpion. "It's my nature."

Though his irrationality, like the scorpion's, may cost him his life, man is his own worst enemy. Undone by the beast within, man self-destructs no matter what form of social organization he adopts.

"Beast from the Air" opens with the sign from the world of grown-ups that answers Ralph's desperate cry for help after the breakup of the assembly. Dropping from the air battle high above the island, a dead parachutist settles on the mountaintop where fitful breezes cause him spasmodically to rise and fall. This grotesque "message" recalls the adult savagery that marooned the boys on the island. Moreover, the boys now take the faraway figure for the beast that haunts their dreams. Confronted by its apparent physical reality even Ralph succumbs to fear. The ironic appropriateness of the man-beast foreshadows Jack's growing power and the final unraveling of the social order. Now that the primary task is to kill the beast, Jack assumes command. Promising hunting and feasting he lures more and more boys into his camp. Man regresses from settler to roving hunter, society from democracy to dictatorship.

It is at this point, shortly after the collapse of social order under the pressures of inherent evil associated with Jack and irrational fear embodied in the beast from the air, that Golding paints his most startling and powerful scene. Simon, the only boy who feels the need for solitude, returns to his place of contemplation, a leafy shelter concealed by the dense growth of the forest. There he witnesses the butchering of a frantically screaming sow, its gutting and dismemberment, and the erection of its bleeding head on a pole. This head, abandoned by the hunters as a "gift" to the beast, presides over a pile of guts that attracts great swarms of buzzing flies. And the Lord of the Flies speaks: "Fancy thinking the Beast was something you could hunt and kill. You knew didn't you? I'm part of you? Close, close, close! I'm the reason why it's no go? Why things are what they are?" Looking into the vast mouth, Simon sees only a spreading blackness into which he falls in a faint.

As previously noted, Golding has called himself a fabulist and his novel a fable. All fables contain morals; and the moral of *Lord of the Flies* is stated most explicitly in the confrontation between Simon and the pig's head. "I included a Christ-figure in my fable. This is the little boy Simon, solitary, stammering, a lover of mankind, a visionary." Since the Lord of the Flies is Beelzebub, the Judeo-Christian prince of devils, the scene dramatizes the clash between principles of good and evil. To accept the consequences of Golding's symbolism is to recognize the inequality of the struggle between Simon and the head. The Lord of the Flies has invaded Simon's forest sanctuary to preach an age-old semon: evil lies within man whose nature is inherently depraved. Simon cannot counter this lesson. Engulfed by the spreading blackness of the vast mouth, he is overwhelmed by Beelzebub's power and loses consciousness. While it does not necessarily follow that Christ's message is similarly overpowered by Satan's, the forest scene strongly implies that innocence and good intentions are lost amidst the general ubiquity of evil. That evil cannot be isolated in Jack or in the beast; it is "close, close, close," a part of all of us.

The Simon who awakens from his faint trudges out of the forest "like an old man," stooping under the heavy burden of revelation. Immediately he comes face-to-face with a second awful symbol of human corruption—the rotting body of the downed parachutist. It, too, has been found by the flies; like the pig's head it too has been reduced to a corrupt and hideous parody of life. Releasing the broken figure from the tangled parachute lines that bind it to the rocks, Simon staggers back down the mountain with this news that the beast is harmless. But he stumbles into the frenzied mob of dancing and chanting boys who take him for the beast, fall upon him, and tear him apart.

The ritual murder of Simon is as ironic as it is inevitable. Ironically, he is killed as the beast before he can explain that the beast does not exist. His horrid death refutes his aborted revelation: the beast exists, all right, not where we thought to find it, but within ourselves. Inevitably, we kill our savior who "would set us free from the repetitive nightmare of history." Unable to perceive his truth, we huddle together in the circle of our fear and reenact his ritual murder, as ancient as human history itself. Golding's murderous boys, the products of centuries of Christianity and Western civilization, explode the hope of Christ's sacrifice by repeating the pattern of his crucifixion. Simon's fate underlines the most awful truths about human nature: its blindness, its irrationality, its blood lust.

That the human condition is hopeless is revealed in the fact that even Ralph and Piggy felt the need to join in the "demented but partly secure society" of the hunters just prior to Simon's murder. Later, they console themselves with the excuse that they remained outside the dancing circle. When Ralph recalls the horror of the murder, Piggy first tries to deny its reality. And when Ralph refuses to drop the subject, Piggy shrills again and again that Simon's death was an accident. His desperate rationalizations point to the inability of human reason to cope with the dark reality of human nature. Piggy's excuses are mere frantic attempts to explain away our basest instincts and actions. Their transparent failure to do so marks the limits of the human intellect. Symbolic of the fall of reason is the loss of Piggy's sight. His broken glasses, the means of fire making, are stolen in a raid by Jack and his hunters. As Jack stalks triumphantly off with the glasses dangling from his hand, the reign of savagery is all but sealed.

Jack's victory comes swiftly in the following chapter, "Castle Rock." Again Golding sets up a contest between pinciples of good and evil. But this time the outcome is a foregone conclusion. The pack of painted savages who blindly murdered Simon has by now abandoned all restraints. Personified by Roger, Jack's fanatical self-appointed "executioner," the hunters turn viciously against Ralph and Piggy and the twins Sam and Eric, the last four remnants of an orderly society. From high atop a cliff Roger pushes a great rock that, gathering momentum, strikes Piggy, killing the fat boy and shattering the conch. Although the conch has long since lost the power to invoke order, its explosion signals the final triumph of lawlessness. Screaming wildly, "I'm chief," Jack hurls his spear at Ralph, inflicting a flesh wound, and forcing the former chief to run frantically for his life.

"Cry of the Hunters," the novel's concluding chapter, marks the final degenerative stage in Golding's fable of man's fall. Ralph's pursuers, freed by Piggy's murder from the faint restraint of reason, have reduced Ralph to their quarry. As the savage pack closes in, the sad lesson of the hunt is inescapable: not that the boys are dehumanized, but that they are all too human. Man's basic instinct is to kill; and the depth of his depravity is measured by the urge to kill his own species. Not only does the metaphor of the hunt complete Golding's definition of the human animal, but it forges a link to analogous hunts in Greek drama that loom in the background of *Lord of the Flies*.

Golding has often acknowledged the formative influence of the ancients. Together with the biblical version of man's fate expressed in the doctrine of original sin, Greek drama fleshes out the myth of the fall. If it is true that a writer's forebears surface most apparently in his early work, then the final hunt of *Lord of the Flies* is second only to Simon's "passion" in fixing the origins of Golding's most cherished ideas. While it is true that Simon's confrontation with the pig's head and his subsequent martyrdom are couched primarily in Christian terms, the Greek influence is also apparent. The pig's head is at once the Judeo-Christian Beelzebub and the king of the Olympian gods. Thus Jean-Paul Sartre's modern reworking of Greek motifs in *The Flies* opens on a public square in Argos, "dominated by a statue of Zeus, god of flies and death. The image has white eyes and blood-smeared cheeks." Zeus himself appears in the play to explain the great swarms of buzzing flies that plague the city. "They are," he says, "a symbol," sent by the gods to "a dead-and-alive city, a carrion city" still festering fifteen years after the original sin of Agamemnon's murder. The citizens of Argos are "working out their atonement." Their "fear and guilty consciences have a good savor in the nostrils of the gods." Zeus implies that man's blood lust is balanced by this reverence for the gods, a view shared by Golding: "As far back as we can go in history we find that the two signs of man are a capacity to kill and a belief in God." Human fear and guilt are perverse affirmations of the gods' existence and therefore find favor with the gods. For Sartre, the existential philosopher, man's awful freedom, won at the expense of breaking his shackles to the gods, is all-important. But for Golding, the Christian believer, man is lost without God. The absence of prayer, even among fearful young choirboys, is one of the darkest aspects of *Lord of the Flies*.

Although *The Flies* may have no direct bearing upon Golding's novel, its title as well as its identification of Zeus as god of flies and death reveal the same backdrop of Greek tradition. At the end of Sartre's play, the hero Orestes, drawn directly from Greek drama, is pursued by the shrieking Furies. No such deities hunt Ralph, only his fellow boys. Yet chase scenes of all kinds fill Greek drama, and Golding the classicist seems indebted not merely to the general metaphor of the hunt but specifically to its powerful treatment in two plays of Euripides: *The Bacchae* and *Iphigenia in Tauris*.

Euripides wrote *The Bacchae*, his greatest and most difficult play, in the wake of a disillusionment with the Peloponnesian War as profound as Golding's with World War II. As skeptical about human nature as Golding, Euripides had already written the most devastating antiwar play that survives from antiquity, *The Trojan Women*. Both *Lord of the Flies* and *The Bacchae* are anthropological passion plays in which individuals—children in Golding, adults in Euripides—revert to savagery and murder during a frenzied ritual. At Thebes, where Dionysus (Bacchus) comes to introduce his worship to Greece, King Pentheus adamantly denies the new religion. To Dionysus's orgiastic revels Pentheus opposes the rule of reason. Yet he is tempted to disguise himself in the fawn skin of a Dionysian follower in order to watch the rites of the female devotees. Spied by the Bacchants, he is hunted down and torn to pieces by the frenzied women, led by his own mother, Agave. Maddened by the god, the hapless Agave bears Pentheus's head, which she imagines is a lion's, triumphantly back to Thebes. There she comes to her senses and awakens to the horrid proof of Dionysus's power. To deny Dionysus is to deny a fundamental force in human nature. That the destruction of Pentheus is so disproportionate to his offense constitutes poetic justice in *The Bacchae*: Pentheus denies the primitive power of unreason only to become its victim. Yet the orgiastic worship that transforms Agave into the unwitting murderess of her son is hardly preferable to Pentheus's denial. Euripides, in dramatizing the clash between emotionalism and rationalism, may be arguing the primacy of neither. However one interprets *The Bacchae*, its affinities with *Lord of the Flies* are striking:

> Specifically, both drama and novel contain three interrelated ritual themes: the cult of a beast-god, a hunt as prefiguration of the death of the scapegoat-figure, and the dismemberment of the scapegoat. Golding deviates in only one respect from Euripides: logically Ralph, the Pentheus in embryo, should be the scapegoat; but the author assigns this role to Simon, allowing Ralph to live instead with his new-found knowledge of "the darkness of man's heart."

Dionysus is the true hero of *The Bacchae*; his merciless destruction of Pentheus is but the opening salvo in his campaign to establish his worship in Hellas. Golding is no less concerned with the primitive force that Dionysus represents; but his primary concern is the impact of that force upon his hero. Ralph, the latter-day Pentheus, must therefore survive the ordeal of the hunt and live with his hard-won knowledge. Against the backdrop of the flaming island, a hell that once was Eden, the savage tribe pursues Ralph until, stumbling over a root, the frantic boy sprawls helplessly in the sand. Staggering to his feet, flinching at the anticipated last onslaught, Ralph looks up into the astonished face of a British naval officer. Ralph's miraculous salvation completes the drama of his initiation as, in a shattering epiphany, he weeps "for the end of innocence, the darkness of man's heart, and the fall through the air of the true wise friend called Piggy."

Although Golding shifts the focus from God's power to man's knowledge he relies on a familiar Euripidian device for ending his novel. Golding calls the timely arrival of the naval officer a "gimmick," a term subsequently used by critics to plague him. Yet the officer is neither more nor less than the Greek deus ex machina in modern uniform. Employed most strikingly by Euripides, the "god" in the machine is hoisted high above the other actors to solve the problems of the preceding action and to supply a happy ending. Most often, when the diety imposes a happy ending, the normal consequences of the action would be disastrous. Neither *The Bacchae* nor Sartre's *The Flies* employs the device in its purest form. In the former, Dionysus resolves the action by heaping even more woe upon the Thebans who denied his god head. In the latter, Sartre's Zeus absents himself from the ending, having already explained its significance. Moreover, both gods take major roles from the outset of their respective plays. Neither makes the single in-the-nick-of-time appearance to reverse the action that generally characterizes the deus ex machina.

In *Iphigenia in Tauris*, however, Euripides relies upon the deus ex machina for a resolution markedly similar to that of *Lord of the Flies*. Iphigenia, her brother Orestes, and his friend Pylades, pursued by the minions of the barbarian king Thoas, reach the seacoast where a Greek ship waits to carry them home. But Thoas's troops control the strait through which the ship must pass; and a strong gale drives the ship back toward the shore. Enter the goddess Athena, who warns Thoas to cease his pursuit. It seems that the fates of Iphigenia and her companions have been foreordained, and against this "necessity" even gods are powerless. Thoas wisely relents, the winds grow favorable, and the ship sails off under Athena's divine protection.

Barbarian pursuit, friendly ship, and miraculous rescue are no less present in Golding's conclusion. And when to these elements are added the hunt for sacrificial victims and the bloody rites of the Taurian religion, the resemblances between *Iphigenia in Tauris* and *Lord of the Flies* seem more than skin deep. Yet the lessons of the two works radically differ. Greek drama is ultimately conditioned by the proximity of the gods: omnipresent yet inscrutable they influence human action and determine human destiny. Since, as Sartre's Zeus admits, the gods need mortals for their worship as much as mortals need objects for their devotion, it follows that Greek drama chronicles this interdependence. In *The Flies*, Sartre's Zeus, the fading though still powerful king of the gods, owes his rule to human fear and superstition and relies upon man's willing servitude. When Orestes finally strides boldy into the sunlight, the spell of the gods is broken; henceforth he will blaze his own trail, acknowledging no law but his own. For Sartre, man's freedom begins with his denial of the gods and his full acceptance of responsibility for his actions and their consequences. And while existential freedom is as fearful as it is lonely, it is infinitely preferable to god-ridden bondage. Whether Dionysus stalking through *The Bacchae*, Athena watching over *Iphigenia in Tauris*, or Zeus brooding in *The Flies*, the gods play a role in the human drama. Note that all three deities carefully define their roles: Dionysus to punish the errant Thebans whose king denied him; Athena to ensure the proper worship of her sister, Artemis; and Zeus to warn the recalcitrant Orestes of the consequences of rebellion. So closely are the gods involved with mortals that their interventions, no matter how arbitrary, take on a certain inevitable logic.

What Golding calls the "gimmicked" ending of *Lord of the Flies* and the Greek deus ex machina used most conventionally in *Iphigenia in Tauris* are alike in their technical function: to reverse the course of impending disaster. Yet their effects are quite different. Athena's wisdom is incontrovertible, her morality unassailable. High above the awed mortals she dispels chaos and imposes ideal order. The very fact of her appearance underlines the role of the gods in shaping human destiny. Golding's spiffy naval officer is, however, no god. Nor does he represent a higher morality. Confronted by the ragtag melee, he can only wonder that English boys hadn't put up a better show, and mistakes their savage hunt for fun and games à la *Coral Island*. While he cannot know the events preceding his arrival, his comments betray the same ignorance of human nature that contributed to the boys' undoing. Commanding his cruiser, the officer will direct a maritime search-and-destroy mission identical to the island hunt. *Lord of the Flies* ends with the officer gazing at the cruiser, preparing to reenact the age-old saga of man's inhumanity to man.

Just as the naval officer cannot measure up to Euripides' Athena, so Ralph falls short of Sartre's Orestes. Orestes strides into the sunlight of his morality to live Sartre's dictum that existence precedes essence. Creating himself anew with each action, he will become his own god. Ralph can only weep for the loss of innocence from the world; he shows no particular signs of coping with his newfound knowledge. To understand one's nature is not to alter it. Morally diseased, mired in original sin, fallen man can rise only by the apparently impossible means of transcending his very nature. In man's apparent inability to re-create himself lies the tragedy of *Lord of the Flies*. The futility of Simon's sacrificial death, the failure of adult morality, and the final absence of God create the spiritual vacuum of Golding's novel. For Sartre the denial of the gods is the necessary prelude to human freedom. But for Golding, God's absence leads only to despair and human freedom is but license. "The theme of *Lord of the Flies* is grief, sheer grief, grief, grief."

# Chronology

1911  William Golding born in Cornwall on September 19, 1911, one of two sons of Alec Golding, mathematics teacher and soon to be senior master of Marlborough Grammar School, and Mildred Golding, an activist for women's suffrage.

1930  Completes secondary school at the Marlborough School, well-educated in science and able to play piano, cello, oboe, violin, and viola. Enters Brasenose College, Oxford, to study science; soon switches to English literature.

1934  A friend sends twenty-nine of Golding's poems to Macmillan; *Poems* published in Contemporary Poets series.

1935  Receives BA in English and diploma in education from Oxford. Writes, acts, and produces for a small, noncommercial theater in London.

1939  Marries Ann Brookfield, an analytical chemist; begins teaching English, Greek literature in translation, and philosophy at Bishop Wordsworth's School in Salisbury. Involved in adult education; teaches in army camps and Maidstone Gaol.

1940–45  Enlists in Royal Navy at start of World War II; works at secret scientific research center, is injured in an explosion and recovers.

Given command of small rocket-launching craft; involved in chase and sinking of the *Bismarck*; takes part in D-Day assault, 1944.

1945 Returns to teach at Bishop Wordsworth's school.

1954 *Lord of the Flies* published by Faber and Faber after being rejected by twenty-one other publishers; retires from teaching to write full time.

1955 *The Inheritors* published; Golding becomes a fellow of the Royal Society of Literature.

1956 *Pincher Martin* published; republished in the United States as *The Two Lives of Christopher Martin*, in 1957.

1958 A play, *The Brass Butterfly*, performed at Oxford and in London.

1959 *Free Fall* published.

1960–62 Becomes frequent contributor of essays and book reviews to the *Spectator*.

1960 April 20, BBC radio script *Miss Pulkinhorn* performed.

1961 Completes master of arts degree at Oxford. March 19, BBC radio script *Break My Heart* performed.

1961–62 Spends year as writer in residence at Hollins College, Virginia, and tours as lecturer at other American colleges.

1963 *Lord of the Flies* produced for film.

1964 *The Spire* published.

1965 A collection of essays, *The Hot Gates* published. Golding made a Commander of the British Empire.

1966 Becomes honorary fellow of Brasenose College, Oxford.

1967 *The Pyramid* published.

| 1970 | Awarded honorary doctor of letters by Sussex University. |
| 1971 | *The Scorpion God: Three Short Novels* published. |
| 1976 | First visit to Egypt. |
| 1979 | *Darkness Visible* published. |
| 1980 | *Rites of Passage* published, wins Booker Prize for fiction. |
| 1982 | A second collection of essays, *A Moving Target*, published. |
| 1983 | Wins Nobel Prize for Literature. |
| 1984 | *The Paper Men* published. |
| 1985 | *An Egyptian Journal* published. |
| 1987 | *Close Quarters*, the second volume of sea trilogy begun with *Rites of Passage*, published. |
| 1989 | *Fire Down Below* published, concludes sea trilogy. |
| 1990 | New film version of *Lord of the Flies*. |
| 1993 | William Golding dies June 19 at Perranaworthal, Cornwall. |

# Contributors

HAROLD BLOOM is Sterling Professor of Humanities at Yale University and Professor of English at New York University. His works include *Shelley's Mythmaking* (1959), *The Visionary Company* (1961), *The Anxiety of Influence* (1973), *Agon: Towards a Theory of Revisionism* (1982), *The Book of J* (1990), *The American Religion* (1992), and *The Western Canon* (1994). His forthcoming books are a study of Shakespeare and *Freud, Transference and Authority*, which considers all of Freud's major writings. A MacArthur Prize Fellow, Professor Bloom is the editor of more than thirty anthologies and general editor of five series of literary criticism published by Chelsea House.

CLAIRE ROSENFIELD is author of *Paradise of Snakes: an Archetypal Analysis of Conrad's Political Novels* (1967).

BERNARD F. DICK has published numerous articles and books on literature, and film history and criticism. His recent works include *City of Dreams: The Making and Remaking of Universal Pictures* (1997), *The Star-Spangled Screen: The American World War II Film* (1996), *Anatomy of Film* (1990), and *Radical Innocence: A Critical Study of the Hollywood Ten* (1988).

BERNARD S. OLDSEY is editor of *British Novelists 1930-1959* (1983) and *Ernest Hemingway, the Papers of a Writer* (1981); and author of *Hemingway's Hidden Craft* (1979) and *Visions and Revisions in Modern American Literary Criticism* (1962).

STANLEY WEINTRAUB has published widely on English literature and history. His works include *Uncrowned King: The Life of Prince Albert* (1997), *Victorian Yankees at Queen Victoria's Court* (1994), *Disraeli: A Biography* (1993), *Victoria: An Intimate Biography* (1987), and studies of the plays of George Bernard Shaw.

MARK KINKEAD-WEEKES has written extensively on the life and works of D.H. Lawrence, as well as studies of the works of Samuel Richardson, William Golding, and Ian Gregor. He is author of *D.H. Lawrence* (1991) and editor, with A. Robert Lee, of *Tensions and Transitions, 1869–1990: the Mediating Imagination for Ian Gregor* (1990).

IAN GREGOR is editor of *Reading the Victorian Novel* (1980) and, with Walter Stein, of *The Prose for God: Religious and Anti-Religious Aspects of Imaginative Literature* (1973). He is author of *The Great Web: The Form of Hardy's Major Fiction* (1974).

LEIGHTON HODSON is lecturer in French at the University of Glasgow. He is editor of *Marcel Proust: The Critical Heritage* (1997), as well as the 1969 *Study of William Golding*.

HOWARD S. BABB is editor of *Essays in Stylistic Analysis* (1972) and author of *Jane Austen's Novels; the Fabric of Dialogue* (1967).

JEANNE DELBAERE-GARANT is Professor of English literature at the University of Brussels and has published articles on James, Lawrence, Ford, Forster, Woolf, Joyce, Waugh, Cary, and Janet Frame. Her books include *The Ring of Fire: Essays on Janet Frame* (1992) and *Henry James: The Vision of France* (1970).

PHILIP REDPATH is author of *Seeing Venus: A Structural Study of William Golding's Fiction* (1984).

ARNOLD JOHNSTON is associate professor of English at Western Michigan University. He has published short stories and poems and two of his plays have been successfully produced. His "Innovation and Rediscovery in Golding's *The Pyramid*" appeared in *Critique*.

JAMES GINDIN has published essays and articles on the works of Galsworthy, Trollope, Hardy, Forster, Woolf, Lawrence, Joyce, and Bellow. Among his recent works is *British Fiction in the 1930's: The Dispiriting Decade* (1992).

PATRICK REILLY is author of *Lord of the Flies: Fathers and Sons* (1993), *Tom Jones: Adventure and Providence* (1991), *Nineteen Eighty-Four: Past, Present, and Future* (1989), and *George Orwell: The Age's Adversary* (1985).

S.J. BOYD is Lecturer in English at the University of St. Andrews.

L(ENORE) L. DICKSON has written widely on the works of William Golding.

LAWRENCE S. FRIEDMAN is author of *The Cinema of Martin Scorsese* (1997), *Understanding Cynthia Ozick* (1991), and *Understanding Isaac Bashevis Singer* (1988).

# Bibliography

Alcantara-Dimalanta, O. "Christian Dimensions in Contemporary Literature," *Unitas* 46 (1973): 213–23.

Anderson, Robert S. " 'Lord of the Flies' on Coral Island," *Canadian Review of Sociology and Anthropology* 4:1 (February 1967): 54–69.

Baker, James R. *William Golding: A Critical Study*. New York: St. Martin's Press, 1965.

———. "The Decline of *Lord of the Flies*," *South Atlantic Quarterly* 69 (1970): 447.

———, and Arthur P. Ziegler, Jr., eds. *Lord of the Flies: Text, Notes and Criticism*. New York: G.P. Putnam's Sons, 1964.

———. "Why It's No Go: A Study of William Golding's *Lord of the Flies*," *Arizona Quarterly* 19 (1963): 293–305.

Biles, Jack I. "Literary Sources and William Golding," *South Atlantic Bulletin* 37 (May 1972): 29–36.

———. *Talk: Conversations with William Golding*. New York: Harcourt Brace Jovanovich, 1970.

———. "Piggy: Apologia Pro Vita Sua," *Studies in the Literary Imagination* 1 (1968): 83–109.

———, and Robert O. Evans, eds. *William Golding: Some Critical Considerations*. Lexington: University of Kentucky Press, 1979.

Boyd, S.J. *The Novels of William Golding*. Brighton: Harvester Press, 1988.

Bufkin, E.C. "*Lord of the Flies*: An Analysis,: *Georgia Review* 19 (Spring 1965): 40–57.

Coskren, Father Thomas M. "Is Golding Calvinistic? A More Optimistic Interpretation of the Symbolism Found in *Lord of the Flies*," *America* 6 (July 1963): 18–20.

Dick, Bernard F. *William Golding*. New York: Twayne, 1967. Rev. ed. 1987.

Ely, Sister M. Amanda. "The Adult Image in Three Novels of Adolescent Life," *English Journal* (November 1967): 1127–31.

Forster, E.M. Introduction to William Golding, *Lord of the Flies*. New York: Coward-McCann, 1962. xiii.

Herndl, George C. "Golding and Salinger: A Clear Choice," *Wiseman Review* 502 (Winter 1964–65): 309–22.

Hollahan, Eugene. "Running in Circles: a Major Motif in *Lord of the Flies*," *Studies in the Novel* 2 (Spring 1970): 22–30.

Karl, Frederick R. "The Novel as Moral Allegory: The Fiction of William Golding," *A Reader's Guide to the Contemporary English Novel*. New York: Noonday Press, 1962. Revised. New York: Farrar, 1972.

Kermode, Frank. "Coral Islands," *Spectator* (August 22, 1958): 257.

——— . "The Later Golding," *Continuities*. London: Routledge & Kegan Paul, 1968.

Lederer, Richard H. "Student Reactions to *Lord of the Flies*," *English Journal* 58 (April 1969): 521.

——— , and Paul Hamilton Beattie. "*African Genesis* and *Lord of the Flies*: Two Studies of the Beastie Within," *English Journal* (December 1969): 1316.

Levitt, Leon. "Trust the Tale: A Second Reading of *Lord of the Flies*," *English Journal* (April 1969): 521.

MacLure, Millar. "Allegories of Innocence," *Dalhousie Review* 40 (Summer 1960): 145–56.

Mitchell, Charles. "*The Lord of the Flies* and the Escape from Freedom," *Arizona Quarterly* 22 (Spring 1966): 27–40.

Mitchell, Juliet. "Concepts and Techniques in William Golding," *New Left Review* (May–June 1962): 63–71.

Moody, Philippa. *A Critical Commentary on William Golding's Lord of the Flies*. London: Macmillan, 1966.

Nelson, William, ed. *William Golding's "Lord of the Flies": A Source Book*. New York: Odyssey, 1963.

Oakland, John. "Satiric Technique in *Lord of the Flies*," *Moderna Sprak* 64 (1970): 14–18.

O'Hara, J.D. "Mute Choirboys and Angelic Pigs: The Fable in *Lord of the Flies*," *Texas Studies in Literature and Language* 7 (Winter 1966): 411–20.

Pritchett, V.S. "Secret Parables," *New Statesman* 56 (August 2, 1958): 146–47.

Rosenberg, Bruce A. "Lord of the Fireflies," *Centennial Review* 11 (1967): 128–39.

Spitz, David. "Power and Authority: An Interpretation of Golding's *Lord of the Flies*," *Antioch Review* 30 (Spring 1970): 21–33.

Sternlicht, Stanford. "A Source for Golding's *Lord of the Flies*: Peter Pan?" *English Record* 14:2 (December 1963): 41–42.

——— . "Songs of Innocence and Songs of Experience in *Lord of the Flies* and *The Inheritors*," *Midwest Quarterly* 9 (July 1968): 383–90.

Talon, Henri A. "Irony in *Lord of the Flies*," *Essays in Criticism* 18 (July 1968): 296–309.

Tanzman, Lea. "The Mulberry in William Golding's Fiction: Emblematic Connotations," *Notes on Contemporary Literature* 21:5 (November 1991): 7–8.

——— . "The Murder of Simon in William Golding's *Lord of the Flies*," *Notes on Contemporary Literature* 17:5 (November 1987): 2–3.

Taylor, Henry H. "The Case Against William Golding's Simon-Piggy," *Contemporary Review* 209:1208 (September 1966): 155–60.

Tiger, Virginia. *William Golding: The Dark Fields of Discovery*. London: Calder and Boyars, 1974.

Townsend, R.C. "*Lord of the Flies: Fool's Gold?*" *Journal of General Education* 16 (July 1964): 153–60.

Veidemanis, Gladys. "*Lord of the Flies* in the Classroom—No Passing Fad," *English Journal* (November 1964): 569–74.

Watson, Kenneth. "A Reading of *Lord of the Flies*," *English* 15 (Spring 1964): 2–7.

White, Robert J. "Butterfly and Beast in *Lord of the Flies*," *Modern Fiction Studies* 1 (1964): 163–70.

Wilson, Angus. "Evil in the English Novel," *Kenyon Review* 19 (Summer 1957): 478–82.

Young, Wayland. "Letter from London, *Kenyon Review* 19 (Summer 1957): 478–82.

# Acknowledgments

"Men of a Smaller Growth": A Psychological Analysis of William Golding's *Lord of the Flies* by Claire Rosenfield from *Literature and Psychology* 11:4 (Autumn 1961): 93–100. Copyright © 1961 by the Modern Language Association.

*Lord of the Flies* and *The Bacchae* by Bernard F. Dick from *The Classical World* 57:4: 1283 (January 1964): 145–46. Copyright © 1964 by The Classical Association of the Atlantic States.

"Beelzebub Revisited: *Lord of the Flies*" by Bernard S. Oldsey and Stanley Weintraub from *The Art of William Golding* by Bernard S. Oldsey and Stanley Weintraub. Copyright © 1965 by Bernard S. Oldsey and Stanley Weintraub.

"Classical Themes in *Lord of the Flies*" by Robert C. Gordon from *Modern Fiction Studies* 11:4 (Winter 1965–1966): 424–27. Copyright © 1966 by the Purdue Research Foundation.

"*Lord of the Flies*" by Mark Kinkead-Weekes from *William Golding, A Critical Study* by Mark Kinkead-Weekes and Ian Gregor. Copyright © 1967, 1984 by Mark Kinkead-Weekes and Ian Gregor.

"The Metaphor of Darkness: *Lord of the Flies*" by Leighton Hodson from *William Golding* by Leighton Hodson. Copyright © 1969 by Leighton Hodson.

"*Lord of the Flies*" by Howard S. Babb from *The Novels of William Golding* by Howard S. Babb. Copyright © 1970 by The Ohio State University Press.

"Rhythm and Expansion in *Lord of the Flies*" by Jeanne Delbaere-Garant from *William Golding: Some Critical Considerations*, edited by Jack I. Biles and Robert O. Evans. Copyright © 1978 by The University Press of Kentucky.

"*Lord of the Flies*: Fable, Myth, and Fiction" by Arnold Johnston from *Earth and Darkness: The Novels of William Golding* by Arnold Johnston. Copyright © 1980 by The Curators of the University of Missouri.

"Doorways Through Walls: *Lord of the Flies* and *The Inheritors*" by Philip Redpath from *William Golding: A Structural Reading of His Fiction*. Copyright © 1986 by Philip Redpath.

"The Fictional Explosion: *Lord of the Flies* and *The Inheritors*" by James Gindin from *William Golding* by James Gindin. Copyright © 1988 by James Gindin.

"*Lord of the Flies*: Beelzebub's Boys" by Patrick Reilly from *The Literature of Guilt from Gulliver to Golding*. Copyright © 1988 by Patrick Reilly.

"The Nature of the Beast: *Lord of the Flies (1954)*" by S.J. Boyd from *The Novels of William Golding* by S.J. Boyd. Copyright © 1988 by S.J. Boyd.

"*Lord of the Flies*" by L.L. Dickson from *The Modern Allegories of William Golding* by L.L. Dickson. Copyright © 1990 by the Board of Regents of the State of Florida.

"Golding's *Lord of the Flies*: Pride as Original Sin" by John F. Fitzgerald and John R. Kayser from *Studies in the Novel* 24:1 (Spring 1992). Copyright © 1992 by the University of North Texas.

"Grief, Grief, Grief: *Lord of the Flies*" by Lawrence S. Friedman from *William Golding* by Lawrence S. Friedman. Copyright © 1993 by Lawrence S. Friedman.

# Index